Contributions to Economics

The series *Contributions to Economics* provides an outlet for innovative research in all areas of economics. Books published in the series are primarily monographs and multiple author works that present new research results on a clearly defined topic, but contributed volumes and conference proceedings are also considered. All books are published in print and ebook and disseminated and promoted globally. The series and the volumes published in it are indexed by Scopus and ISI (selected volumes).

Wanglin Ma • Dil B. Rahut
Bambang Brodjonegoro
Editors

E-Commerce for Inclusive Rural and Agricultural Development

Springer

ADBInstitute

Editors
Wanglin Ma
Lincoln University
Christchurch, Canterbury, New Zealand

Dil B. Rahut
Asian Development Bank Institute (ADBI)
Tokyo, Japan

Bambang Brodjonegoro
Asian Development Bank Institute (ADBI)
Tokyo, Japan

ISSN 1431-1933 ISSN 2197-7178 (electronic)
Contributions to Economics
ISBN 978-981-92-5236-7 ISBN 978-981-92-5237-4 (eBook)
https://doi.org/10.1007/978-981-92-5237-4

This Springer imprint is published by the registered company Springer Nature Singapore Pte Ltd.
The registered company address is: 152 Beach Road, #21-01/04 Gateway East, Singapore 189721, Singapore

Preface

Digital technologies are reshaping economies and societies worldwide, and e-commerce has emerged as one of the most powerful instruments driving this transformation. For rural and agricultural communities, in particular, e-commerce offers new opportunities to overcome geographic isolation, reduce transaction costs, expand market access, and improve livelihoods. Yet, despite its promise, the benefits of e-commerce have been unevenly distributed. Structural barriers, digital divides, and institutional constraints continue to limit participation by smallholders, rural workers, women, and other disadvantaged groups. Ensuring that e-commerce contributes to inclusive rural and agricultural development, therefore, remains a pressing challenge for policymakers and researchers alike.

This book, "*E-Commerce for Inclusive Rural and Agricultural Development*," brings together a carefully selected set of chapters that collectively advance understanding of how e-commerce can foster rural transformation while addressing issues of equity, access, and inclusion. A distinctive strength of this book is its explicit focus on inclusion. Rather than treating e-commerce adoption as an end in itself, the chapters examine who participates, who benefits, and who risks being left behind. Issues such as unequal access, uneven gains, gender disparities, and the persistent disadvantages faced by smallholders and rural workers are brought to the forefront. By integrating insights from systematic reviews, micro-level econometric analysis, and qualitative case studies, the book provides a nuanced understanding of how digital transformation interacts with existing socioeconomic structures in rural areas.

The insights offered in this book are highly relevant for policymakers, development practitioners, and scholars. They underscore that promoting rural e-commerce is not merely a technological challenge but a broader development task that requires coordinated policies across infrastructure, education, finance, and agricultural systems. More importantly, the evidence presented in this book highlights that inclusive outcomes are not automatic: they must be deliberately designed and supported.

Christchurch, New Zealand Wanglin Ma
Tokyo, Japan Dil B. Rahut
Tokyo, Japan Bambang Brodjonegoro

Acknowledgments The editors gratefully acknowledge the reviewers who carefully reviewed the chapters before their acceptance and the former staff member Adam Majoe of the Asian Development Bank Institute (ADBI) for coordinating the editing and production process. They also thank Dr Raja Rajendra Timilsina, Dr Ngawang Dendup, Prof. Song Soo Lim, Mami Nomoto, and Chiisye Toki of ADBI for their invaluable support in organizing the international conference "*Innovations for Sustainable Agriculture and Rural Development*," held on September 22–24, 2025. The papers in this book were presented during the Part 2 Session, themed on "*E-commerce for Rural and Agricultural Development*," on Day 3 of the conference. Other people who contributed to the conference were also greatly acknowledged.

Introduction and Summary

Across the rapidly evolving digital economies, the promise of e-commerce to transform rural livelihoods is expanding fastest in regions where structural constraints remain most pronounced. In many developing countries, smallholder farmers and rural workers still rely on traditional markets characterized by geographic isolation, information asymmetries, and limited bargaining power. Digital platforms have the potential to bridge these gaps by connecting producers directly with consumers, expanding market access, improving price transparency, and diversifying income opportunities. Evidence from Asia and other developing regions shows that rural e-commerce can increase household income, reduce poverty, stimulate the adoption of improved agricultural practices, and enhance rural development outcomes. Yet the benefits of digital transformation remain unevenly distributed. Rural areas continue to face persistent barriers, including inadequate digital infrastructure, limited internet connectivity, high transaction costs, low digital literacy, and institutional constraints that hinder farmers' integration into online markets.

These structural challenges interact with demographic and socioeconomic inequalities that shape who participates in the digital economy and who benefits from it. In countries such as India and Indonesia, rural households often experience lower returns to digital resources due to gaps in education, gender disparities, and occupational constraints. Even where internet access has expanded rapidly, many farmers lack the skills, financial resources, or logistical support needed to engage effectively in e-commerce. In addition, regional disparities in infrastructure quality, platform access, and regulatory support further reinforce digital divides between urban and rural populations. As a result, while digitalization offers unprecedented opportunities for rural transformation, it also risks amplifying existing inequalities unless supportive policies and institutional frameworks are in place.

To fully realize the transformative potential of rural e-commerce, solutions must address two interconnected challenges. The first involves structural barriers that limit digital participation, including gaps in infrastructure, logistics, digital literacy, and regulatory frameworks. The second concerns inclusive participation and equitable outcomes, encompassing gender disparities, unequal access to digital skills and assets, and the uneven distribution of economic gains from digital markets.

Addressing both challenges simultaneously is essential to ensure that digital transformation contributes not only to economic efficiency but also to inclusive and sustainable rural development.

Building on these twin challenges, this book aims to provide a clear and practice-oriented overview of how rural e-commerce can support agricultural transformation and improve rural livelihoods in developing economies. It integrates evidence from systematic literature reviews, cross-country empirical analyses, and detailed case studies to identify the drivers, barriers, and impacts of digital market participation. By synthesizing insights from multiple countries and methodological approaches, the book highlights what works in promoting inclusive rural digitalization and how policy frameworks can enable farmers and rural workers to participate more effectively in emerging digital economies. The goal is to translate growing interest in rural e-commerce into actionable strategies and policy recommendations for researchers, policymakers, and practitioners seeking to foster inclusive and sustainable rural development through digital innovation.

Chapter 1, "*E-Commerce as a Driver of Rural Transformation: Insights from a Systematic Review*," provides a comprehensive synthesis of the existing literature on how e-commerce contributes to rural transformation. Drawing on a systematic review of 95 empirical studies, the chapter examines the impacts of e-commerce across three interrelated dimensions: household livelihoods, agricultural production, and broader rural development. The evidence suggests that e-commerce participation can enhance rural incomes, reduce income inequality, improve consumption and subjective well-being, and stimulate the adoption of sustainable agricultural practices. At the community level, it contributes to human capital accumulation, improved financial access, and broader economic development. The chapter also highlights the key role of national policies and digital infrastructure in facilitating these outcomes while identifying important research gaps, including the lack of cross-country comparative evidence and limited analysis of mechanisms and cost–benefit implications. By providing a multidimensional framework that links micro-level household outcomes with macro-level policy initiatives, this chapter establishes the conceptual foundation for the book's subsequent analyses of rural e-commerce and agricultural transformation.

Chapter 2, "*Pathways to Rural E-Commerce: A Systematic Review of Drivers, Barriers, and Policy Implications*," examines the key drivers and barriers shaping rural e-commerce development through a systematic review of 105 studies published between 2015 and 2026. The chapter identifies a wide range of determinants, including human capital, social capital, digital infrastructure, online platform development, government policies, and technological innovation. It further highlights how demographic and socioeconomic characteristics—such as age, gender, land ownership, and household economic status—can have dual effects on e-commerce adoption, either facilitating or constraining participation depending on context. The chapter also develops a comprehensive conceptual definition of rural e-commerce. It situates the discussion within several theoretical frameworks, including human capital theory, social capital theory, transaction cost economics, and household livelihood frameworks. By synthesizing the diverse determinants documented in previous studies, the chapter provides an integrated framework for understanding how rural e-commerce can support poverty reduction, sustainable agricultural production, and long-term rural development.

Chapter 3, "*Unequal Access, Uneven Gains: Demographic and Structural Barriers to Rural E-Commerce Adoption in India*," focuses on the persistent rural–urban digital divide in India and explores the demographic and structural barriers that limit rural households' participation in e-commerce. Using nationally representative household data from the Consumer Pyramids Household Survey covering more than 100,000 households, the chapter applies a multi-method empirical framework—including fixed-effects regression, Oaxaca-Blinder decomposition, and quantile regression—to analyze how demographic characteristics shape digital expenditure and e-commerce engagement. The results reveal that rural households face both endowment disadvantages and lower returns from digital resources, particularly in education and occupation. Distributional analysis further shows that digitally excluded groups are concentrated among lower-income households, reinforcing structural inequalities in access to the digital economy. The chapter highlights the importance of targeted digital literacy programs, gender-responsive platform design, and improved rural digital infrastructure to ensure that e-commerce development is inclusive and equitable.

Chapter 4, "*From Farm to Online Market: Analyzing E-Commerce Adoption Trends and Drivers for Indonesian Farmers*," investigates trends and determinants of e-commerce adoption among rural farmers in Indonesia, a country experiencing rapid digital transformation but persistent rural digital divides. Using three waves of nationally representative survey data combined with village-level infrastructure statistics, the chapter analyzes spatial disparities in internet access and farmer participation in e-commerce. The findings indicate that although internet penetration among farmers has increased substantially in recent years, participation in e-commerce remains relatively low. Key barriers include limited digital literacy, uneven internet quality, high access costs, and socioeconomic inequalities across regions. Education and digital skills emerge as critical determinants of adoption, while disparities across gender and age groups highlight persistent structural barriers. The chapter concludes that expanding high-quality internet infrastructure and strengthening digital training programs are essential to enabling smallholder farmers to fully benefit from digital markets.

Chapter 5, "*Digital Inclusion and Rural Earnings in Indonesia: Evidence from E-Commerce Adoption Across Sectors*," explores how e-commerce adoption influences rural earnings and income inequality in Indonesia. Using nationally representative labor force data from 2018 to 2024, the chapter employs several econometric techniques—including endogenous switching regression, propensity score matching, and inverse probability weighting—to evaluate the income effects of digital participation. The findings show that education, training, and sectoral affiliation significantly influence the likelihood of adopting e-commerce, with adoption rates remaining lower among agricultural workers. Importantly, participation in e-commerce is associated with substantial income gains across both agricultural and non-agricultural sectors, particularly among employers and lower-income workers.

However, gender disparities persist, suggesting that digital adoption alone is insufficient to eliminate structural income inequalities. The chapter highlights the need for inclusive digital policies that combine infrastructure investments with digital literacy programs and gender-sensitive interventions to ensure equitable rural development.

Chapter 6, "*Policy- and Household-Level Challenges of E-Commerce for Smallholder Agriculture in Vietnam*," examines the policy and household constraints that limit the expansion of e-commerce in smallholder agriculture in Vietnam. Using case studies of fruit farmers in peri-urban Hanoi and rural Son La Province, the chapter analyzes both policy frameworks and farmers' experiences with digital marketing platforms. The findings reveal that although several national and provincial policies support e-commerce development, only a few explicitly target smallholder agriculture. At the household level, farmers face substantial barriers, including limited technical knowledge, inadequate digital skills, and difficulties complying with certification and quality standards required for online markets. Peri-urban farmers benefit from closer proximity to urban markets and stronger connections with traders, while rural farmers face greater logistical and information constraints. The chapter emphasizes the need for targeted agricultural e-commerce policies, improved infrastructure, and trust-building mechanisms between farmers and consumers to unlock the full potential of digital markets for smallholder agriculture.

Contents

About the Editors

Wanglin Ma is Full Professor of Applied Economics at the Department of Global Value Chains and Trade, Faculty of Agribusiness and Commerce, Lincoln University, New Zealand. His research spans agricultural and development economics, with a strong emphasis on identifying strategies that enhance farm performance, strengthen the sustainability of the agrifood systems, improve household welfare and farmers' subjective well-being, and promote sustainable rural and agricultural development. He earned his PhD in Agricultural Economics from the University of Kiel, Germany, and has authored 160 Scopus-indexed articles in leading international journals.

Dil B. Rahut is Vice Chair of Research at the Asian Development Bank Institute (ADBI). He was a Sr. Global Program Manager for the International Maize and Wheat Improvement Centre's (CIMMYT). He also worked in the Research and Statistics Department of the Royal Monetary Authority of Bhutan, the WorldFish Centre as a senior fellow and Japan chair at the Indian Council for Research in International Economic Relations, chief of research, planning, and monitoring at the Bank of Bhutan Ltd, and assistant professor of development economics at South Asian University. He has a PhD in development economics from the University of Bonn's Center for Development Research, Germany. He has over 260 peer-reviewed publications in Scopus-indexed journals and several books focusing on development issues.

Bambang Brodjonegoro an Indonesian national, is the Dean and CEO of the Asian Development Bank Institute (ADBI). Before joining ADBI in April 2025, he was Special Advisor to the President of the Republic of Indonesia for Economic Affairs and National Development. He served the Government of Indonesia in several senior leadership roles from 2011. He was Indonesia's Minister of Finance (2014–2016), Minister of National Development Planning (2016–2019), and Minister of Research and Technology (2019–2021). Besides government and academic, he also served as Director General of the Islamic Research and Training Institute (IRTI), Islamic Development Bank (IsDB) (2009–2010). Dean Brodjonegoro holds a doctorate and master's degree in urban and regional planning from the University of Illinois at Urbana-Champaign and a bachelor's degree in economics from the Faculty of Economics and Business, University of Indonesia, where he was a full Professor and served as Dean during 2005–2009.

List of Figures

List of Tables

Chapter 1
E-Commerce as a Driver of Rural Transformation: Insights from a Systematic Review

Hongyun Zheng, Wanglin Ma, Jingyi Li, and Bambang Brodjonegoro

1.1 Introduction

Agricultural producers in underdeveloped and developing countries have long relied on traditional marketing channels, including local markets, wholesale intermediaries, and producer cooperatives (Dey and Singh 2023; Tabe Ojong et al. 2022). While these channels provide access to nearby consumers, they are often constrained by geographic reach and asymmetric market information. Such inefficiencies can limit farmers' bargaining power and reduce incentives to upgrade product quality (Chiaverina et al. 2023; Tuni et al. 2022). In some remote rural areas, limited physical infrastructure and the dominance of intermediaries further exacerbate these constraints, restricting household livelihood improvements, discouraging investments in agricultural production, and slowing broader rural development.

Digital technology—particularly E-commerce—offers the potential to shift how agricultural goods are marketed, priced, and delivered to consumers (Abate et al. 2023; Baumüller et al. 2023; Nogueira et al. 2025; Zant 2023). E-commerce refers to the sale or purchase of goods and services conducted through digital or electronic networks—including the Internet, mobile platforms, and other online systems—where order placement is carried out electronically, while payment and delivery may occur either online or offline (Huang et al. 2022; Li 2017; OECD 2011). Rural

H. Zheng (✉) · J. Li
College of Economics and Management, Huazhong Agricultural University, Wuhan, China
e-mail: Hongyun.Zheng@mail.hzau.edu.cn

W. Ma
Department of Global Value Chains and Trade, Faculty of Agribusiness and Commerce, Lincoln University, Christchurch, New Zealand
e-mail: Wanglin.Ma@lincoln.ac.nz

B. Brodjonegoro
Asian Development Bank Institute, Tokyo (ADBI), Japan

W. Ma et al. (eds.), *E-Commerce for Inclusive Rural and Agricultural Development*, Contributions to Economics,
https://doi.org/10.1007/978-981-92-5237-4_1

households can bypass traditional intermediaries by leveraging online platforms and accessing real-time price information. This digital market integration has the potential to lower search and negotiation costs and improve price transparency. However, these benefits are not always guaranteed, as E-commerce development can potentially lead to market concentration and logistical vulnerabilities.

Globally, Reardon et al. (2021) noted that E-commerce is spreading rapidly across developing regions. Although its share in modern retail remains modest, it has expanded quickly in Asia and Latin America, is emerging in Africa, and is most advanced in China. For example, in China, rural ICT development was first incorporated into the National Economic and Social Development Five-Year Plan in 2001 (Huang et al. 2022), followed in 2009 by the launch of the National E-commerce Demonstration Cities (NEDC) program. By 2017, 70 pilot cities had been approved. Taobao village is a designation introduced by the Alibaba Research Institute in 2013, and—despite being unofficial—remains a widely recognized and authoritative benchmark for rural E-commerce development in China (Ali Research 2022). In 2014, the Ministry of Finance and the Ministry of Commerce introduced the National Rural E-commerce Comprehensive Demonstration County (NRECDC) initiative to extend E-commerce development in rural areas. Collectively, these initiatives have accelerated the adoption of rural E-commerce. By 2021, the number of officially recognized Taobao Villages had reached 7023 (Ali Research 2022). In 2024, China's rural retail sales totaled 6.67 trillion yuan (approximately USD 936 billion, 1 USD = 7.12 Yuan), up 4.3% year-on-year, while rural online retail sales grew by 6.4%; notably, online agricultural product sales increased by 15.8% (Ministry of Commerce 2025).

An increasing number of empirical studies have investigated the impacts of E-commerce development on rural transformation, with China serving as the most intensively examined case. These studies consistently converge around three interrelated dimensions: (1) household livelihoods, focusing on income, poverty alleviation, consumption, and subjective well-being (e.g., Gao et al. 2025; Wen et al. 2024; Zhang et al. 2025a), (2) agricultural production, including land use, input management, technology adoption, productivity, and price realization (e.g., Lu et al. 2025; Yang et al. 2025), and (3) broader rural development, covering human capital formation, labor allocation, economic development, and environmental sustainability (e.g., Qin et al. 2023; Qin and Fang 2022). While these strands provide valuable insights, the literature remains fragmented in scope and uneven in coverage. Very few studies systematically integrate micro- and macro-level outcomes (Cordes and Marinova 2023; Haji 2021), underscoring the need for a comprehensive review that organizes dispersed findings into a coherent framework and identifies priorities for future research.

This study addresses these gaps by conducting a systematic review of 95 empirical studies on the role of E-commerce development in rural transformation. Our review makes two contributions. First, this review provides a comprehensive synthesis of how E-commerce development influences household livelihoods, agricultural production, and broader rural development. By integrating evidence across these three interconnected domains, it offers a holistic and multidimensional understanding of E-commerce's transformative potential—moving beyond the fragmented, outcome-specific focus that characterizes much of the existing literature. Second, this review offers a multilevel perspective largely absent in the existing literature by systematically linking top-down policy initiatives—such as NRECDC—with bottom-up evidence from rural households. This integration enables us to examine how national E-commerce strategies translate into welfare outcomes.

Theoretically, E-commerce development can influence rural and agricultural transformation through two channels: purchasing and sales channels. On the consumption side, participation in E-commerce as buyers affects household welfare through mechanisms consistent with consumer choice theory, which posits that expanded product variety and reduced search costs shift household expenditure patterns and utility. By increasing access to diverse goods and services, E-commerce participation may enhance subjective well-being (Wei et al. 2024a; Zheng and Ma 2021), improve dietary diversity and quality (Ma et al. 2022; Shen et al. 2023), and increase early human capital investment (Zheng and Ma 2025).

Meanwhile, participation in E-commerce as sellers operates through mechanisms grounded in market participation theory, which highlights how reductions in transaction and information costs influence farmers' decisions to enter markets. Expanded digital sales channels can increase market access and alter production behavior (Cordes and Marinova 2023; Tang and Zhu 2020; Wang et al. 2021). At the macro level, policy-driven E-commerce initiatives—such as Taobao Villages, NEDC, and NRECDC—further lower entry barriers by providing digital infrastructure and institutional support, amplifying these micro-level effects.

The remainder of the paper is structured as follows: Sect. 1.2 details the literature collection strategy and presents descriptive statistics. Section 1.3 synthesizes the evidence on the impact of E-commerce development on rural transformation. Section 1.4 highlights the research gaps and identifies future research directions. The final Sect. 1.5 concludes the paper and offers policy recommendations.

1.2 Literature Collection and Descriptive Statistics

1.2.1 Literature Collection

This review adheres to the PRISMA (Preferred Reporting Items for Systematic Reviews and Meta-Analyses) framework to ensure transparency and reproducibility in the assessment of the literature (Lee and Gambiza 2022). The process involved four main stages: (1) formulating precise research questions, (2) identifying relevant studies using predefined inclusion and exclusion criteria, (3) screening and removing non-eligible records, and (4) synthesizing the retained studies to minimize potential selection bias. The overall workflow for literature identification and selection is presented in Fig. 1.1.

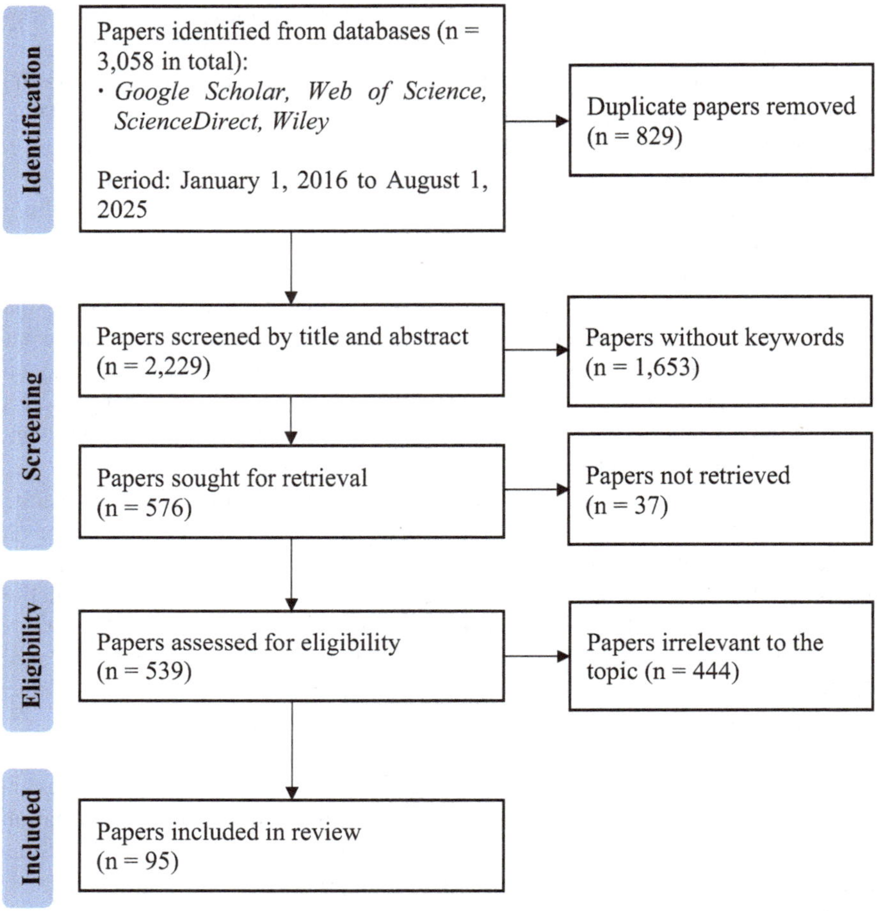

Fig. 1.1 Flow diagram of the literature selection. Source: Authors

In compiling the literature for this review, we consulted a diverse range of sources, including peer-reviewed journal articles, book chapters, policy reports, and working papers—as commonly practiced in systematic reviews (Li et al. 2024a; Meinzen-dick et al. 2019; Siegle et al. 2024). The search covered the period from January 1, 2016, to August 1, 2025, to capture early developments and the most recent evidence on rural E-commerce development. We first identified a set of core keywords, encompassing *rural E-commerce, online agricultural sales, Taobao village, NEDC, NRECDC,* and related synonyms. We constructed search strings using these keywords by combining terms and their synonyms with Boolean operators. The initial search syntax was refined during a pilot phase to ensure coverage of all relevant literature. Searches were conducted using *Google Scholar, Web of Science, ScienceDirect,* and *Wiley*, as these are widely recognized platforms for retrieving peer-reviewed literature (Salemink et al. 2017; Wever et al. 2024; Zangue et al.

2022). To ensure that studies were directly relevant, we required at least one core term to appear in the title, abstract, or keywords. We adopted a hybrid strategy, combining TITLE-ABS-KEY searches with full-text searches when necessary, which we found balanced sensitivity and specificity in identifying eligible studies.

Our initial search identified 3058 records covering the period. After removing 829 duplicates, 2229 unique records remained for title and abstract screening. The research team jointly completed the literature screening process to ensure consistency and accuracy. At this stage, 1653 papers were excluded because they contained no core keywords, leaving 576 studies for retrieval. Of these, 37 could not be accessed in full text, resulting in 539 papers for detailed eligibility assessment. The inclusion criteria included that a study: (1) examine E-commerce development in the context of agricultural and/or rural development; (2) focus on either micro-level participation (e.g., rural households as sellers) or macro-level policy initiatives (e.g., Taobao village or NEDC); (3) provide evidence, either quantitative or qualitative, rather than purely conceptual discussions. Qualitative studies can also provide valid evidence on E-commerce development impacts—for example, through case-based identification of mechanisms—without relying on econometric estimation (e.g., Huang et al. 2020; Zapata et al. 2016); and (4) report measurable outcomes focused on this study. During full-text screening, 444 papers were excluded for reasons including a lack of direct relevance to E-commerce development. This left 95 studies that met all criteria.

1.2.2 *Definition of E-Commerce Development*

Existing studies define E-commerce development at multiple levels, including the household, village, and macro (policy) levels (see Table 1.1). At the household-level, a total of 29 studies define E-commerce participation—typically for rural producers—as a dummy variable indicating whether a household sells any products via online platforms (e.g., Taobao, Douyin, and Pinduoduo) (e.g., Chen et al. 2022; Liu et al. 2024a). At the village level, the most common focus is on Taobao villages (13 studies). In these cases, E-commerce development is operationalized in several ways: as a dummy variable indicating whether a household resides in a Taobao village (Qi et al. 2019) or whether any Taobao village exists within the local county (Zhang et al. 2024); as a censored variable representing the proportion of Taobao villages among all villages in a county (Liu et al. 2025c); or as a continuous variable capturing the absolute number of Taobao villages in a locality (Lin and Li 2023). In addition, two studies define E-commerce participation intensity as the share of households engaged in E-commerce within a village (Li and He 2024; Liu et al. 2025b), and four studies measure village-level E-commerce development,

Table 1.1 Typical definitions of E-commerce development in the reviewed literature

Measurement	Descriptions
Household level	
E-commerce participation	Whether households sell any products via online platforms (e.g., Taobao, Douyin, and Pinduoduo)
Village level	
Taobao village	Whether the village was identified as a Taobao village
E-commerce participation intensity	Share of households that participated in E-commerce within households
E-commerce service	Whether the village has an E-commerce service center
Macro level	
NRECDC	Whether the county was identified as a National Rural E-commerce Comprehensive Demonstration County (NRECDC)
NEDC	Whether the city was identified as a National E-commerce demonstration city (NEDC)
E-commerce development level	The index derived from the synthesis of various indicator systems

Source: Authors

such as the presence of delivery stations (e.g., Cao et al. 2024; Cao and Li 2025; Wang et al. 2023).

At the macro level, E-commerce development is frequently defined through the lens of policy initiatives and regional development indicators. A total of 29 studies examined the NRECDC program (e.g., Cui 2025; Wang et al. 2025b), while six focused on the NEDC initiative (e.g., Di and Qiu 2023; Wang et al. 2025a). A total of seven studies construct composite indicators of E-commerce development using metrics such as the density of E-commerce businesses (Hou and Liu 2024; Mei et al. 2025). In addition, one study investigated policies on cross-border E-commerce (He et al. 2024), and four analyzed different types of E-commerce platforms (Huang et al. 2020; Liao et al. 2023; Mei et al. 2020; Zapata et al. 2016).

1.2.3 Descriptive Statistics

We provide descriptive statistics for the reviewed studies, organized into four dimensions: country distribution, data type, research method, and publication year. Only one study is set in Indonesia (Permani 2023) and one in the United States (Zapata et al. 2016), while the remaining 93 focus on China, underscoring China's role as both a policy laboratory and a primary context for rural E-commerce development. In terms of data type, a total of 33 studies rely on cross-sectional datasets, typically drawn from household-level surveys such as the China Rural Revitalization

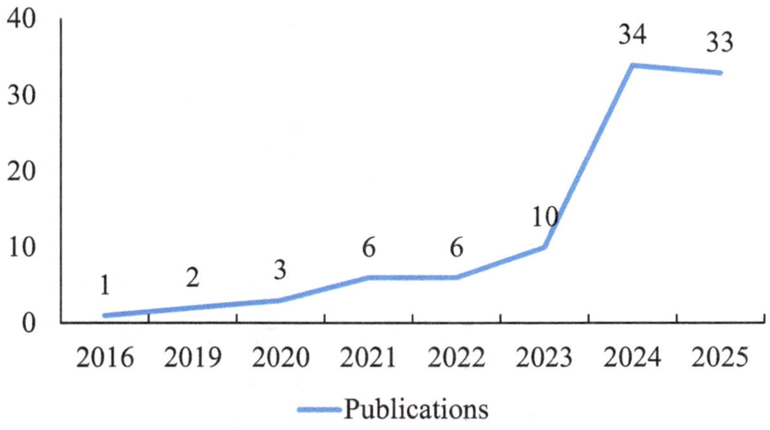

Fig. 1.2 Number of reviewed literature (2016–2025). Source: Authors

Survey (CRRS) (e.g., Luo et al. 2025; Zhou et al. 2024), whereas 62 employ panel data, including both micro-level sources like the China Family Panel Studies (CFPS) (e.g., Mei et al. 2025; Wang et al. 2025b) and county- or city-level statistical records (e.g., Ji et al. 2023; Lu and Yan 2025).

Methodologically, studies using cross-sectional data often apply propensity score matching (PSM) (e.g., Jin et al. 2020; Li et al. 2025b) or endogenous switching regression (ESR) (e.g., Liu et al. 2021; Wang et al. 2024b) to address the endogeneity of household E-commerce adoption, while panel data analyses predominantly use difference-in-differences (DID) models (e.g., Wang et al. 2025c; Wei et al. 2024a) and conventional panel regressions (e.g., Mei et al. 2025; Wang and Wu 2025). In addition, a subset of studies investigating spatial spillover effects adopts spatial econometric techniques (e.g., Han et al. 2023; Hou and Liu 2024). While only a handful of studies appeared before 2021, the number increased sharply thereafter, reaching ten in 2023, 34 in 2024, and 33 in 2025 (see Fig. 1.2).

Figure 1.3 presents the thematic distribution of the 95 studies reviewed, categorized into three domains. Household livelihoods are the most extensively examined topic, with 44 papers—of which 32 focus on income-related outcomes, six on poverty-related measures, five on consumption-related outcomes, and three on subjective well-being. Agricultural production is covered in 24 papers, examining land management issues (nine papers), input management (five papers), technology adoption (six papers), farm performance (five papers), and market performance outcomes (four papers). Rural development is addressed in 27 papers, focusing on human capital development (11 papers), labor allocation decisions (4 papers), credit and financial accessibility (3 papers), broader economic growth in agricultural and non-agricultural sectors (6 papers), and environmental sustainability outcomes (5 papers).

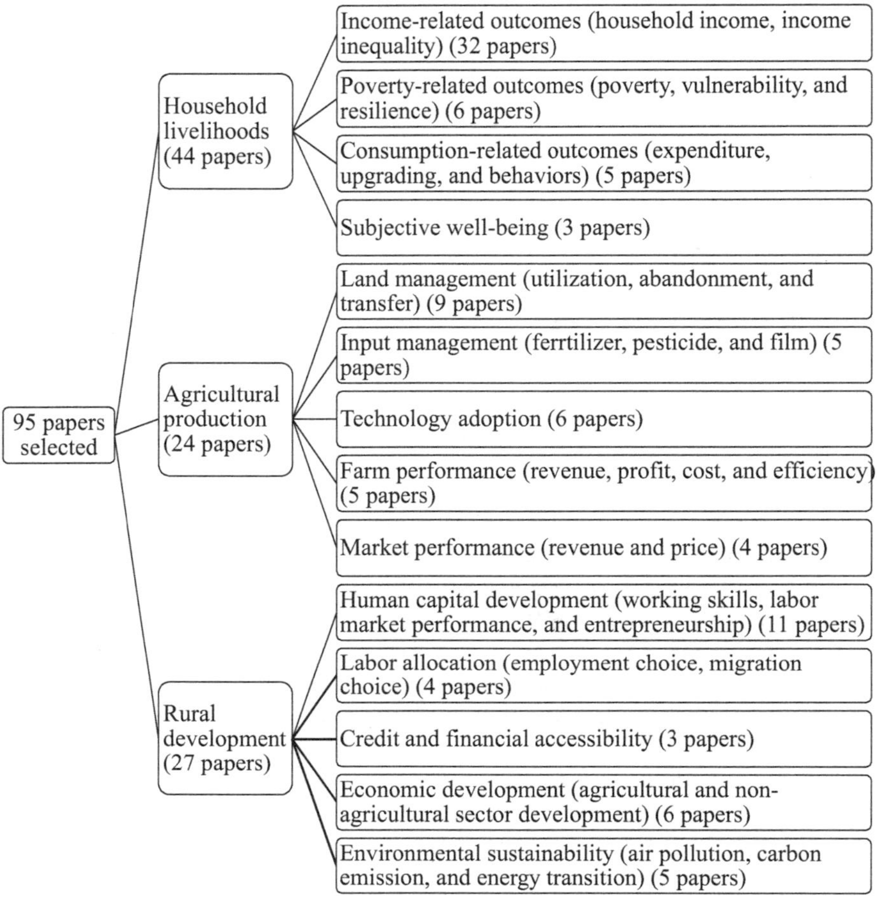

Fig. 1.3 Distributions of reviewed literature. Note: the reference may overlap across categories. Source: Authors

We employed VOSviewer[1] software to visualize a bibliometric network of keyword co-occurrence, applying a fractional counting method and setting the minimum occurrence threshold at 2. Of the 281 keywords, 44 meet the threshold. Figure 1.4 displays the distribution and interconnections of keywords. The most central terms are E-commerce, rural E-commerce, China, and rural China. Surrounding these core nodes are clusters of keywords related to research methods (e.g., propensity score matching and treatment effect models), thematic concentrations (e.g., poverty reduction and subjective well-being), and policy initiatives (e.g., Taobao Village and national E-commerce demonstration city), reflecting the multidimensional nature of research.

[1] Please see https://www.vosviewer.com/ for detailed information.

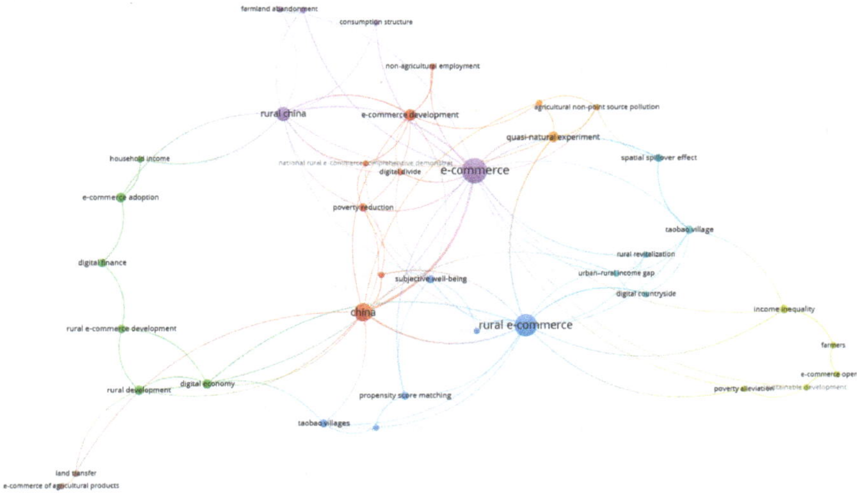

Fig. 1.4 Distributions and connections of the keywords in the reviewed literature. Source: Authors

1.3 Impact of E-Commerce Development on Rural Transformation

1.3.1 Impact of E-Commerce Development on Household Livelihoods

Household livelihoods represent the most immediate area in which the effects of rural E-commerce development can be observed. To capture this multidimensional influence, we organize the review into four subsections: income-related outcomes, poverty-related outcomes, consumption-related outcomes, and subjective well-being (See Table 1.2).

1.3.1.1 Income-Related Outcomes

Income remains the most visible measure of E-commerce development's contribution to rural development. Existing studies assess overall household income gains and explore how these benefits are distributed—both within rural areas and between rural and urban residents.

E-commerce development can increase household income by expanding market access, reducing transaction costs, and enhancing sales revenues. Policy initiatives such as Taobao Villages, NRECDC, and NEDC further reinforce these effects by improving infrastructure and logistics. Most studies report significant income gains from E-commerce participation (e.g., Li et al. 2021c; Lyu et al. 2022; Qiu et al. 2024b; Wang et al. 2025c), as well as from residence in Taobao Villages (Li and Qin

Table 1.2 Overview of literature examining the impact of E-commerce development on household livelihoods

Category	Literature and findings
Income-related indicators	
Household income	Increase • E-commerce participation (Chen et al. 2023; Li and He 2024; Li et al. 2021c; Liu et al. 2025a,; Lyu et al. 2022; Qiu et al. 2024b; Wang et al. 2025c; Zheng et al. 2024) • Taobao village (Li and Qin 2022; Zhang et al. 2024) • NRECDC (Cui 2025; Gao et al. 2025; He et al. 2024; Wang et al. 2024b; Wang and Zhang 2025; Wen et al. 2024; Ye et al. 2024; Zhang et al. 2025a) • NEDC (Wang et al. 2025a) Decrease (Li et al. 2025a) Insignificant (Tang et al. 2022)
Income inequality	Decrease (Gao et al. 2025; Guan et al. 2024; Luo et al. 2025; Mei et al. 2025; Qiu et al. 2025a; Sun et al. 2025; Wei et al. 2025a; Zhang et al. 2025b) Increase (Li et al. 2025a) Insignificant (Ma and Komatsu 2025)
Urban-rural income gap	Increase (He et al. 2024; Li et al. 2021b; Liu and Zhou 2023) Decrease (Wei et al. 2024b)
Poverty-related indicators	
Poverty	Decrease (Cao and Li 2025; Hou and Liu 2024)
Poverty vulnerability	Decrease (Tang et al. 2024)
Resilience	Increase (Huang et al. 2024; Li et al. 2024c)
Food security	Increase (Permani 2023)
Consumption-related indicators	
Consumption expenditure	Increase (Wang et al. 2025c)
Purchasing power	Increase (Liu et al. 2025c)
Consumption upgrading	Increase (Chen and Li 2025)
Online shopping	Increase (Liu et al. 2025a)
Digital payment	Increase (Su et al. 2021; Wang et al. 2025c)
Subjective well-being	
Happiness	Increase (Jin et al. 2020; Wang et al. 2025b; Wei et al. 2024a)

2022; Zhang et al. 2024), NRECDC counties (Gao et al. 2025; He et al. 2024; Wang et al. 2024b), and NEDC cities (Wang et al. 2025a). Exceptions include a significant income decline (Li et al. 2025a) and no significant effect (Tang et al. 2022). From a mechanism perspective, Gao et al. (2025) found that the NRECDC program increases household income by enhancing both digital capital and social capital. Heterogeneity may stem from differences in income composition—e.g., wage income decreases while business income increases as reported (Li et al. 2025a). Tang et al. (2022) reported that the positive effect of E-commerce development on rural residents' per capita disposable income becomes marginally significant only after control variables are included in the regression, suggesting that the income effect may be limited or highly context-dependent.

In addition to household income, several studies have examined the effects of E-commerce development on income inequality (Gao et al. 2025; Guan et al. 2024; Li et al. 2025a; Luo et al. 2025; Ma and Komatsu 2025; Mei et al. 2025; Qiu et al. 2025a; Sun et al. 2025; Wei et al. 2025a; Zhang et al. 2025b). E-commerce development can narrow disparities by expanding market access and generating entrepreneurial opportunities for rural households. However, unequal access to digital infrastructure and capital may reinforce existing divides. The majority of studies suggest that E-commerce development reduces overall income inequality (e.g., Gao et al. 2025; Guan et al. 2024; Sun et al. 2025), though studies offer contrasting evidence. Li et al. (2025a) reported an increase in inequality. In contrast, Ma and Komatsu (2025) found that the effect is heterogeneous across regions—E-commerce tends to widen income inequality in more developed countries but to alleviate it in less developed ones, with no significant effect overall. Zhang et al. (2025b) also highlighted mixed outcomes: E-commerce development increases wage income inequality but reduces operating income inequality.

Although the urban–rural income gap is a key component of overall income inequality, it warrants separate attention due to its distinct policy relevance and the unique structural factors shaping income growth across urban and rural areas. E-commerce development could narrow the income gap between urban and rural residents by integrating rural producers into broader markets and enhancing rural earning opportunities; however, it may also widen disparities if urban areas adopt digital technologies more rapidly or capture a disproportionate share of the value added. Empirical evidence is mixed: several studies report an increase in the gap (He et al. 2024; Li et al. 2021b; Liu and Zhou 2023), while Wei et al. (2024b) showed a decrease. Liu and Zhou (2023) found that Taobao Villages widen the urban–rural income gap by promoting migration flows across income groups. However, they also show that this widening effect weakens as the degree of spatial agglomeration increases.

1.3.1.2 Poverty-Related Outcomes

E-commerce development can alleviate poverty by expanding market access and creating non-farm employment opportunities. Empirical evidence shows that E-commerce participation reduces poverty incidence (Cao and Li 2025; Hou and Liu 2024) and lowers poverty vulnerability (Tang et al. 2024). Cao and Li (2025) found that E-commerce development reduces rural poverty by strengthening collective action, increasing commercialization, and facilitating farmers' participation in pension insurance. It has also been found to enhance household resilience (Huang et al. 2024; Li et al. 2024c) and improve food security (Permani 2023). These findings suggest that E-commerce development can play a complicated role in lifting households out of poverty and enhancing their capacity to tackle future risks.

1.3.1.3 Consumption-Related Outcomes

E-commerce development expands rural households' ability to spend and reshapes what they consume and how they consume it. Empirical evidence suggests that E-commerce participation increases overall consumption expenditure (Wang et al. 2025c) and increases purchasing power (Liu et al. 2025c). It may also encourage consumption upgrading (Chen and Li 2025). In addition, E-commerce development can reshape rural consumption patterns by promoting the adoption of online shopping and digital payment systems. Empirical studies have shown that E-commerce participation increases the likelihood of online shopping (Liu et al. 2025a) and accelerates the adoption of digital payment tools (Su et al. 2021; Wang et al. 2025c). Liu et al. (2025a) showed that the REDC program promotes online shopping by increasing the availability of service provision, logistics support, training opportunities, and marketing assistance.

1.3.1.4 Subjective Well-Being

While income, poverty, and consumption are easily observable and therefore frequently examined, subjective well-being is often overlooked in empirical research. E-commerce development can enhance subjective well-being by improving income opportunities and facilitating social connections through digital platforms. Empirical evidence shows that E-commerce participation is positively associated with higher levels of reported happiness (Jin et al. 2020; Wang et al. 2025b; Wei et al. 2024a), suggesting that its benefits extend beyond material gains to broader life satisfaction.

1.3.2 Impact of E-Commerce Development on Agricultural Production

E-commerce development influences agricultural production through various channels that shape the utilization of land, inputs, technology, and markets. To capture these diverse effects, this section reviews the literature across five dimensions: land management, input management, technology adoption, farm performance, and market performance (See Table 1.3).

1.3.2.1 Land Management

E-commerce development can influence land use decisions by increasing the profitability of specific crops and facilitating specialization. Empirical evidence shows that it promotes the shift toward high-value cash crop production (Lu et al. 2025;

Table 1.3 Overview of literature examining the impact of E-commerce development on agricultural production

Indicators	Literature and findings
Land management	
High-value (cash) crop production	Increase (Lu et al. 2025; Yang et al. 2025)
Grassland utilization pressure	Decrease (Tian and Wu 2024)
Large-scale farming land	Increase (Liao et al. 2023; Zang et al. 2025)
Land abandonment	Increase (Zhou et al. 2024) Decrease (Wang et al. 2023)
Land transfer	Increase (Wang et al. 2024e; Zheng et al. 2025)
Input management	
Chemical fertilizer	Decrease (Cheng et al. 2024; Ji et al. 2023; Qiu et al. 2025b; Wang et al. 2022)
Organic fertilizer	Increase (Li et al. 2025b)
Pesticide	Decrease (Cheng et al. 2024; Wang et al. 2022)
Film consumption	Decrease (Cheng et al. 2024; Wang et al. 2022)
Technology adoption	
Awareness of green production	Increase (Wang et al. 2024a)
Green production technology	Increase (Li et al. 2021a, 2025b; Qiu et al. 2024a)
Mechanization	Increase (Lu and Yan 2025)
Water-saving irrigation	Increase (Cheng et al. 2024)
Farm performance	
Farm revenue	Increase (Yang et al. 2025)
Profit	Increase (Liu et al. 2024b)
Production cost	Increase (Liu et al. 2021, 2024b)
Technical efficiency	Increase (Chen et al. 2022; Yan and Liu 2023)
Market performance	
Market revenue	Increase (Liu et al. 2021, 2024b; Zapata et al. 2016)
Selling price	Increase (Liu et al. 2021, 2024a)

Source: Authors

Yang et al. 2025), reduces pressure on grassland utilization (Tian and Wu 2024), and supports the expansion of large-scale farming land (Liao et al. 2023; Zang et al. 2025). In addition, findings on the relationship between E-commerce development and land abandonment are mixed. Zhou et al. (2024) reported that E-commerce participation may increase abandonment. In contrast, Wang et al. (2023) found the opposite. Evidence on land transfer is more consistent. Studies show that E-commerce development facilitates land transfer (Wang et al. 2024e; Zheng et al. 2025), with more land flowing in and less flowing out (Wang et al. 2024e). This shift reflects how digital market opportunities can reshape land allocation within rural communities.

1.3.2.2 Input Management

Inputs in this review primarily refer to intermediate inputs such as chemical fertilizers, pesticides, and plastic film. A recurring pattern in the literature is that E-commerce development tends to reduce chemical fertilizer use while encouraging the adoption of organic alternatives. Several studies attribute the decline in chemical inputs (Cheng et al. 2024; Ji et al. 2023; Qiu et al. 2025b; Wang et al. 2022) to producers' incentives to adopt more sustainable practices. Evidence from Li et al. (2025b) suggests an increase in the use of organic fertilizers. As with fertilizer use, E-commerce participation is often linked to pesticide application and reductions in plastic film consumption. Two studies suggest that access to more discerning markets encourages farmers to limit the use of pesticides and film (Cheng et al. 2024; Wang et al. 2022).

1.3.2.3 Technology Adoption

Evidence consistently links E-commerce development to the adoption of modern and sustainable production technologies. Studies highlight that it enhances farmers' awareness of green production practices (Wang et al. 2024a) and promotes the actual adoption of environmentally friendly methods (Li et al. 2021a, 2025b; Qiu et al. 2024a). Li et al. (2025b) showed that E-commerce participation promotes the adoption of green production technologies by enhancing farmers' cognition and awareness of green production practices. In addition, E-commerce participation has been found to increase the use of agricultural mechanization (Lu and Yan 2025) and encourage broader implementation of water-saving irrigation systems (Cheng et al. 2024).

1.3.2.4 Farm Performance

E-commerce development appears to enhance multiple aspects of farm performance. Studies document increases in farm revenue (Yang et al. 2025) and profitability (Liu et al. 2024b), alongside gains in technical efficiency (Chen et al. 2022; Yan and Liu 2023). However, evidence also suggests higher production costs (Liu et al. 2021, 2024b), which may result from investments in quality improvement and technology adoption necessary to meet the standards of online markets. The literature suggests that while E-commerce development can improve farm performance, these gains may come at a higher cost.

1.3.2.5 Market Performance

The literature suggests that E-commerce participation can enhance market performance by expanding sales channels and improving price realization. Studies show increases in market revenue (Liu et al. 2021, 2024b; Zapata et al. 2016) and selling prices (Liu et al. 2021, 2024a), as well as growth in high-quality agricultural exports (Li et al. 2024b). Liu et al. (2024a) found that E-commerce participation increases farm-gate prices by extending the sales time and lengthening the sales period for agricultural products.

1.3.3 Impact of E-Commerce Development on Rural Development

E-commerce development shapes rural transformation beyond household- and farm-level outcomes. Its influence extends to broader dimensions of rural development, including human capital formation, labor allocation, sectoral economic development, and environmental sustainability. This section reviews the literature along these four dimensions (See Table 1.4).

Table 1.4 Overview of literature examining the impact of E-commerce development on rural development

Indicators	Literature and findings
Human capital development	
Work skills	Increase (Huang et al. 2020)
Non-agricultural employment	Increase (Qin et al. 2023; Zang et al. 2025) Decrease (Qi et al. 2019)
Employment quality	Increase (Wang and Wu 2025)
Entrepreneurship	Increase (Chang et al. 2024; Mei et al. 2020)
Women part-time employment	Increase (Li and Zhou 2025)
Women entrepreneurship	Increase (Dong et al. 2024)
Women empowerment	Decrease (Yu and Cui 2019) Increase (Wang et al. 2024c)
Labor allocation	
Local employment	Increase (Tao et al. 2025)
Return migration intention	Increase (Wang et al. 2024d)
Settlement intentions	Increase (Wei et al. 2025b)
Rural depopulation	Decrease (Zhao et al. 2024)

(continued)

Table 1.4 (continued)

Indicators	Literature and findings
Credit and financial accessibility	
Digital credit	Increase (Su et al. 2021; Yu and Xiang 2021)
Digital wealth management	Increase (Su et al. 2021)
Digital inclusive finance	Increase (Zhang and Zhao 2025)
Economic development	
Family farms	Increase (Lin and Li 2023)
Primary industry development	Increase (Qin et al. 2023; Qin and Fang 2022)
Village development	Increase (Zang et al. 2025)
Non-agricultural industry development	Increase (Hong and Su 2024)
Urban-rural integration	Increase (Bai et al. 2025)
Environmental sustainability	
Air pollution	Increase (Duan et al. 2024)
Agricultural non-point source pollution	Decrease (Han et al. 2023)
Carbon emissions	Decrease (Di and Qiu 2023; Du et al. 2023)
Clean energy transition	Increase (Cao et al. 2024)

Source: Authors

1.3.3.1 Human Capital Development

E-commerce development can enhance rural human capital by fostering new skills and reshaping labor-market participation. Evidence suggests that it enhances work-related skills (Huang et al. 2020) and promotes shifts toward non-agricultural employment (Qin et al. 2023; Zang et al. 2025), although some studies report the opposite effect, with reduced off-farm employment opportunities (Qi et al. 2019). Additionally, E-commerce participation is associated with improved employment quality (Wang and Wu 2025).

E-commerce development can stimulate entrepreneurial activity in rural areas by lowering market entry barriers and providing new sales channels. Studies report that it raises learning aspirations (Liu et al. 2025b) and increases overall entrepreneurship (Chang et al. 2024; Mei et al. 2020), including growth in women-led businesses (Dong et al. 2024). Beyond entrepreneurship, Li and Zhou (2025) showed that E-commerce development facilitates women's part-time employment, thereby diversifying labor opportunities. However, its impact on women's empowerment is not uniformly positive—Yu and Cui (2019) reported a decline.

1.3.3.2 Labor Allocation

E-commerce development influences where and how rural labor is allocated by creating local economic opportunities. Studies show that it boosts local employment (Tao et al. 2025) and strengthens rural settlement intentions (Wei et al. 2025b), while also increasing return migration intentions (Wang et al. 2024d). These dynamics contribute to declining rural depopulation rates (Zhao et al. 2024). Zhao et al. (2024) demonstrated that the REDC program increases rural income by creating employment opportunities and improving local public infrastructure and services, thereby facilitating labor mobility.

1.3.3.3 Economic Development

E-commerce development can stimulate growth in the agricultural sector by enhancing market connectivity and supporting rural industrial upgrading. Evidence shows that it promotes the expansion of family farms (Lin and Li 2023), fosters the development of the primary industry (Qin et al. 2023; Qin and Fang 2022), and contributes to broader village-level economic growth (Zang et al. 2025). Beyond agriculture, E-commerce development also contributes to the growth of rural non-agricultural industries. Studies indicate it supports non-agricultural industry development (Hong and Su 2024) and advances urban–rural integration (Bai et al. 2025). Bai et al. (2025) found that the pilot program promotes labor inflows into rural areas and increases investment in rural regions, thereby fostering more integrated urban–rural development at the county level. These findings highlight the role of E-commerce development as a driver of diversified economic development.

1.3.3.4 Environmental Sustainability

E-commerce development influences environmental sustainability by altering production practices, energy use, and market incentives for sustainability. While Duan et al. (2024) showed that it can exacerbate air pollution—possibly due to increased logistics and packaging—other studies report environmental benefits, including reductions in agricultural non-point source pollution (Han et al. 2023) and carbon emissions (Di and Qiu 2023; Du et al. 2023), as well as progress in the transition to clean energy (Cao et al. 2024).

1.4 Identifying Potential Research Gaps and Future Research Directions

While existing studies provide valuable insights, three key gaps remain. First, the reviewed literature is concentrated on China, limiting cross-country generalizability. Second, most studies examine only farmers' online sales while overlooking the roles of other stakeholders. Third, few studies assess the mechanisms underlying the impacts of E-commerce.

1.4.1 Cross-Country Comparative Studies

Nearly all reviewed studies (93 of 95) are based in China, with only isolated cases from Indonesia and the United States. While China provides a valuable policy laboratory—primarily through large-scale programs such as the NRECDC and Taobao Villages—the heavy concentration on a single country raises concerns about external validity. It remains unclear whether digital infrastructure, institutional arrangements, or platform-driven market integration operate similarly in other contexts. Moreover, theoretical pathways, such as reductions in transaction costs or gains in information efficiency, may differ across institutional settings. Future research should therefore draw on multi-country datasets or comparative frameworks to test the robustness of these mechanisms across diverse rural economies.

1.4.2 The Roles of Diverse Stakeholders

Many existing studies narrowly define E-commerce participation as farmers' online sales, often captured through a simple binary indicator. However, rural E-commerce ecosystems depend on a broader set of actors, including digital platforms, cooperatives, logistics and delivery networks, financial service providers, and local governments. These stakeholders influence heterogeneity in E-commerce outcomes by shaping information flows, entry barriers, and market access. Future studies should adopt more comprehensive measures of E-commerce participation and employ empirical strategies that explicitly account for stakeholder interactions and distributional consequences.

1.4.3 Mechanisms Underlying E-Commerce Impacts

Although numerous studies document positive or mixed effects of E-commerce development on household livelihoods, agricultural production, and rural development, the underlying mechanisms remain insufficiently examined. Most papers identify associations—for example, higher income or improved market access—without rigorously testing the channels through which these outcomes arise. Future research should therefore adopt clearer conceptual frameworks and empirical strategies to test how E-commerce development exerts its influence, distinguish competing pathways, and examine why impacts vary across contexts and population groups.

1.5 Conclusions and Implications

1.5.1 Conclusions

E-commerce development has emerged as a transformative force, reshaping household livelihoods, agricultural production, and broader rural development. This review systematically reviewed 95 studies to map the current evidence base. Diverse data types and methodological approaches characterize the selected literature.

Our synthesis across three domains reveals several clear patterns. At the household level, E-commerce participation tends to increase income, reduce poverty, improve consumption, and enhance subjective well-being, though the distribution of benefits varies across groups and regions. From the agricultural production perspective, E-commerce encourages the adoption of modern production technologies, improves input-use efficiency, and strengthens both farm and market performance. At the rural development level, E-commerce contributes to human capital enhancement, supports labor reallocation toward higher-productivity activities, and promotes the growth of both agricultural and non-agricultural sectors, while its environmental effects remain mixed across contexts.

1.5.2 Policy Implications

The analysis yields several actionable policy implications. First, although evidence on inequality and the urban–rural income gap is mixed, there is consistent heterogeneity in who benefits from E-commerce development. This suggests that policies should focus on removing participation barriers for vulnerable groups and lagging regions—for example, through targeted digital infrastructure investment and tailored platform-access support—to ensure a more inclusive distribution of E-commerce gains. Second, E-commerce development enhances farm and market performance, but it may also raise production costs. Policymakers should therefore support cost management and sustainable practices through measures such as logistics subsidies in remote areas, training on efficient use of inputs, and incentives to adopt environmentally friendly production methods. Third, since E-commerce development stimulates both agricultural and non-agricultural rural industries, policies should integrate E-commerce development with broader rural revitalization strategies. This includes strengthening entrepreneurship programs, upgrading local industries through digital technologies, and aligning E-commerce expansion with green transition initiatives to maximize long-term benefits for rural development.

Despite this review's strengths, it still has certain limitations. This review includes only studies published in English; relevant research in Chinese-language journals was not covered, potentially leading to partial omission of evidence from China. In addition, we could not pool them for a meta-analysis of their estimates because of significant heterogeneity across the identified studies. Future research could address this gap by providing a quantitative synthesis of the impacts of E-commerce development using formal meta-analytic methods.

Acknowledgements Hongyun Zheng acknowledges the financial support from the National Natural Science Foundation of China (72303076).

Data Availability Statement The data supporting this study's findings are available from Hongyun Zheng upon request.

Conflict of Interests There is no conflict of interest.

Ethics Statement Not applicable.

References

Abate, G.T., Abay, K.A., Chamberlin, J., Kassim, Y., Spielman, D.J., Paul Jr Tabe-Ojong, M., 2023. Digital tools and agricultural market transformation in Africa: Why are they not at scale yet, and what will it take to get there? *Food Policy* 116(March), 102439.

Ali Research, 2022. List of Taobao Villages in 2021. http://www.aliresearch.com/EN/index

Bai, Q., Zang, D., Zhang, J., Zhang, K., Chen, H., Pan, Y., Shen, Q., 2025. "Bridging the urban-rural divide": evaluating the impact of e-commerce pilots on urban-rural integration — evidence from a quasi-natural experiment in China's rural e-commerce construction policy. *Electronic Commerce Research* 1–33.

Baumüller, H., Ikpi, U., Jumpah, E.T., Kamau, G., Kergna, A.O., Mose, L., Nientao, A., Omari, R., Phillip, D., Salasya, B., 2023. Building digital bridges in African value chains: Exploring linkages between ICT use and social capital in agricultural marketing. *Journal of Rural Studies* 100(January), 103002.

Cao, A., Li, H., 2025. Revolutionizing Rural Poverty Reduction in China: The Impact of E-Commerce Strategies. *Agribusiness* (Steal 1972), 1–22.

Cao, A., Su, M., Li, H., 2024. Digitizing the green revolution: E-commerce as a catalyst for clean energy transition in rural China. *Energy Economics* 137(July), 107778.

Chang, Q., Wang, L., Li, J., 2024. Has e-commerce program affected the development of agribusiness in rural China, AgEcon Search. 1-23.

Chen, C., Gan, C., Li, J., Lu, Y., Rahut, D., 2023. Linking farmers to markets: Does cooperative membership facilitate e-commerce adoption and income growth in rural China? *Economic Analysis and Policy* 80(August), 1155–1170.

Chen, D., Guo, H., Zhang, Q., Jin, S., 2022. E-commerce Adoption and Technical Efficiency of Wheat Production in China. *Sustainability (Switzerland)* 14(3), 1–18.

Chen, W., Li, J., 2025. Digital finance, rural E-commerce development and consumption upgrading. *International Review of Financial Analysis* 104(May), 104351.

Cheng, X., Lv, H., Wang, Z., 2024. Enhancing environmental sustainability in transferred farmlands through rural e-commerce: insights from China. *Environmental Science and Pollution Research* 31(17), 25388–25405.

Chiaverina, P., Drogué, S., Jacquet, F., Lev, L., King, R., 2023. Does short food supply chain participation improve farm economic performance? A meta-analysis. *Agricultural Economics (United Kingdom)* (December 2022), 400–413.

Cordes, D.L., Marinova, D., 2023. Systematic literature review of the role of e-commerce in providing pathways to sustainability for poverty alleviation in Sub-Saharan Africa. *Discover Sustainability*, 4(1), 7.

Cui, Y., 2025. Influence of E-commerce on rural residents' income: a multi-time difference-in-differences model. *Electronic Commerce Research*, 1-19.

Dey, S., Singh, P.K., 2023. Role of market participation on smallholder vegetable farmers' wellbeing: Evidence from matching approach in Eastern India. *Agribusiness* 39(4), 1217–1237.

Di, L., Qiu, Z.-P., 2023. Can e-commerce reduce urban CO2 emissions? Evidence from National E-commerce Demonstration Cities policy in China. *Environmental Science and Pollution Research* 30(20), 58553–58568.

Dong, S., Wang, N., Fan, C., Chen, S., Zhang, L., 2024. E-commerce and rural women entrepreneurship — Based on the quasi-natural experiment of "comprehensive demonstration policy" for E-commerce in rural areas. *Economic Analysis and Policy* 83(July), 749–765.

Du, L., Wang, X., Zhang, S., 2023. Can rural e-commerce contribute to carbon reduction? A quasi-natural experiment based on China's e-commerce demonstration counties. *Environmental Science and Pollution Research* 30(47), 104336–104349.

Duan, W., Jiang, M., Qi, J., 2024. Poverty or pollution: The environmental cost of E-commerce for poverty reduction in China. *Journal of Environmental Economics and Management* 127(April), 103029.

Gao, Y., Yang, J., Zhao, J., Peng, H., 2025. Impact of developmental social policy on household welfare: Evidence from China's comprehensive demonstration policy for e-commerce in rural areas. *Economic Analysis and Policy* 86(February), 1820–1838.

Guan, X., He, L., Hu, Z., 2024. Impact of Rural E-Commerce on Farmers' Income and Income Gap. *Agriculture (Switzerland)* 14(10), 1–22.

Haji, K., 2021. E-commerce development in rural and remote areas of BRICS countries. *Journal of Integrative Agriculture* 20(4), 979–997.

Han, A., Liu, P., Wang, B., Zhu, A., 2023. E-commerce development and its contribution to agricultural non-point source pollution control: Evidence from 283 cities in China. *Journal of Environmental Management* 344(July), 118613.

He, B., Xu, D., Nan, G., Zhang, X., Yu, X., 2024. Does the cross-border e-commerce comprehensive pilot zones policy affect the urban–rural income gap in China? *American Journal of Economics and Sociology* 83(4), 773–792.

Hong, Q., Su, J., 2024. The impact of rural e-commerce platforms on the transformation of industrial structure: Evidence from China. *Review of Development Economics* 28(3), 1267–1291.

Hou, J., Liu, Y., 2024. Assessing the impact of rural E-commerce on regional poverty alleviation: A spatial spillover analysis. *International Review of Economics and Finance* 94(June), 103399.

Huang, C.C., Jin, H., Zhang, J., Zheng, Q., Chen, Y., Cheung, S., Liu, C., 2020. The effects of an innovative e-commerce poverty alleviation platform on Chinese rural laborer skills development and family well-being. *Children and Youth Services Review* 116(June), 105189.

Huang, J., Su, L., Huang, Q., Liu, X., 2022. Facilitating inclusive ICT application and e-Commerce development in rural China. *Agricultural Economics (United Kingdom)* 53(6), 938–952.

Huang, Z., Wang, L., Meng, J., 2024. Does rural e-commerce improve the economic resilience of family farms? *International Review of Economics and Finance* 95(August), 103505.

Ji, X., Xu, J., Zhang, H., 2023. Environmental effects of rural e-commerce: A case study of chemical fertilizer reduction in China. *Journal of Environmental Management* 326, 116713.

Jin, H., Li, L., Qian, X., Zengd, Y., 2020. Can rural e-commerce service centers improve farmers' subject well-being? A new practice of 'internet plus rural public services' from China. *International Food and Agribusiness Management Review* 23(5), 681–695.

Lee, M., Gambiza, J., 2022. The adoption of conservation agriculture by smallholder farmers in southern Africa: A scoping review of barriers and enablers. *Journal of Rural Studies* 92(September 2021), 214–225.

Li, A.H.F., 2017. E-commerce and Taobao Villages. *China Perspectives* 2017(3), 57–62.

Li, B., Xu, C., Zhu, Z., Kong, F., 2021a. Does e-commerce drive rural households engaged in non-timber forest product operations to adopt green production behaviors? *Journal of Cleaner Production* 320(November 2020), 128855.

Li, G., Qin, J., 2022. Income effect of rural E-commerce: Empirical evidence from Taobao villages in China. *Journal of Rural Studies* 96(December 2020), 129–140.

Li, Junpeng, Ma, W., Zhu, H., 2024a. A systematic literature review of factors influencing the adoption of climate-smart agricultural practices. *Mitigation and Adaptation Strategies for Global Change* 29(1), 1–38.

Li, Jia, Shi, J., Cao, R., Wu, J., Liu, J., 2024b. How e-commerce can boost China's high-quality agricultural exports. *Frontiers in Sustainable Food Systems*, 8, 1372129.

Li, L., Zeng, Y., Ye, Z., Guo, H., 2021b. E-commerce development and urban-rural income gap: Evidence from Zhejiang Province, China. *Papers in Regional Science* 100(2), 475–494.

Li, Q., Xie, M., Tang, Y., 2025a. Do the E-commerce-induced business clusters increase the income of local rural households? *Economic Analysis and Policy* 86(May), 1510–1526.

Li, W., He, W., 2024. Revenue-increasing effect of rural e-commerce: A perspective of farmers' market integration and employment growth. *Economic Analysis and Policy* 81(November 2023), 482–493.

Li, X., Guo, H., Jin, S., Ma, W., Zeng, Y., 2021c. Do farmers gain internet dividends from E-commerce adoption? Evidence from China. *Food Policy* 101(April 2020), 102024.

Li, X., Li, Y., Chen, Z., 2024c. Impact of Rural E-Commerce Participation on Farmers' Household Development Resilience: Evidence from 1229 Farmers in China. *Agriculture (Switzerland)* 14(5), 692.

Li, Y., Zhou, L., 2025. E-commerce development, time allocation and the gender division of labour: evidence from rural China. *Applied Economics Letters* 32(3), 373–378.

Li, Z., Gao, K., Qiao, G., 2025b. From Online Markets to Green Fields: Unpacking the Impact of Farmers' E-Commerce Participation on Green Production Technology Adoption. *Agriculture (Switzerland)* 15(14), 1–31.

Liao, Y., Wu, G., Huang, J., 2023. The Impact of Rural E-Commerce Environment Development on Orchard Expansion from the Perspective of Tele-Coupling: The Case of Pinghe County in Southeast China. *Land* 12(11), 1991.

Lin, Y., Li, C., 2023. Does rural e-commerce agglomeration help expand family farms' size? Evidence from Taobao villages in China's Yangtze River Delta. *Electronic Commerce Research* 23(3), 1731–1752.

Liu, M., Liu, T., Ren, Y., Wu, L., 2024a. How Does the Adoption of e-Commerce Impact the Selling Prices of Agricultural Products? Empirical Evidence From Apple Farmers in China. *Review of Development Economics* 1–22.

Liu, M., Min, S., Ma, W., Liu, T., 2021. The adoption and impact of E-commerce in rural China: Application of an endogenous switching regression model. *Journal of Rural Studies* 83(3), 106–116.

Liu, S., Jin, Y., Zheng, F., 2024b. Did product certification and e-commerce benefit agricultural producers in China? *Food Policy* 127(July), 102688.

Liu, Xinyu, Li, S., Huang, J., Xiao, H., 2025a. Transforming consumption: How E-commerce reshape online shopping behavior and household spending. *China Economic Review* 92(May), 102444.

Liu, Xiaotong, Ma, Y., Li, Y., Li, B., Xia, Y., 2025b. Shaping learning aspirations: the influence of E-commerce clusters on rural entrepreneurs. *Electronic Commerce Research*, 1-30.

Liu, Y., Zhou, M., 2023. Can rural e-commerce narrow the urban–rural income gap? Evidence from coverage of Taobao villages in China. *China Agricultural Economic Review* 15(3), 580–603.

Liu, Y., Zhou, M., Li, Q., 2025c. How penetration of e-commerce in rural areas drives consumption in China. *China Agricultural Economic Review* 17(2), 339–357.

Lu, F., Yan, L., 2025. Rural E-Commerce and Agricultural Mechanization. *Applied Spatial Analysis and Policy* 18(2), 61.

Lu, H., Sun, G., Zhou, L., Zhang, W., Zou, J., 2025. The impact and mechanism of E-commerce of agricultural products on nongrain production of cultivated land in rural China. *Journal of Environmental Management* 373, 123639.

Luo, Y., Zhou, L., Zhang, W., 2025. Can e-commerce bring dividends to rural households? New evidence from the income inequality perspective. *Economic Analysis and Policy* 86(January), 363–379.

Lyu, D., Zhou, L., Ma, X., 2022. Income-increasing effect of e-commerce of agricultural products based on IT absorptive theory. *Wireless Networks* 28(5), 2337–2344.

Ma, W., Vatsa, P., Zheng, H., Guo, Y., 2022. Does online food shopping boost dietary diversity? Application of an endogenous switching model with a count outcome variable. *Agricultural and Food Economics* 10(1), 30.

Ma, X., Komatsu, S., 2025. Impact of e-commerce on income inequality: evidence from rural China based on cross-county panel data. *Information Technology for Development* 31(3), 635–663.

Mei, Y., Lin, N., Hu, B., Zhang, X., 2025. Is e-commerce widening or narrowing the income distribution gap among Chinese households? *China Agricultural Economic Review* 17(4), 589-606.

Mei, Y., Mao, D., Lu, Y., Chu, W., 2020. Effects and mechanisms of rural E-commerce clusters on households' entrepreneurship behavior in China. *Growth and Change* 51(4), 1588–1610.

Meinzen-dick, R., Quisumbing, A., Doss, C., Theis, S., 2019. Women ' s land rights as a pathway to poverty reduction : Framework and review of available evidence. *Agricultural Systems* 172(November 2017), 72–82.

Ministry of Commerce, 2025. The director of the Commerce Ministry's Department of Circulation Development talked about the development situation of the wholesale and retail industries in China in 2024. [WWW Document].

Nogueira, G.P.M., Silva, S.V., Hasenclever, L., de Assis Rangel, J.J., 2025. Sustainability in B2C e-commerce: a literature review and future research opportunities in last-mile deliveries. *Environment, Development and Sustainability*, 27(6), 12415-12436.

OECD, 2011. OECD guide to measuring the information society 2011.

Permani, R., 2023. Do online agri-food sellers contribute to food security in Indonesia? A PCA-based composite index and a Tobit approach. *Food Security* 15(6), 1541–1561.

Qi, J., Zheng, X., Cao, P., Zhu, L., 2019. The effect of e-commerce agribusiness clusters on farmers' migration decisions in China. *Agribusiness* 35(1), 20–35.

Qin, Q., Guo, H., Shi, X., Chen, K., 2023. Rural E-commerce and County Economic Development in China. *China and World Economy* 31(5), 26–60.

Qin, Y., Fang, Y., 2022. The Effects of E-Commerce on Regional Poverty Reduction: Evidence from China's Rural E-Commerce Demonstration County Program. *China and World Economy* 30(3), 161–186.

Qiu, H., Deng, H., Lu, M., Luo, L., Chen, X., Wang, Z., 2025a. The Impact of Rural E-Commerce on Farmers' Income Gap: Implications for Farmers' Sustainable Development. *Sustainability (Switzerland)* 17(9), 1–23.

Qiu, H., Huang, Y., Zhang, W., He, B., Yuan, R., Wang, Z., 2025b. E-commerce operation empowers green agriculture: implication for the reduction of farmers' fertilizer usage. *Frontiers in Sustainable Food Systems* 9, 1557224.

Qiu, H., Tang, W., Huang, Y., Deng, H., Liao, W., Ye, F., 2024a. E-commerce operations and technology perceptions in promoting farmers' adoption of green production technologies: Evidence from rural China. *Journal of Environmental Management* 370(1101), 122628.

Qiu, H., Zhang, X., Feng, M., Zhang, Z., Wang, J., Wang, Z., 2024b. Exploring the Income-Increasing Benefits of Rural E-Commerce in China: Implications for the Sustainable Development of Farmers. *Sustainability (Switzerland)* 16(17), 7437.

Reardon, T., Belton, B., Liverpool-Tasie, L.S.O., Lu, L., Nuthalapati, C.S.R., Tasie, O., Zilberman, D., 2021. E-commerce's fast-tracking diffusion and adaptation in developing countries. *Applied Economic Perspectives and Policy* 43(4), 1243–1259.

Salemink, K., Strijker, D., Bosworth, G., 2017. Rural development in the digital age: A systematic literature review on unequal ICT availability, adoption, and use in rural areas. *Journal of Rural Studies* 54, 360–371.

Shen, J., Zhu, Z., Qaim, M., Fan, S., Tian, X., 2023. E-commerce improves dietary quality of rural households in China. *Agribusiness* 39(S1), 1495–1511.

Siegle, J., Astill, G., Plakias, Z., Tregeagle, D., 2024. Estimating perennial crop supply response: A methodology literature review. *Agricultural Economics (United Kingdom)* 55(2), 159–180.

Su, L., Peng, Y., Kong, R., Chen, Q., 2021. Impact of e-commerce adoption on farmers' participation in the digital financial market: Evidence from rural China. *Journal of Theoretical and Applied Electronic Commerce Research* 16(5), 1434–1457.

Sun, Y., Yuan, Y., Wang, L., 2025. Build or Break? The Impact of Rural E-Commerce on Household Income Inequality in China. *Review of Development Economics* 1–21.

Tabe Ojong, M.P.J.R., Hauser, M., Mausch, K., 2022. Does Agricultural Commercialisation Increase Asset and Livestock Accumulation on Smallholder Farms in Ethiopia? *Journal of Development Studies* 58(3), 524–544.

Tang, K., Xiong, Q., Zhang, F., 2022. Can the E-commercialization improve residents' income? -- Evidence from "Taobao Counties" in China. *International Review of Economics and Finance* 78(September 2021), 540–553.

Tang, L., Chen, M., Tang, Y., Xiong, Y., 2024. Can E-commerce development alleviate farm household poverty vulnerability: Evidence from rural China. *Cities* 153(November 2023), 105297.

Tang, W., Zhu, J., 2020. Informality and rural industry: Rethinking the impacts of E-Commerce on rural development in China. *Journal of Rural Studies* 75, 20–29.

Tao, S., Wang, Q., Zhu, T., 2025. The Role of E-Commerce in Promoting Sustainable Local Employment in Rural Areas: Evidence from China. *Sustainability (Switzerland)* 17(12). 5641.

Tian, M., Wu, Y., 2024. E-Commerce Participation, Subjective Norms and Grassland Utilization Pressure: An Empirical Evidence of Herdsmen in Inner Mongolia, China. *Agriculture (Switzerland)* 14(5), 690.

Tuni, A., Rentizelas, A., Chipula, G., 2022. Barriers to commercialise produce for smallholder farmers in Malawi: An interpretive structural modelling approach. *Journal of Rural Studies* 93(May), 1–17.

Wang, B., Liu, P., Han, A., 2025a. Can E-commerce development improve farmers' incomes? Evidence from prefecture-level data and the spatial difference-in-difference approach. *Australian Journal of Agricultural and Resource Economics* 69(2), 344–368.

Wang, C., Tong, Q., Xia, C., Shi, M., Cai, Y., 2024a. Does participation in e-commerce affect fruit farmers' awareness of green production: evidence from China. *Journal of Environmental Planning and Management* 67(4), 809–829.

Wang, C.C., Miao, J.T., Phelps, N.A., Zhang, J., 2021. E-commerce and the transformation of the rural: The Taobao village phenomenon in Zhejiang Province, China. *Journal of Rural Studies* 81(September 2020), 159–169.

Wang, H., Fang, L., Mao, H., Chen, S., 2022. Can e-commerce alleviate agricultural non-point source pollution? — A quasi-natural experiment based on a China's E-Commerce Demonstration City. *Science of the Total Environment* 846(July), 157423.

Wang, L., Lyu, S., Zhou, L., 2025b. Rural e-commerce and happiness: evidence from China. *Electronic Commerce Research*, 1-41.

Wang, M., Ding, X., Cheng, P., 2024b. Exploring the income impact of rural e-commerce comprehensive demonstration project and determinants of county selection. *Humanities and Social Sciences Communications* 11(1). 1-11.

Wang, Xinya, Liu, S., Liu, R., 2024c. E-commerce development and women's family empowerment: evidence from China. *Applied Economics Letters,* 33(1), 1-5.

Wang, Xiumei, Yi, F., Cai, Y., 2024d. The effect of rural e-commerce development on return migration intentions: evidence from the China migrants dynamic survey. *Applied Economics Letters* 31(20), 2104–2109.

Wang, Y., Wang, W., Jiang, X., Wang, H., 2024e. The Impact of Farmers' E-Commerce Adoption on Land Transfer: Evidence from Ten Provinces across China. *Land* 13(7), 1066.

Wang, Y., Wu, Y., 2025. Digital Economy, Rural E-Commerce Development, and Farmers' Employment Quality. *Sustainability (Switzerland)* 17(7), 1–20.

Wang, Y., Yang, A., Li, Y., Yang, Q., 2023. Effect of e-commerce popularization on farmland abandonment in rural China: Evidence from a large-scale household survey. *Land Use Policy* 135(September), 106958.

Wang, Y., Zhang, Z., 2025. Start a business or get a job? Rethinking the impacts of e-commerce on household income in China. *Applied Economics*, 1–18.

Wang, Z.Y., Zhou, J., Wang, Q.J., Zheng, M.T., 2025c. Foster the household consumption of rural residents: does the rural e-commerce matter?, *Electronic Commerce Research*, 1-31.

Wei, B., Luo, M., Zhao, C., 2025a. Bridging the gap: the effect of rural e-commerce development on internal income inequality in China. *Applied Economics* 57(27), 3776–3795.

Wei, B., Zhao, C., Cai, W., Luo, M., 2025b. Online markets, offline homes: E-commerce development and rural migrant workers' urban settlement intentions in China. *Cities* 161(483), 105867.

Wei, B., Zhao, C., Luo, M., 2024a. Online markets, offline happiness: E-commerce development and subjective well-being in rural China. *China Economic Review* 87(August), 102247.

Wei, X., Yang, Z., Yan, Y., Sun, J., 2024b. Rural E-commerce, Digital finance, and urban–rural common prosperity: A Quasi-natural Experiment Based on China's Comprehensive Demonstration of E-commerce Entering Rural Areas Policy. *Finance Research Letters* 69(PB), 106237.

Wen, H., Qiu, A., Huang, Y., 2024. Impact of e-commerce development on rural income: Evidence from counties in revolutionary old areas of China. *Economic and Labour Relations Review* 345–367.

Wever, H., Michels, M., Musshoff, O., 2024. Unearthing the behavioural factors influencing commodity futures contracts adoption in agriculture—A systematic literature review. *Australian Journal of Agricultural and Resource Economics* 68(4), 931–947.

Yan, B., Liu, T., 2023. Can E-Commerce Adoption Improve Agricultural Productivity? Evidence from Apple Growers in China. *Sustainability (Switzerland)* 15(1), 1–16.

Yang, Y., Wang, F., Tang, B., 2025. The impact and mechanism of e-commerce on rural agriculture: Evidence from China. *NJAS: Impact in Agricultural and Life Sciences* 97(1), 2523380.

Ye, Y., Fang, J., Ye, J., 2024. Does E-Commerce Construction Boost Farmers' Incomes? Evidence from China. *Sustainability (Switzerland)* 16(11), 4595.

Yu, G., Xiang, H., 2021. Rural E-commerce development and farmers' digital credit behavior: Evidence from China family panel studies. *PLoS ONE* 16(10 October), 1–21.

Yu, H., Cui, L., 2019. China's E-Commerce: Empowering Rural Women? *China Quarterly* 238(February), 418–437.

Zang, Y., Hu, S., Li, J., Lv, L., Man, Z., Tan, Y., 2025. Reconfiguring rural development: Spatial diffusion of E-Commerce and its multifaceted effects. *Habitat International* 163(8), 103496.

Zangue, Y.D., Melot, R., Martin, P., 2022. Diversity of farmland management practices (FMP) and their nexus to environment: A review. *Journal of Environmental Management* 302(November 2021), 114059.

Zant, W., 2023. Mobile Phones and Mozambique Traders: Size, Composition and Distribution of Reduced Transaction Costs. *Food Policy* 116(February), 102423.

Zapata, S.D., Isengildina-Massa, O., Carpio, C.E., Lamie, R.D., 2016. Does E-Commerce Help Farmers' Markets? Measuring the Impact of MarketMaker. *Journal of Food Distribution Research* 47(2), 1–18.

Zhang, H., Millan, E., Money, K., Guo, P., 2025a. E-commerce development, poverty reduction and income growth in rural China. *Journal of Strategy and Management* 18(1), 148–176.

Zhang, N., Yang, W., Ke, H., 2024. Does rural e-commerce drive up incomes for rural residents? Evidence from Taobao villages in China. *Economic Analysis and Policy* 82(November 2023), 976–998.

Zhang, Y., Wu, X., Cai, R., 2025b. The effects of rural e-commerce on income inequality: evidence from the National Rural E-Commerce Comprehensive Demonstration policy in China. *Economic Analysis and Policy* 87(May), 221–234.
Zhang, Y.F., Zhao, H., 2025. The effect of E-commerce on digital inclusive finance: evidence from the E-commerce boom in rural China. *Cogent Economics and Finance* 13(1), 2460082.
Zhao, J., Zheng, J., Li, T., 2024. Does e-commerce offer a solution to rural depopulation? Evidence from China. *Cities* 152(November 2023), 105155.
Zheng, H., Ma, W., 2025. Online food shopping and nutrition inequality among rural children. *Review of Economics of the Household*, 1-18.
Zheng, H., Ma, W., 2021. Click it and buy happiness: does online shopping improve subjective well-being of rural residents in China? *Applied Economics* 53(36), 4192–4206.
Zheng, L., Li, L., Jin, S., 2025. Opening the Village Door: China's Agricultural E-Commerce Facilitates the Transformation of Land Rental Markets. *Agricultural Economics (United Kingdom)* (2), 1–15.
Zheng, S., Yu, L., Fu, H., 2024. Has Rural E-Commerce Increased Potato Farmers' Income? Evidence from the Potato Home of China. *Potato Research* 67(1), 15–35.
Zhou, R., Ji, M., Zhao, S., 2024. Does E-Commerce Participation among Farming Households Affect Farmland Abandonment? Evidence from a Large-Scale Survey in China. *Land* 13(3), 376.

Chapter 2
Pathways to Rural E-Commerce: A Systematic Review of Drivers, Barriers, and Policy Implications

Junpeng Li, Wanglin Ma, Die Hu, and Dil B. Rahut

2.1 Introduction

It is a pressing and arduous task to reduce poverty, promote sustainable agriculture, and improve people's objective and subjective well-being in rural areas. In particular, around 79% of the world's impoverished population lives in rural areas, and the poverty incidence rate in rural areas is 17.2%, which is over three times that of urban areas (UNDP 2021). However, the process of overcoming rural poverty is constrained by resource scarcity, environmental degradation, and stagnation in human development (Li et al. 2025b). As it stands, strategies that can simultaneously achieve poverty mitigation, sustainable agricultural production, and long-term human development are necessary.

Advancing rural e-commerce is considered a complementary strategy (Cui et al. 2019). In particular, e-commerce effectively connects smallholder farmers with markets, enabling them to optimize their agricultural inputs and product sales (Gao and Liu 2020). This can render agricultural production both economically viable and sustainable in the long run. Moreover, e-commerce allows farmers to diversify

J. Li
Business School, Huaiyin Normal University, Huai'an, People's Republic of China

W. Ma (✉)
Department of Global Value Chains and Trade, Faculty of Agribusiness and Commerce, Lincoln University, Christchurch, New Zealand
e-mail: Wanglin.Ma@lincoln.ac.nz

D. Hu
School of International Communication, Wuhan Business University, Wuhan, Hubei, People's Republic of China

D. B. Rahut
Asian Development Bank Institute (ADBI), Tokyo, Japan
e-mail: drahut@adbi.org

W. Ma et al. (eds.), *E-Commerce for Inclusive Rural and Agricultural Development*, Contributions to Economics,
https://doi.org/10.1007/978-981-92-5237-4_2

their income sources (Liu et al. 2025), enhancing their economic performance and resilience. Previous studies have confirmed that rural e-commerce is effective in increasing agricultural income (Komatsu and Suzuki 2025), reducing rural poverty (Qin and Fang 2022), improving farmers' subjective well-being (Li et al. 2023), and averting environmental degradation induced by agricultural production (Wang et al. 2023a, b). Accordingly, it is urgently necessary to penetrate e-commerce in rural areas (Li et al. 2021a, b). Therefore, identifying pathways to rural e-commerce development is crucial.

A growing body of literature has investigated the determinants of rural e-commerce development from multiple dimensions. For instance, Chen et al. (2021a, b) found that education is positively correlated with farmers' adoption of e-commerce in rural China. Raza et al. (2025) suggested that farmers' digital literacy drives them to participate in e-commerce in Pakistan. Gao and Qiao (2025) found that enriching farmers' social capital can promote their adoption of e-commerce in China. There is no doubt that previous studies have successfully unlocked strategies to advance rural e-commerce. However, the penetration rate of rural e-commerce in most developing countries remains low. For instance, Ariansyah et al. (2021) found that the rural e-commerce adoption rate in Indonesia reached only 28.80%. The proportion of e-commerce adopters in the Quang Doan et al. (2024) sample from Northern Vietnam was 50.71%. Wang et al. (2024a, b) reported that 67.30% of their sample from rural China used e-commerce. Accordingly, more effort is urgently needed to develop effective strategies to popularize rural e-commerce in developing settings.

To a great extent, synthesizing existing findings is more significant than conducting new research. For rural e-commerce development, reviewing previous studies on its determinants can help identify and formulate effective channels to improve it. Several studies have devoted considerable effort to this point (Altarturi et al. 2025; Cordes and Marinova 2023; Gupta and Sharma 2018; Loo et al. 2024; Nogueira et al. 2025; Soleimani 2022; Thenoz et al. 2024). For instance, Nogueira et al. (2025) examined the determinants of rural e-commerce, with a special emphasis on delivery services. Soleimani (2022) and Thenoz et al. (2024) reviewed the literature on the impact of trustworthiness, institutional factors, and farmers' organizations, respectively. Unarguably, prior literature reviews help deepen people's knowledge of the determinants of rural e-commerce development. However, one has to admit that they only focus on a typical aspect of rural e-commerce. Thus, a comprehensive literature review of the factors influencing rural e-commerce development is currently absent.

Our study expands the scope of existing studies in four key areas. First, we provide a systematic review of the determinants of rural e-commerce development. By doing so, our study can significantly enhance our understanding of the factors influencing rural e-commerce development. More importantly, our study can refine practical strategies to advance rural e-commerce. Second, our study proposes a comprehensive definition of rural e-commerce. In our humble view, a comprehensive definition of rural e-commerce has yet to be established in academic research. Our study fills this gap, clarifying the focal points of research and policy design.

Third, we traced and discussed the theoretical foundations of rural e-commerce determinants. This can facilitate a deeper understanding of the association between determinants and rural e-commerce development. Fourth, our study also highlights gaps in the prior literature. This can not only clarify the future research priorities but also facilitate the government in designing suitable policy instruments to foster rural e-commerce development.

To achieve this, our study reviewed 105 literature published between 2015 and 2026 obtained from publicly accessible sources (e.g., Google Scholar, ScienceDirect, and academic journal websites). The determinants of rural e-commerce development were discussed under three categories: individual and household characteristics, institutional factors, and other factors. As a result, drivers of rural e-commerce development were comprehensively identified. Meanwhile, this study also summarized the research gaps existing in previous studies. With these efforts, the present study can effectively support policymakers and scholars in pursuing targeted endeavors to boost rural e-commerce development.

The remaining parts of the paper are structured as follows. Section 2.2 provides a brief introduction to the definition of rural e-commerce. Section 2.3 details the theoretical foundations, process of literature collection, and descriptive analysis. Section 2.4 discusses the representative determinants of rural e-commerce development as documented in previous studies, followed by an interpretation of the research gaps and future research recommendations in Sect. 2.5. Finally, Sect. 2.6 highlights the conclusions, policy implications, and research limitations.

2.2 Rural e-Commerce Definition

Clearly defining the rural e-commerce streamlines our literature collection and helps sharpen the focus of our research. In our humble view, there is no universally agreed-upon definition of rural e-commerce. In response, we follow Yildirim (2022) and use the inductive approach to define rural e-commerce comprehensively. This strategy contains two steps. The first step is to assemble the characteristics of rural e-commerce. In the next step, the definition of rural e-commerce can be refined by integrating its defining characteristics.

According to reality and existing literature, rural e-commerce possesses four typical characteristics. First, rural e-commerce transactions encompass agricultural production inputs, services, and products, as well as goods essential for the daily lives of rural residents (Chen and Li 2025). Second, rural e-commerce is driven by information and communication technologies (ICTs), including the internet, smartphones, and online platforms (Rahayu and Day 2015). Third, rural e-commerce operates irrespective of temporal and spatial constraints but relies heavily on transportation and delivery services (Huang et al. 2024a, b). Fourth, rural e-commerce connects smallholder farmers to the broader market (Ma et al. 2019), which is facilitated by rural residents or their agents (e.g., farmers' organizations).

Based on its characteristics, we can define rural e-commerce as:

Rural e-commerce refers to the ICT-enabled trading of agricultural and daily-life goods and services by rural residents or their agents, operating beyond temporal and spatial constraints, and connecting rural economies with broader markets, underpinned by transportation infrastructure and logistics.

2.3 Literature Collection and Descriptive Statistics

2.3.1 Theoretical Foundations

Articulating the relevant theoretical foundations can provide a clearer roadmap for collecting and analyzing the literature. Overall, the human capital theory, social capital theory, transaction cost economics, and the household production and livelihood framework serve as the four theoretical pillars of the literature on the determinants of rural e-commerce participation and performance. In particular, rural e-commerce is a knowledge and technology-intensive activity that requires farmers to acquire, process, and apply market and platform-related information. For instance, effectively using e-commerce platforms requires farmers to have the knowledge and skills to promote their products, publish product information, and analyze supply–demand conditions (Doanh et al. 2022). Thus, the human capital theory can be used to select and discuss related literature.

Essentially, e-commerce participation is a behavior that involves establishing contact with the outside world (Chen et al. 2023). For instance, effective connections among supervisors, buyers, and peers are considered a prerequisite for adopting e-commerce (Shiu et al. 2023). Therefore, the impact of social connection-related factors on rural e-commerce can be explained by the social capital theory.

The profit from rural e-commerce is primarily subject to transaction costs. Thus, as widely observed, one of the most important tasks for stakeholders (e.g., the government, farmers, and farmers' organizations) is to reduce the transaction costs of rural e-commerce. Accordingly, the theory of transaction cost economics provides the theoretical foundation for the literature focusing on the determinants of rural e-commerce (Li and He 2024; Liu et al. 2021).

In reality, farmers' participation in specific economic activities depends on their pursuit of maximizing utility. In this case, farmers' behavior, such as participation in rural e-commerce, tends to be determined by their household resource endowment and external shocks that shape constraints and incentives (Bozzola and Finger 2021; Keenan et al. 2024). Thus, the related literature can be included within the scope of household production and the livelihood framework.

2.3.2 Literature Collection

The literature discussed in this study is drawn from open, publicly accessible sources, including Google Scholar, ScienceDirect, Web of Science, and relevant journal websites (e.g., Electronic Commerce Research and the Journal of Rural Studies). We followed the Preferred Reporting Items for Systematic Reviews and Meta-Analysis (PRISMA) 2020 guidelines to enhance the transparency and reproducibility of the literature considered in our study. Figure 2.1 illustrates the process of literature collection and cleaning.

First, to center our discussion on the determinants of rural e-commerce development, we search for literature according to the following criteria: First, the literature should focus on rural e-commerce development; Second, the literature should contain considerable content to discuss the pathway to advance rural e-commerce; Third, the literature should be publicly published and accessible; Fourth, to ensure the timeliness of our study, we mainly comb literature published between 2015 and 2026. We select 2015 as the starting year of our study period for two main reasons. One reason is that 2015 is recognized as a global turning point where mobile broadband and smartphones reached mass diffusion in developing countries, making rural e-commerce feasible (Zeng 2015). Another reason is that the post-2015 SDG agenda triggered a surge of empirical work treating rural e-commerce as a key development instrument (Li et al. 2021a, b; Liu et al. 2021). Fifth, keywords including "rural e-commerce", "determinants", "factors", "online sales", "e-commerce entrepreneurship", "e-commerce adoption", "e-commerce participation", and "e-commercialization" were used to identify and download literature. Initially, we obtained 150 journal articles.

Second, we conduct an explicit literature review to ensure that the literature aligns with our topic. The inclusion criteria include: (1) papers focusing on rural e-commerce or closely related forms of digital platforms connecting rural producers to markets; (2) papers investigating the determinants, drivers, and barriers of rural e-commerce development, adoption, and participation; (3) papers offering empirical or theoretical evidence related to our research objective. The exclusion criteria include: (1) conceptual papers provide no clear implications to rural e-commerce; (2) studies pertain to general digitalization without rural or e-commerce components; (3) commentaries, news pieces, and editorials; and (4) duplicates. In practice, 23 records were excluded (e.g., because they did not focus on rural contexts, did not address e-commerce, or did not discuss determinants). The full texts of the remaining 127 records were then assessed in detail, leading to the exclusion of an additional 22 records due to insufficient information on determinants or irrelevance to our research questions. As a result, 105 literature items are reviewed in the present study.

To reduce selection bias, three researchers independently screened all titles/abstracts and full texts.[1] Discrepancies were discussed and resolved by consensus, and, where necessary, a third senior researcher was consulted.

[1] In addition to the first author, two co-authors were involved in the processes of literature collection and cleaning.

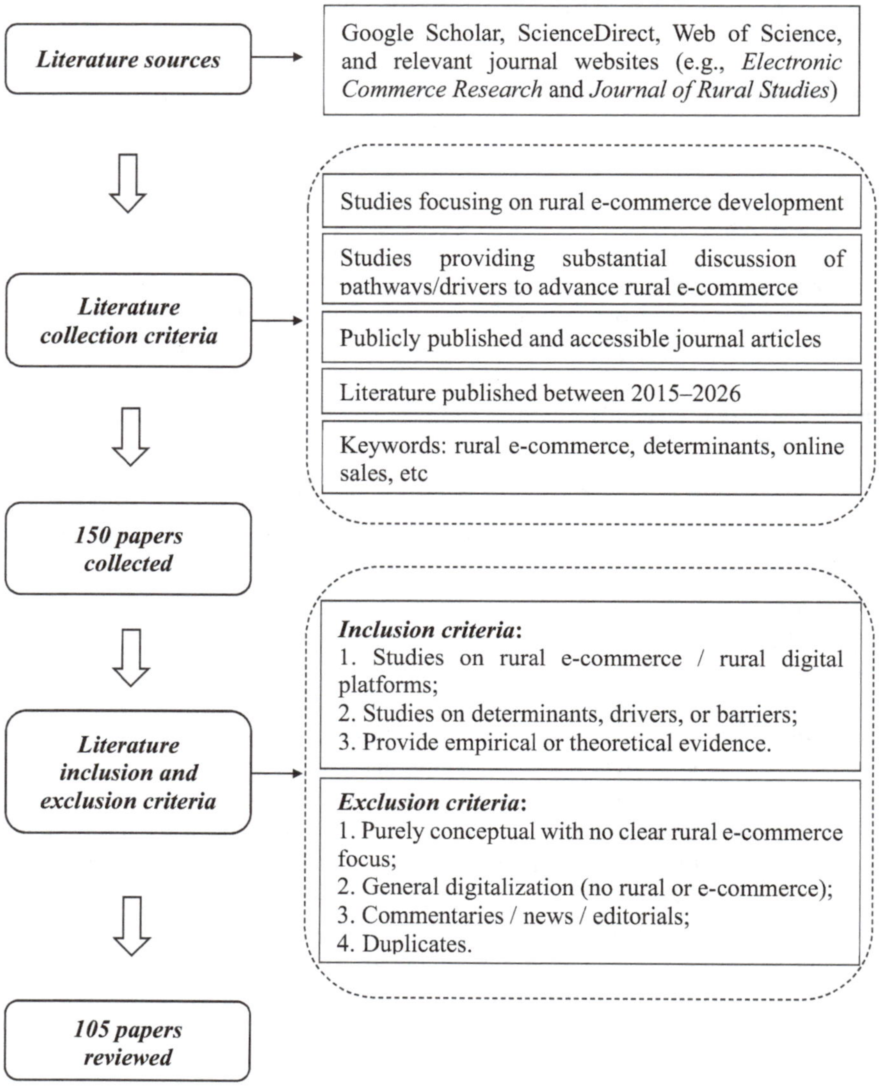

Source: Authors.

Fig. 2.1 The process of literature collection and cleaning. Source: Authors

2.3.3 *Descriptive Statistics*

Figure 2.2 illustrates the distribution of literature across the study period. Generally, publications on the determinants of rural e-commerce development show an upward trend from 2015 to 2026. Especially after 2020, the number of literature published increased from under 4 to over 10 per year. In 2024 and 2025, the literature on the topic reached 19 and 23, respectively. In early 2026, 3 studies focusing on the determinants of rural e-commerce were published. At this pace, about 36 relevant studies are expected to be published in 2026. This strongly suggests that scholars worldwide are increasingly committed to exploring effective strategies for advancing rural e-commerce development.

More importantly, the substantial increase in literature publication after 2020 is consistent with reality. That is, the COVID-19 pandemic outbreak at the end of 2019 restricted people's mobility and increased demand for online transactions (Chmielarz et al. 2022). Put another way, the COVID-19 pandemic is regarded as a pivotal point in the development of rural e-commerce. To improve the development of rural e-commerce, an increasing number of scholars have been involved in investigating its determinants. Considering the long publication cycle, it is understandable why the relevant literature experienced a substantial surge in 2021.

Figure 2.3 presents the types of literature involved in this study, along with their respective proportions. As shown, the econometric literature constitutes the majority of the considered literature, accounting for 80.00%. The second most cited literature in our study is descriptive analysis (10.00%), followed by qualitative analysis (8.00%). In contrast, the literature on literature reviews accounts for only 7.00% of the studies considered in our study. This aligns with the quantitative trend in

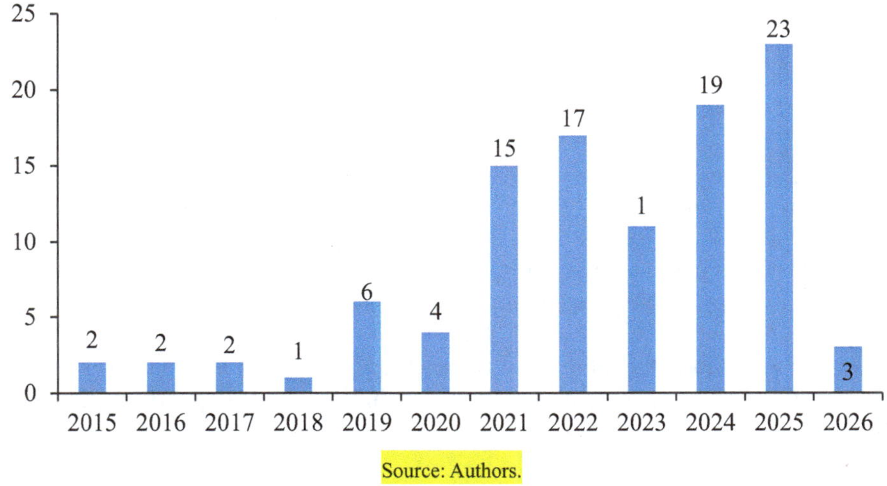

Fig. 2.2 Number of studies published on the factors influencing rural e-commerce development (2015–2026). Source: Authors

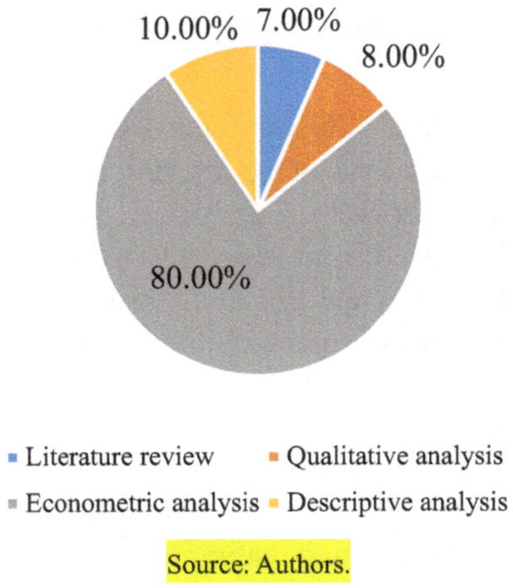

Fig. 2.3 Distribution of types of considered literature. Source: Authors

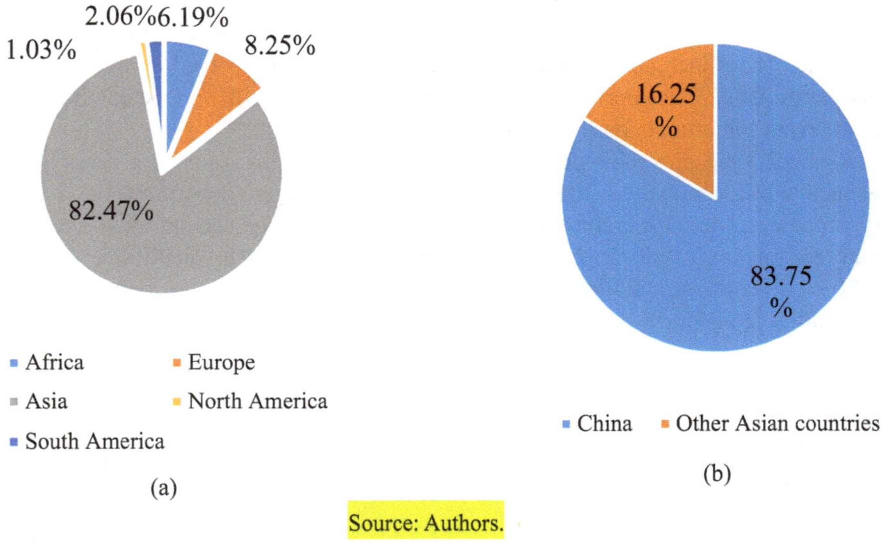

Fig. 2.4 Distribution of literature across regions: (a) distribution across continents; (b) distribution within Asia. Source: Authors

academic research. Econometric analysis can precisely identify the determinants of rural e-commerce development and evaluate their impact magnitudes, which scholars prefer.

Figure 2.4a shows the ratio of the considered literature across the study regions. Generally, related studies covered the following regions: Asia, Africa, Europe, North America, and South America. Among them, studies on Asian countries accounted for the largest share, at 82.47% of the considered literature. Literature from Europe accounted for the second-largest share (8.25%), followed by that from Africa (6.19%). Additionally, the proportions of literature derived from South and

North America were 2.06% and 1.03%, respectively. As shown in the figure, the major fraction of the literature was conducted in Asia. This is because governments in such regions place great importance on e-commerce in their efforts to enhance rural development (Arromdee and Suntrayuth 2020; Qiu et al. 2024).

Figure 2.4b also provides a closer look at the distribution of literature within Asia. It shows that 83.75% of the literature was from China, while the remaining 16.25% came from other Asian countries, such as India and Thailand. In recent years, e-commerce has been widely promoted in China as a means to alleviate poverty, narrow income gaps, and foster rural development (Li et al. 2023; Qin and Fang 2022). This country's rural areas are witnessing a rich array of explorations and experiments in e-commerce. Therefore, China provides a compelling case study for exploring the determinants of rural e-commerce development.

2.4 Determinants of Rural e-Commerce Development

In reality, rural e-commerce development is a complex process deeply associated with multiple factors. Regarding this, prior literature has conducted extensive analyses and documented numerous factors influencing rural e-commerce development. Generally, relevant factors can be categorized into three main groups: individual and household characteristics, institutional factors, and other factors. To properly identify pathways for advancing rural e-commerce, we will discuss relevant factors in the following categories.

2.4.1 Individual and Household Characteristics

Rural households constitute the most fundamental unit in the development of rural e-commerce. As we all know, farmers' adoption of improved practices is often influenced by their individual and household characteristics, such as age, social capital, land endowment, and household economic status. Logically, these characteristics are considered critical factors affecting their participation in e-commerce. In general, existing studies have comprehensively investigated the role of age, gender, human capital, social capital, land, and household economic status in fostering rural e-commerce development.

2.4.1.1 Age

As shown in Table 2.1, 11.4% of the considered literature identified age as an important determinant of rural e-commerce. Age is not only a concept of knowledge but also a proxy of life and production experience (Li et al. 2023a). Thus, the human

Table 2.1 Distribution of literature across determinants

Determinants	Number of literature	Ratio of literature (%)
Individual and household characteristics		
Age	12	11.4
Gender	6	5.7
Human capital	11	10.5
Social capital	11	10.5
Land	9	8.6
Household economic status	9	8.6
Institutional factors		
Infrastructure construction	24	22.9
Online platform development	6	5.7
Subsidy provision	6	5.7
Laws and regulations	8	7.6
Other factors		
E-commerce awareness	18	17.1
Technology innovation and adoption	17	18.1
External shocks: COVID-19	6	5.1
Traditional culture	8	7.6

Source: Authors

capital theory suggests that age is an important component of individuals' human capital, with a complex impact on farmers' adoption of e-commerce. On the one hand, people's capacity for knowledge absorption degrades with age (Li et al. 2025a). Therefore, older farmers often lack essential knowledge and skills for e-commerce, such as market research, business arrangements, and advertising. Understandably, age-related factors slow the development of rural e-commerce (Ariansyah et al. 2021; Quang Doan et al. 2024; Wang et al. 2024a, b). On the other hand, people's human capital, in terms of life and production experiences, accumulates with age (Li et al. 2025a), enabling them to readily recognize the significance of e-commerce in enhancing their agricultural performance and quality of life. Therefore, the age factor is also documented as a driver of rural e-commerce development (Ji et al. 2024; Song et al. 2024a; Žukovskis et al. 2023). Additionally, prior literature also noted that people's labor endowment decreases with their age (Smith and Ehrenberg 2016). Accordingly, older people are less likely to meet the labor demand of e-commerce and are therefore less likely to engage in e-commerce. Put another way, age tends to hinder farmers' adoption of e-commerce (Li et al. 2021a, b). This phenomenon is more pronounced in countries facing a continuously deepening aging problem, such as China (Huang et al. 2022a, b). In summary, the impact of farmers' age on rural e-commerce development remains inconclusive.

2.4.1.2 Gender

Table 2.1 shows that 5.7% of the 105 collected literature focuses on the role of gender in rural e-commerce adoption. According to theories of social capital and human capital, males and females differ in social capital, labor endowment, and financial management (Milazzo and Goldstein 2019; Shen et al. 2025). In particular, compared to males, females are disadvantaged in social networks and labor supply, while they tend to be more adept at financial management. Since e-commerce participation involves social connections, labor input, and financial management, the gender variable tends to have a dual impact on rural e-commerce development. The majority of the existing literature suggests that male farmers experience greater convenience and a higher probability of success in e-commerce than females (Chen et al. 2021a, b; Ünver and Alkan 2021). This is because, compared to females, male farmers' rich social capital provides them with essential market information and seed capital. Meanwhile, the labor endowment of male farmers satisfies the labor demand of e-commerce engagement.

It is worth noting that the thriving feminist movement has enhanced women's status within their households, which helps unlock their strengths in financial management (Shen et al. 2025). This creates opportunities for female farmers to play an indispensable role in rural e-commerce development. Consistently, the work of Li et al. (2021a, b) and Altarturi et al. (2025) has documented that the gender factor (1 = females; 0 = males) has a significant, positive influence on the adoption of e-commerce by rural households.

2.4.1.3 Human Capital

Notably, the human capital theory suggests that human capital directly drives the adoption of knowledge- and skill-intensive practices, such as rural e-commerce (Ma et al. 2019). For instance, the operation of online platforms requires farmers to possess the abilities of promotion, information collection, and financial management. 10.5% of the considered literature (see Table 2.1) has assessed the impact of human capital in terms of education and health on rural e-commerce development. Good education not only inspires farmers to recognize the importance of e-commerce in improving their lives but also enhances their ability to acquire knowledge and skills for participation in e-commerce (Raza et al. 2025). Therefore, education is regarded as a significant driver of rural e-commerce development (Chen et al. 2021a, b; Gudele and Rivza 2015; Liu et al. 2021). For instance, Liu et al. (2021) found that higher levels of education among farmers can promote their adoption of e-commerce in China. More importantly, the literature also shows that better education is associated with higher levels of e-commerce participation and performance, including online sales scale (Liu et al. 2021).

A good health status ensures a stable labor supply (Smith and Ehrenberg 2016) and helps alleviate farmers' liquidity constraints by reducing medical expenses (Li et al. 2024). Accordingly, a good health status can meet the demand for labor and capital inputs in e-commerce. Thus, prior literature has concluded that health status is a factor that promotes farmers' participation in e-commerce (Gao and Qiao 2025; Gunay et al. 2024; Qiu et al. 2024; Song et al. 2024a).

2.4.1.4 Social Capital

According to social capital theory, farmers' social connections can effectively support their acquisition of information and resources (Quang Doan et al. 2024), thereby promoting their participation in e-commerce. In particular, strong social capital helps farmers promptly access market information and related resources (e.g., financial support), enabling them to accurately perceive market demand (Sevigny et al. 2025). Meanwhile, social capital eases "Learning by doing" through information sharing and peer imitation (Bailey et al. 2022), thereby facilitating farmers' acquisition of related skills and access to sales channels. As a result, social capital can effectively lower the barriers to e-commerce adoption, improve e-commerce performance, and reduce the risk of failure. In this case, as shown in Table 2.1, 10.5% of the literature in our study found that social capital is beneficial for rural e-commerce development (Gao and Qiao 2025; Huang et al. 2022a, 2026; Lin et al. 2021; Liu et al. 2021; Wang et al. 2024a, b). For instance, Geng et al. (2024) argued that interpersonal trust can help mitigate information asymmetry and enhance farmers' confidence in participating in e-commerce. More direct evidence suggests that their peers' adoption positively influences farmers' adoption of e-commerce (Wang et al. 2025; Xiang et al. 2022). In summary, enriching rural residents' social capital is recognized as a promising strategy for accelerating rural e-commerce development.

2.4.1.5 Land

9 studies, accounting for 8.6% of the considered literature, documented the impact of land (see Table 2.1). The household production and livelihood framework indicates that farmers' economic behavior is primarily determined by their resource endowment (Ho et al. 2022). That is, farmers with rich resource endowments are more likely to adopt improved practices. As we all know, land is a very fundamental resource for farmers. Thus, expanding farmers' land is a significant precondition for farmers' participation in e-commerce (Chen et al. 2021a, b; Huang et al. 2022a, b; Liu et al. 2021, 2024a, b; Qiu et al. 2024; Wang et al. 2023a, b). For instance, Qiu et al. (2024) found a positive correlation between land size and farmers' participation in e-commerce in China. However, it is worth noting that large-scale farmland cultivation requires a relatively substantial budget for agricultural inputs and service purchases (Li et al. 2023b). This can inevitably lead to liquidity shortages, hindering farmers' adoption of e-commerce. For instance, Zhang and Zhang (2024) found that large landholdings reduce farmers' willingness to adopt e-commerce in China.

2.4.1.6 Household Economic Status

Improved household economic status is not only the ultimate goal of rural e-commerce development, but also its foundation. Referring to the household production and livelihood framework, economic status provides the foundation for farmers to participate in economic activities (Ndlovu et al. 2021). In particular, a favorable economic status strengthens farmers' financial capacity to bear the costs of e-commerce start-up and operation. It enhances their resilience to fluctuations and potential failures in e-commerce activities (Yang et al. 2021). Building on this logic, 8.6% of the considered literature classified household economic status (e.g., income and asset ownership) as rural e-commerce drivers (e.g., Gao 2022; Haji 2021; Li et al. 2025; Misra and Pandey 2022). For instance, Misra and Pandey (2022) found that income has a positive impact on people's e-commerce adoption. However, some scholars recognize the nonlinear relationship between household economic conditions and farmers' adoption of e-commerce. That is, exceeding a specific level, the increase in household income can reduce the need to adopt e-commerce (Chen et al. 2021a, b; Zhang et al. 2025; Zhang and Zhang 2024). For instance, Zhang and Zhang (2024) found a negative association between household income and farmers' willingness to adopt e-commerce in rural China.

2.4.2 *Institutional Factors*

As mentioned earlier, advancing e-commerce is regarded as a viable strategy for achieving rural development. Thus, governments worldwide have devoted massively to promoting rural e-commerce (Cui et al. 2017; Li et al. 2022; Phiri 2019). As suggested by prior literature, governments' efforts—institutional factors—to promote rural e-commerce development can be categorized into infrastructure development, online platform development, subsidy provision, and laws and regulations.

2.4.2.1 Infrastructure Construction

The literature on infrastructure construction constitutes the major part of the literature considered in this section, accounting for 22.9% of the total. The theory of transaction cost economics indicates that appropriate infrastructure can help lower transaction costs, like search costs, transportation costs, and bargaining and contracting costs, and thus expand the profit space for sellers and buyers. Accordingly, infrastructure construction is recognized as an important driver of rural commercialization. In fact, stable information flow, convenient delivery of goods, and low transaction costs are three crucial physical prerequisites for rural e-commerce (Gao et al. 2025; Huang et al. 2022a, b). Accordingly, a sound internet network, efficient logistics, and accessible transportation are fundamental to the functioning of e-commerce (Ji et al. 2024; Liu et al. 2020; Wang et al. 2024a, b). In practice, a reliable internet network enables e-commerce executives to collect market information and release product details, facilitates consumers in obtaining suitable goods, and enables smooth online transactions. Therefore, improving internet infrastructure construction is documented as an important engine for rural e-commerce development (Chen and Bashir 2022; Jabbouri et al. 2023; Liu et al. 2024a, b; Song et al. 2024b; Ünver and Alkan 2021). Complete logistics delivers products purchased online to consumers, helping to accomplish the last mile of rural e-commerce (Altarturi et al. 2025; El Aissoug et al. 2024; Tang 2016). In particular, e-commerce entrepreneurs must overcome the high transportation costs resulting from the spatially dispersed distribution of consumers and minimize product losses (Luo and Niu 2019). By leveraging specialized division of labor and economies of scale, the logistics system has created opportunities to overcome the challenges above (Tang 2016). Undoubtedly, logistics plays a critical role in driving rural e-commerce development (Barata et al. 2024; Chen and Li 2025; El Aissoug et al. 2024; Li et al. 2021a, b; Lu et al. 2023; Qiu et al. 2024).

Transportation infrastructure supports the effectiveness of logistics (Nogueira et al. 2025). Meanwhile, improved transportation infrastructure plays a central role in reducing product delivery costs and shortening transportation time. Donaldson (2018) found that railroad construction significantly reduces trade costs and interregional price gaps. Thus, constructing and improving transportation infrastructure is favorable to rural e-commerce development (Chen et al. 2021a, b; Cui et al. 2019; Nogueira et al. 2025; Wang 2015). For instance, Cui et al. (2019) suggested that the construction of transportation infrastructure empowers rural e-commerce development.

2.4.2.2 Online Platform Development

Among the 105 considered literature, 5.7% discuss the impact of online platforms on rural e-commerce. It is well documented that spatial and temporal constraints induce high transaction costs. For instance, long-distance transactions incur substantial transportation costs for goods. According to transaction cost economics, optimizing the organizational form of trade can reduce transaction costs. Online platforms, particularly online transaction and payment platforms, are the carriers of rural e-commerce (Duan et al. 2023; Vavekanand and Kumar 2024). In particular, online platforms open multiple channels between product sellers and consumers, ensuring the sale and revenue of agricultural products. Also, online platforms streamline the trading of agricultural products by removing spatial and temporal constraints, thereby effectively reducing transaction costs for both parties and achieving a Pareto improvement (Geng et al. 2024; Shiu et al. 2023). Vavekanand and Kumar (2024) suggested that online platforms are a significant precondition for farmers participating in rural e-commerce. Chen et al. (2023) and Gao and Qiao (2025) also observed a similar phenomenon in rural China. It is worth noting that certain livestreaming platforms have increasingly been functioning as a new form of e-commerce platform. Compared with conventional online platforms, livestreaming platforms are more appealing as they integrate cultural performances, product presentations, and online transaction functions (Shiu et al. 2023). Duan et al. (2023) found that streamlining platforms are a pivotal driver of farmers' participation in rural e-commerce in Huaiyang, China.

2.4.2.3 Subsidy Provision

5.7% of the considered literature is categorized as studies on the role of subsidy provision in rural e-commerce development. From the perspective of transaction cost economics, when rural e-commerce generates positive externalities, but farmers receive no compensation, the gap between private and social returns acts as an additional transaction cost, discouraging adoption (Livernois 2024; Paniagua and Rayamajhee 2024). Liquidity constraints aggravate this problem. Well-designed subsidies can both internalise these externalities and relax farmers' liquidity constraints by covering part of the fixed and variable transaction costs. The existing literature generally agrees that rural e-commerce development generates substantial benefits, including employment opportunities, income growth, and sustainable agricultural development (Komatsu and Suzuki 2025; Liu et al. 2025). Thus, adopting e-commerce is a typical behavior with positive externalities, whose persistence heavily hinges on whether targeted reimbursements are received. Moreover, substantial capital is required to start and operate an e-commerce business (Li et al. 2025). For instance, registering with online platforms and leasing storage facilities entail significant capital commitments. However, farmers often face liquidity constraints (Melkani et al. 2025). External monetary support is warranted for farmers who are willing to adopt e-commerce. The provision of subsidies helps farmers handle capital shortage and smooth their budgets for e-commerce operations. On the other hand, it allows e-commerce executors to gain rewards from their positive externalities. Therefore, subsidies help boost rural e-commerce penetration (Chen et al. 2024; Li et al. 2025; Zhong et al. 2021). For instance, Zhong et al. (2021) noted that government subsidy plays a critical role in promoting rural e-commerce adoption in China.

2.4.2.4 Laws and Regulations

Due to information asymmetry, e-commerce is prone to fraud and moral hazard issues (Penagos et al. 2025). This, in turn, increases transaction costs, such as consumers' information search costs and sellers' product promotion expenses, which obstruct market development. In response, the government needs to step in to correct it. Enacting laws and regulations is a reliable strategy for the government to address market disruptions (Geng et al. 2024; Zhang 2021). The former sets the rules, while the latter implements them. In particular, a sound legal framework and stringent regulations can effectively prevent fraudulent activities and ensure their prompt rectification—through penalties and compensation—when they occur. Thus, appropriate laws and regulations are pivotal for reducing transaction costs. Aligning with this, 7.6% of the considered literature has confirmed that laws and regulations are effective in promoting rural e-commerce development (e.g., Ariansyah et al. 2021; Arromdee and Suntrayuth 2020; Chatterjee 2019; Jabbouri et al. 2023; Zhang 2021). Arromdee and Suntrayuth (2020) noted that improving targeted laws and regulations is urgently essential to popularize e-commerce among farmers in Thailand. Duan et al. (2023) argued that standardized online platforms can accelerate rural e-commerce in China.

2.4.3 Other Factors

Beyond the determinants discussed above, prior literature also highlighted the significant roles of farmers' e-commerce awareness, technological innovation and adoption, external shocks such as COVID-19, and traditional culture in the development of rural e-commerce. Among them, 17.1% and 18.1% of the literature considered in our study focus on the impact of e-commerce awareness and technology innovation and adoption, respectively. In comparison, those on the impact of COVID-19 and traditional culture only account for 5.1% and 7.6% of the 105 literature, respectively.

2.4.3.1 E-Commerce Awareness

According to the human capital theory, human behavior is driven by the awareness of things—a key dimension of human capital (Lusardi and Mitchell 2023). Positive awareness of things induces related behaviors and *vice versa* (Hassan and Lee 2021; Sundjaja et al. 2020; Yang et al. 2025). Some studies have concluded that farmers' awareness of improved agricultural practices elevates the likelihood of adopting them (Alavion et al. 2017; Yu and Zhang 2022). This is because full awareness of things effectively lowers the adoption barriers and failure risks associated with improved practices, thereby strengthening farmers' confidence in adopting them (Huang et al. 2021; Wang and Zhang 2023). E-commerce adoption also follows the same logic (Fadzillah et al. 2024; Mollick et al. 2023; Sundermeier and Kummer 2022; Utami and Alamanda 2022). Previous studies have found that a strong knowledge base and positive impression of e-commerce can significantly increase the odds of farmers adopting it (Chatterjee 2019; Chov and Ou 2022; Mollick et al. 2023; Wang 2015; Zhu et al. 2024). For instance, Chatterjee (2019) suggested that enhancing farmers' awareness of e-commerce is effective in penetrating this business mode. In a similar vein, Ünver and Alkan (2021) and Klein and Popp (2022) argued that a lack of knowledge about e-commerce is a key obstacle to farmers' adoption of e-commerce in Turkey and Germany, respectively.

2.4.3.2 Technology Innovation and Adoption

In reality, e-commerce relies on related technologies (e.g., the internet, big data, and artificial intelligence) and devices (e.g., smartphones and computers) (Jia et al. 2024; Vavekanand and Kumar 2024; Yang et al. 2020). As suggested by the theory of transaction cost economics, incomplete and asymmetric information is a root cause of transaction costs (Liu and Liang 2025). Essentially, technological innovation can continuously eliminate incomplete information and information asymmetry, thereby reducing transaction costs. Therefore, from a macro perspective, fostering technology innovation is beneficial for e-commerce penetration in rural areas. Previous studies have confirmed this point (Chen et al. 2026; Gao and Liu 2020; Li and Gan 2025; Onjewu et al. 2022). Gao and Liu (2020) found that ICT innovation can help achieve inclusive rural e-commerce development in China. Onjewu et al. (2022) also proposed a similar conclusion in their work on the UK, Jordan, and Nigeria.

From a micro perspective, the effectiveness of technological innovation mainly stems from farmers' adoption of related technologies and devices (Hossain et al. 2025; Leong et al. 2016; Lyu et al. 2022). That is, farmers' adoption enables them to practice related technologies and devices in the e-commerce process. Accordingly, penetrating the adoption of related technologies and devices among farmers is regarded as a reliable channel to promote rural e-commerce development (Huang et al. 2022a, b; Jabbouri et al. 2023; Liu et al. 2021, 2024a, b; Ma et al. 2019; Song et al. 2024b; Ünver and Alkan 2021; Xie 2026). Liu et al. (2021) found that smartphone use incites farmers to adopt e-commerce in China. Jabbouri et al. (2023) suggested that internet access leads to more e-commerce adoption among farmers in the Moroccan Kingdom.

2.4.3.3 External Shocks: COVID-19

Within the household production and livelihood framework, farmers' participation in economic activities tends to be influenced by external shocks (Natarajan et al. 2022). Accordingly, rural e-commerce development is conditioned by external shocks such as the COVID-19 pandemic. As we all know, the COVID-19 pandemic has constrained people's offline shopping. To cope with this, people tend to purchase online, which has opened new opportunities for rural e-commerce development. Previous studies have documented substantial changes in rural e-commerce before and after the COVID-19 pandemic (Chen and Bashir 2022; Chmielarz et al. 2022; Onjewu et al. 2022; Penagos et al. 2025; Yu and Zhang 2022). For instance, Chen and Bashir (2022) argued that the COVID-19 pandemic led to an increase in rural e-commerce in China. Penagos et al. (2025) concluded that the COVID-19 pandemic has, objectively, accelerated the development of rural e-commerce in Latin American countries. Moreover, Chmielarz et al. (2022) found that the incidence of COVID-19 strengthens the sustainability of rural e-commerce in Poland, Turkey, and China.

2.4.3.4 Traditional Culture

Traditional culture, which is driven, shaped, and transmitted through social capital, governs the allocation of resources, the flow of information, and the sharing of risks among farmers, thereby influencing their adoption of improved agricultural practices (Gu et al. 2021; Lavoie and Wardropper 2021). Thus, traditional culture is regarded as a key factor influencing rural e-commerce development (Barretta et al. 2025; Chen et al. 2021a, b; Ramesh 2025). In particular, traditional culture in some Asian countries requires farmers to abide by tradition and experience. Evidently, this can hinder farmers from adopting e-commerce as a means of income generation (Huang et al. 2024a, b; Ramesh 2025). Ramesh (2025) found that traditional culture plays an unfavorable role in the development of rural e-commerce. Huang et al. (2024a, b) also suggested that traditional culture reinforces gender inequality in rural China and reduces women's participation in e-commerce. However, it can not be ignored that traditional culture can also accelerate rural e-commerce development. That is, some excellent traditional culture (such as beautiful legends) endows agricultural products with certain cultural connotations, which can facilitate sales through e-commerce platforms (Barretta et al. 2025; Chen et al. 2021a, b; Yongdi 2025). For instance, Barretta et al. (2025) documented that traditional culture influences consumers' attitudes towards Canastra cheese and improves the e-commercialization of this product in Brazil. In sum, traditional culture can exert a dual impact on the penetration of rural e-commerce.

2.4.4 A Summary

Thus far, we have combed through the typical determinants of rural e-commerce development documented in previous studies. Drawing on the human capital theory, the social capital theory, the theory of transaction cost economics, and the household production and livelihood framework, we summarize the relevant determinants to provide a comprehensive view of rural e-commerce development.

Overall, as shown in Table 2.2, related determinants can be divided into two categories: the positive effect group and the dual effect group. For the positive effect group, determinants such as human capital (i.e., education and health status), social capital, infrastructure development, online platform development, subsidy provision, laws and regulations, e-commerce awareness, technology innovation and adoption, and COVID-19 are documented as drivers of rural e-commerce development. In contrast, variables for age, gender, land, traditional culture, and household economic status tend to have a dual impact on rural e-commerce development. Moreover, discussions grounded in related theories reveal the reasons for the drivers' positive impact and the specific conditions under which the double-edged factors can act as promoters. That significantly deepens our understanding of the factors affecting rural e-commerce development.

Table 2.2 A summary of the impact of selected factors of rural e-commerce development

Determinants	Impact directions	Representative literature
Individual and household characteristics		
Age	±	Ariansyah et al. (2021), Ji et al. (2024)
Gender	±	Altarturi et al. (2025), Li et al. (2021a, b)
Human capital (education and health status)	+	Gudele and Rivza (2015), Ünver and Alkan (2021)
Social capital	+	Wang et al. (2025), Xiang et al. (2022)
Land	±	Qiu et al. (2024), Zhang and Zhang (2024)
Household economic status	±	Misra and Pandey (2022), Zhang et al. (2025)
Institutional factors		
Infrastructure construction	+	Luo and Niu (2019), Nogueira et al. (2025)
Online platform development	+	Duan et al. (2023), Vavekanand and Kumar (2024)
Subsidy provision	+	Chen et al. (2024), Li et al. (2025), Zhong et al. (2021)
Laws and regulations	+	Arromdee and Suntrayuth (2020), Duan et al. (2023)
Other factors		
E-commerce awareness	+	Chatterjee (2019), Klein and Popp (2022)
Technology innovation and adoption	+	Jabbouri et al. (2023), Onjewu et al. (2022)
External shocks: COVID-19	+	Chmielarz et al. (2022), Penagos et al. (2025)
Traditional culture	±	Barretta et al. (2025), Ramesh (2025)

Source: Authors

That is, whether these determinants serve as drivers or hindrances depends on specific conditions. Obviously, this highlights the priority area in which the government should take cautious steps.

2.5 Research Gaps

It is critical to note that the prior literature also leaves substantial room for further analysis. This helps highlight the focus of future research, but also facilitates policymakers in designing precise measures to improve rural e-commerce. Accordingly, we summarize the research gaps that exist in the prior literature in this section.

2.5.1 Gaps in Theoretical and Conceptual Analyses

Our review indicates that the existing literature in the field is characterized by fragmented concepts and relatively weak theoretical anchoring. First, previous studies have not reached an agreement on the definition of rural e-commerce. As aforementioned, the majority of existing literature implicitly equates rural e-commerce with general e-commerce, ICT use, or online sales, without clearly specifying the distinctive features of rural contexts, such as the role of agricultural value chains, logistics constraints, and smallholder producers. This not only makes it difficult to compare the findings across the literature but also hinders the long-term development of rural e-commerce.

Second, most empirical studies are largely data-driven and rely on ad hoc explanatory variables, rather than being theoretically grounded. Even though some classic theories, such as human capital theory, social capital theory, and transaction cost economics, can be used to explore the determinants of rural e-commerce, studies driven by these theories remain thin. Consequently, biases in the identification of determinants can be observed. That is, the determinants of rural e-commerce can not be systematically and accurately identified.

Third, the mechanisms through which the determinants influence rural e-commerce remain unclear. As shown, previous studies have mainly examined whether specific factors influence the development of rural e-commerce, while largely leaving the underlying mechanisms unexplored. As a result, relevant policy instruments are often poorly targeted.

2.5.2 Gaps in the Measurements of Rural e-Commerce

Figure 2.5 shows the distribution of the reviewed literature across the measurement constructs of rural e-commerce. Part (a) of the figure suggests that the most popular measurement of rural e-commerce is manifested as dummy indicators (e.g., e-commerce adoption, e-commerce participation, and e-commerce entrepreneurship), accounting for 75.90% of the considered literature. Meanwhile, 9.64% of the considered literature uses single continuous indicators (e.g., e-commerce adoption ratio and online sales volume) as measures. Moreover, approximately 14.46% of the considered literature measured rural e-commerce using multiple indicators. In particular, part (b) of the figure, which measures rural e-commerce using multiple discrete indicators, accounts for 10.84% of the literature reviewed. Only 3.61% of the literature considered measured rural e-commerce by integrating multiple indicators into a single index.

Common sense suggests that dummy indicators can provide very limited information, as they only indicate whether the event (i.e., rural e-commerce) occurred (Li et al. 2023b). Compared with dummies, continuous indicators can provide more information about rural e-commerce, such as its intensity and frequency. However,

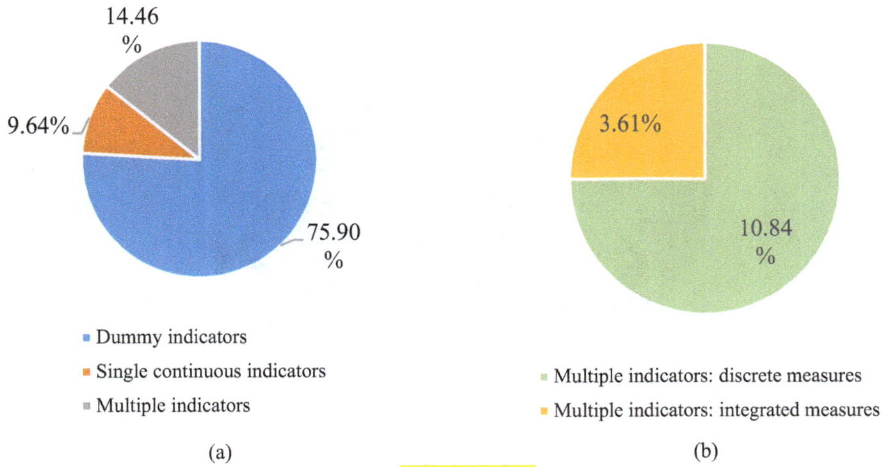

Source: Authors.

Fig. 2.5 Measurements of rural e-commerce development used in prior literature: (a) distribution by indicator type; (b) composition of multiple-indicator measures. Source: Authors

a single continuous indicator captures only one specific dimension of rural e-commerce and cannot provide a comprehensive measure. In contrast, jointly using multiple indicators can capture the multiple dimensions of rural e-commerce, leading to a comprehensive measurement. Importantly, combining multiple indicators into a single measure can provide a continuous assessment of rural e-commerce. However, the majority of prior literature used dummy indicators to measure rural e-commerce, while a relatively small part employed multiple indicators. Thus, future research should endeavor to develop more sophisticated methods and composite indices that measure rural e-commerce by involving multiple indicators.

2.5.3 Gaps in the Identification of Influencing Factors

Figure 2.6 presents the categories of econometric methods used to identify the determinants of rural e-commerce. In particular, among the literature conducting econometric analysis, methods (e.g., Logit, Probit, and panel Probit models) that cannot address endogeneity issues of explanatory variables account for 69.49% of the literature considered. Correspondingly, the proportion of econometric methods addressing endogeneity accounted for 30.51% of those used in the considered literature. Specifically, 27.12% of the considered literature applied methods (e.g., structural equation models and an instrumental-variable-based fixed-effect model) that can address both observed and unobserved endogeneity. Only 3.39% of the literature used methods (e.g., propensity score matching) to address observed endogeneity.

It is widely acknowledged that certain determinants, such as human capital, social capital, and e-commerce awareness, are difficult to quantify, which can

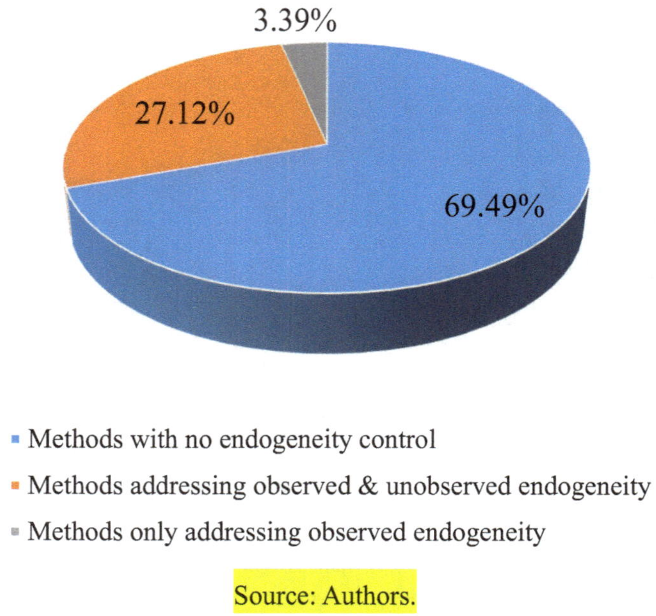

Fig. 2.6 Econometric methods used in related literature. Source: Authors

induce measurement bias. Meanwhile, some potential determinants (e.g., human capital) are influenced by both observed factors (e.g., income and location) and unobserved factors (e.g., motivations and managerial skills). Moreover, it is normal for some determinants to be reversely determined by rural e-commerce. For instance, the development of rural e-commerce can improve farmers' economic conditions. Taken together, relevant determinants are likely to be affected by observed and unobserved endogeneities, which can bias their impact on rural e-commerce development. To rigorously identify the determinants of rural e-commerce, econometric methods that account for both observed and unobserved endogeneities are warranted. However, as mentioned above, such methods are relatively rarely applied in previous studies. Thus, future work should put special emphasis on addressing the observed and unobserved endogeneity issues.

2.5.4 Gaps in the Scope of Determinants of Rural e-Commerce

As suggested, previous studies have largely expanded our knowledge of the determinants of rural e-commerce development. However, over time and as environmental conditions evolve, the influence of several factors previously overlooked in the literature has become increasingly evident.

The first neglected factor is climate change. We have inevitably entered an era of climate change. The increasing impact of climate change induces frequent variations in agricultural outputs (Li et al. 2025a), reshapes the agricultural production mode (Lawson et al. 2020), and even changes people's consumption preferences (Saiful et al. 2022), which can have a substantial impact on the development of rural e-commerce. However, dedicated discussions on the impact of climate change on rural e-commerce development remain scarce.

The second category of factors to be studied is geographical factors. Geographical factors such as distance to urban centers and terrain have shaped farmers' access to agricultural inputs and marketing channels. That is, geographical factors constitute the precondition of rural e-commerce development. Put another way, geographical factors are potential determinants of rural e-commerce development. However, the association between geographical factors and rural e-commerce development is unclear.

Another neglected factor is the development of other industries. Other industries, such as manufacturing and tourism, are important links in the agricultural product sales chain and can serve as potential determinants of rural e-commerce development. In our humble opinion, there are few systematic discussions about the impact of other industries on rural e-commerce.

2.5.5 *Future Research Recommendations*

Our study underscores several points for future research as follows. First, future studies should devote greater effort to accurately defining rural e-commerce, testing classical theories, and uncovering the mechanisms underlying its key determinants. Second, research should focus on developing and applying indices that integrate multiple indicators to produce comprehensive measurements of rural e-commerce development. Third, future research should place greater emphasis on rigorously diagnosing potential endogeneity in the determinants of rural e-commerce and on the broader adoption of appropriately specified econometric strategies to correct for such biases. Fourth, scholars in the field of rural e-commerce are expected to give due consideration to the impacts of climate change, geographical factors, and the development of other industries on rural e-commerce.

2.6 Conclusions, Policy Implications, and Research Limitations

Developing rural e-commerce is widely regarded as a promising strategy to enhance farmers' economic performance, reduce rural poverty, promote sustainable agricultural practices, and achieve long-term rural development. Regarding this, a substantial body of literature has investigated the factors influencing the development of rural e-commerce. However, the adoption rate of rural e-commerce in some developing regions stagnates at an unacceptably low level. Therefore, it is necessary to synthesize the influencing factors identified in existing studies to unlock the developmental pathways.

To this end, this study reviewed 105 studies derived from publicly accessible sources. Drawing on the reviewed literature, this study summarizes the determinants of rural e-commerce along three dimensions: individual and household characteristics, institutional factors, and other factors. One important finding of our study is the systematic assessment of the key drivers of rural e-commerce, namely human capital (education and health status), social capital, infrastructure development, online platform development, subsidy provision, laws and regulations, e-commerce awareness, technological innovation and adoption, and the COVID-19 pandemic. Obviously, these drivers have direct policy implications, as they provide clear guidance for governments' efforts to advance rural e-commerce. The more important finding of the present study is the identification of several double-edged factors—age, gender, land, traditional culture, and household economic status—that tend to exert both positive and negative impacts on rural e-commerce development. That is, the impacts of these double-edged factors depend on certain conditions. When conditions are favorable, these factors function as drivers; otherwise, they turn into barriers. This not only reminds policymakers to proceed cautiously in developing rural e-commerce but also highlights the most challenging frontier of this agenda. Thus, this finding has more profound implications for the development of rural e-commerce compared with the former one.

Evidently, rural e-commerce is increasingly a promising strategy to combat poverty, promote sustainable agriculture, and achieve long-term rural development. Thus, advancing rural e-commerce penetration is regarded as an urgent task. Our study reviews the determinants of rural e-commerce and identifies practical channels to accelerate its development. In particular, regarding drivers, the government should implement policies to amplify their positive impact on rural e-commerce development. That is, policies are expected to focus on the accumulation of human and social capital, the construction of infrastructure and online platforms, the provision of subsidies, the strengthening of laws and regulations, and the promotion of innovation. More importantly, regarding the determinants that have a dual impact on rural e-commerce, the government should design targeted policies to harness their positive effects while mitigating their negative effects. Among them, the government is advised to place special emphasis on the role of traditional culture. Specifically, the government should distil and promote the finest elements of traditional culture, integrating them into the marketing of agricultural products to foster the development of rural e-commerce.

Last but not least, we must admit that our study has two main limitations. First, meta-analysis is excluded from our study. As we all know, meta-analysis can help quantitatively and accurately comb through the determinants of rural e-commerce documented in previous literature. However, since our original objective is to identify the determinants of rural e-commerce and, more importantly, to reveal the economic mechanisms behind them, we did not consider this strategy. Thus, our future research will use this method to deepen our knowledge of the determinants of rural e-commerce. Second, our study focused only on the literature examining the determinants of rural e-commerce and did not incorporate studies on its effectiveness. The positive outcomes of rural e-commerce have already attracted widespread attention from the academic community. Reviewing related literature can effectively solidify our understanding of the development of rural e-commerce. Therefore, we should focus our future research on reviewing the literature on the effectiveness of rural e-commerce.

Acknowledgements The authors gratefully acknowledge the financial support from the Ministry of Education of China Project of Humanities and Social Sciences (Project No.: 21YJC630062), the National Statistical Science Research Project (Project No.: 2023LY033), and the 2024 Jiangsu Higher Education "Qinglan Project".

Data Availability Statement The data supporting this study's findings are available from Junpeng Li upon request.

Conflict of Interests There is no conflict of interest.

References

Alavion, S.J., Allahyari, M.S., Al-Rimawi, A.S., Surujlal, J., 2017. Adoption of Agricultural E-Marketing: Application of the Theory of Planned Behavior. J. Int. Food Agribus. Mark. 29, 1–15. https://doi.org/10.1080/08974438.2016.1229242

Ali Raza; Xueyan Liu; Abdul Qadeer khan, 2025. E-commerce in Agriculture : A Study on Adoption Intentions and Challenges for Farmers in Pakistan. Econ. Bus. Manag. 37–51. https://doi.org/10.63313/EBM.9055

Altarturi, H.H.M., Nor, A.R.M., Jaafar, N.I., Anuar, N.B., 2025. A bibliometric and content analysis of technological advancement applications in agricultural e-commerce, Electronic Commerce Research. Springer US. doi:https://doi.org/10.1007/s10660-023-09670-z

Ariansyah, K., Sirait, E.R.E., Nugroho, B.A., Suryanegara, M., 2021. Drivers of and barriers to e-commerce adoption in Indonesia: Individuals' perspectives and the implications. Telecomm. Policy 45, 102219. doi:https://doi.org/10.1016/j.telpol.2021.102219

Arromdee, J., Suntrayuth, S., 2020. E-commerce adoption for rice selling in Thailand: An empirical study. Thail. World Econ. 38, 88–118.

Bailey, M., Johnston, D.M., Kuchler, T., Stroebel, J., Wong, A., 2022. Peer Effects in Product Adoption. Am. Econ. J. Appl. Econ. 14. doi:https://doi.org/10.2139/ssrn.3409131

Barata, S.F.P.G., Ferreira, F.A.F., Carayannis, E.G., Ferreira, J.J.M., 2024. Determinants of E-Commerce, Artificial Intelligence, and Agile Methods in Small- and Medium-Sized Enterprises. IEEE Trans. Eng. Manag. 71, 6903–6917. doi:https://doi.org/10.1109/TEM.2023.3269601

Barretta, L., Salomão David, M.L., Lourenção, M., 2025. Tales or labels? The impact of storytelling and geographical indication label on consumers' attitudes towards brazilian canastra cheese. Food Qual. Prefer. 134. doi:https://doi.org/10.1016/j.foodqual.2025.105683

Bozzola, M., Finger, R., 2021. Stability of risk attitude, agricultural policies and production shocks: Evidence from Italy. Eur. Rev. Agric. Econ. 48, 477–501. doi:https://doi.org/10.1093/erae/jbaa021

Chatterjee, S., 2019. Developing Rural E-commerce: Trends and Challenges The current article draws on the findings of an ongoing three-year MI project on Rural E-Commerce Development in the.

Chen, C., Gan, C., Li, J., Lu, Y., Rahut, D., 2023. Linking farmers to markets: Does cooperative membership facilitate e-commerce adoption and income growth in rural. Econ. Anal. Policy 80, 1155–1170. doi:https://doi.org/10.1016/j.eap.2023.09.040

Chen, G., Tan, W., Zhang, S., Yan, B., 2021a. Influence of Interpersonal and Institutional Trust on the Participation Willingness of Farmers in E-Commerce Poverty Alleviation. Front. Psychol. 12, 1–12. doi:https://doi.org/10.3389/fpsyg.2021.727644

Chen, M., Bashir, R., 2022. Role of e-commerce and resource utilization for sustainable business development: goal of economic recovery after Covid-19. Econ. Chang. Restruct. 55, 2663–2685. doi:https://doi.org/10.1007/s10644-022-09404-5

Chen, P., Al Mamun, A., Hoque, M.E., Yang, Q., Masud, M.M., 2026. From data to decisions: the role of digital marketing analytics in fashion e-commerce performance. J. Fash. Mark. Manag. 1–24. doi:https://doi.org/10.1108/JFMM-05-2025-0245

Chen, S., Liu, W., Song, H., Zhang, Q., 2024. Government-led e-commerce expansion project and rural household income: Evidence and mechanisms. Econ. Inq. 62, 150–174. doi:https://doi.org/10.1111/ecin.13167

Chen, W., Li, J., 2025. Digital finance, rural E-commerce development and consumption upgrading. Int. Rev. Financ. Anal. 104. doi:https://doi.org/10.1016/j.irfa.2025.104351

Chen, Z., Shu, W., Guo, H., Pan, C., 2021b. The spatial characteristics of sustainable development for agricultural products e-commerce at county-level: Based on the empirical analysis of china. Sustain. 13. doi:https://doi.org/10.3390/su13126557

Chmielarz, W., Zborowski, M., Xuetao, J., Atasever, M., Szpakowska, J., 2022. Covid-19 Pandemic as Sustainability Determinant of e-Commerce in the Creation of Information Society. Procedia Comput. Sci. 207, 4378–4389. doi:https://doi.org/10.1016/j.procs.2022.09.501

Chov, B., Ou, P., 2022. Determinants of the consumer's adoption of the next-generation mobile payments and banking: a case study of the Bakong system, SN Business and Economics. Springer International Publishing. doi:https://doi.org/10.1007/s43546-022-00345-9

Cordes, D.L., Marinova, D., 2023. Systematic literature review of the role of e-commerce in providing pathways to sustainability for poverty alleviation in Sub-Saharan Africa. Discov. Sustain. 4. doi:https://doi.org/10.1007/s43621-022-00109-3

Cui, M., Pan, S.L., Cui, L., 2019. Developing community capability for e-commerce development in rural China: A resource orchestration perspective. Inf. Syst. J. 29, 953–988. doi:https://doi.org/10.1111/isj.12241

Cui, M., Pan, S.L., Newell, S., Cui, L., 2017. Strategy, Resource Orchestration and E-commerce Enabled Social Innovation in Rural China. J. Strateg. Inf. Syst. 26, 3–21. doi:https://doi.org/10.1016/j.jsis.2016.10.001

Doanh, N.K., Do Dinh, L., Quynh, N.N., 2022. Tea farmers' intention to participate in Livestream sales in Vietnam: The combination of the Technology Acceptance Model (TAM) and barrier factors. J. Rural Stud. 94, 408–417. doi:https://doi.org/10.1016/j.jrurstud.2022.05.023

Donaldson, D., 2018. Railroads of the Raj: Estimating the impact of transportation infrastructure. Am. Econ. Rev. 108, 899–934. doi:https://doi.org/10.1257/aer.20101199

Duan, S., Lin, J., van Dijck, J., 2023. Producing new farmers in Chinese rural live E-commerce: platformization, labor, and live E-commerce sellers in Huaiyang. Chinese J. Commun. 16, 250–266. doi:https://doi.org/10.1080/17544750.2023.2203939

El Aissoug, C., Kim, T.Y., Wang, X.Q., Choi, D.H., 2024. Cross-cultural exploration of determinants of e-commerce adoption: Perspectives from logistics service quality and payment driver. J. Retail. Consum. Serv. 81. doi:https://doi.org/10.1016/j.jretconser.2024.104033

Fadzillah, S., Rahman, A., Tan, P., Isa, A., 2024. Technology Adoption Readiness Among Fresh Agricultural Traders in Using E-Commerce Platform in Malaysia 13.

Gao, K., Qiao, G., 2025. How Social Capital Drives Farmers' Multi-Stage E-Commerce Participation: Evidence from Inner Mongolia, China. Agric. 15, 1–22. doi:https://doi.org/10.3390/agriculture15050501

Gao, P., Liu, Y., 2020. Endogenous inclusive development of e-commerce in rural China: A case study. Growth Change 51, 1611–1630. doi:https://doi.org/10.1111/grow.12436

Gao, T., Feng, H., Lu, Q., Qu, M., 2025. Digital agriculture extension boosts E-commerce participation: evidence from China's yellow river provinces, Electronic Commerce Research. Springer US. doi:https://doi.org/10.1007/s10660-025-09998-8

Gao, X., 2022. Qualitative Analysis of the Key Influencing Factors of Farmers Participate in Agricultural Products E-Commerce to Help Rural Revitalization. Acad. J. Bus. Manag. 4, 121–130. https://doi.org/10.25236/ajbm.2022.041716

Geng, Xianhui, Xu, Xia, Jin, Shanshan and Kiprop, E., 2024. Platform Certification and Reputation: Their Role in Boosting E-commerce Sales of Agricultural Products. SSRN.

Gu, R., Peng, C., Zhang, W., 2021. The Gender Gap in Household Bargaining Power: A Revealed-Preference Approach. SSRN Electron. J. 00, 1–43. doi:https://doi.org/10.2139/ssrn.3814200

Gudele, I., Rivza, B., 2015. Factors Influencing E-Commerce Development in Baltic Rural Areas. 25th Congr. -Nordic View to Sustain. Rural Dev. 496–500.

Gunay, S., Prentice, C., Sraieb, M., 2024. Do major health shocks affect the interconnectedness of E-commerce and electronic payment markets? a regional analysis. Electron. Commer. Res. 24, 2353–2379. doi:https://doi.org/10.1007/s10660-022-09669-y

Gupta, R., Sharma, P.K., 2018. Scope of E-Commerce in Agri-Business in India : An Overview. Int. J. Adv. Sci. Res. Manag. 99–104.

Haji, K., 2021. E-commerce development in rural and remote areas of BRICS countries. J. Integr. Agric. 20, 979–997. doi:https://doi.org/10.1016/S2095-3119(20)63451-7

Hassan, M.M., Lee, G., 2021. Online Payment Options and Consumer Trust: Determinants of E-Commerce in Africa. Int. J. Entrep. Knowl. 9, 1–13. https://doi.org/10.37335/ijek.v9i2.121

Ho, T.D.N., Tsusaka, T.W., Kuwornu, J.K.M., Datta, A., Nguyen, L.T., 2022. Do rice varieties matter? Climate change adaptation and livelihood diversification among rural smallholder households in the Mekong Delta region of Vietnam. Mitig. Adapt. Strateg. Glob. Chang. 27. doi:https://doi.org/10.1007/s11027-021-09978-x

Hossain, M.B., Dewan, N., Senin, A.A., Illes, C.B., 2025. Evaluating the utilization of technological factors to promote e-commerce adoption in small and medium enterprises. Electron. Commer. Res. 25, 349–368. doi:https://doi.org/10.1007/s10660-023-09692-7

Huang, J., Su, L., Huang, Q., Liu, X., 2022a. Facilitating inclusive ICT application and e-Commerce development in rural China. Agric. Econ. (United Kingdom) 53, 938–952. doi:https://doi.org/10.1111/agec.12728

Huang, L., Huang, Y., Huang, R., Xie, G., Cai, W., 2022b. Factors Influencing Returning Migrants' Entrepreneurship Intentions for Rural E-Commerce: An Empirical Investigation in China. Sustain. 14. doi:https://doi.org/10.3390/su14063682

Huang, L., Huang, Y., Rong, Z., Xie, G., 2026. Knowledge and drivers of rural e-commerce entrepreneurial vibrancy: A fuzzy-set qualitative comparative analysis study. J. Innov. Knowl. 12, 100911. doi:https://doi.org/10.1016/j.jik.2025.100911

Huang, L., Tan, J., Xie, G., Tian, Y., 2024a. The driving pathways for the construction of rural e-commerce entrepreneurial ecosystem based on the TOE framework. Humanit. Soc. Sci. Commun. 11, 1–14. doi:https://doi.org/10.1057/s41599-024-04072-4

Huang, Y., Li, X., Zhang, G., 2021. The Impact of Technology Perception and Government Support on E-Commerce Sales Behavior of Farmer Cooperatives: Evidence From Liaoning Province, China. SAGE Open 11. doi:https://doi.org/10.1177/21582440211015672

Huang, Y., Yang, Z., Chang, K., 2024b. Mobile immobility: an exploratory study of rural women's engagement with e-commerce livestreaming in China. J. Chinese Sociol. 11. doi:https://doi.org/10.1186/s40711-023-00204-6

Jabbouri, I., Jabbouri, R., Bahoum, K., El Hajjaji, Y., 2023. E-commerce adoption among Moroccan agricultural cooperatives: Between structural challenges and immense business performance potential. Ann. Public Coop. Econ. 94, 1145–1171. doi:https://doi.org/10.1111/apce.12406

Ji, C., Dong, X., Lin, W., 2024. The effects of e-commerce adoption on the financial performance of agri-food enterprises in China. Electron. Commer. Res. doi:https://doi.org/10.1007/s10660-024-09810-z

Jia, F., Yang, X., Jiang, Y., Chen, X., 2024. ICT-empowered rural e-commerce development in China: an adaptive structuration perspective. Int. J. Technol. Manag. 95, 90–119. doi:https://doi.org/10.1504/ijtm.2024.10062290

Keenan, M., Fort, R., Vargas, R., 2024. Shocked into side-selling? Production shocks and organic coffee farmers' marketing decisions. Food Policy 125. doi:https://doi.org/10.1016/j.foodpol.2024.102631

Klein, P., Popp, B., 2022. Last-Mile Delivery Methods in E-Commerce: Does Perceived Sustainability Matter for Consumer Acceptance and Usage? Sustain. 14. doi:https://doi.org/10.3390/su142416437

Komatsu, S., Suzuki, A., 2025. Impact of the Development of Rural E-Commerce on Rural Income and Urban–Rural Income Inequality in China: A Panel Data Analysis. Asia. Pac. Econ. Lit. doi:https://doi.org/10.1111/apel.70007

Lavoie, A., Wardropper, C.B., 2021. Engagement with conservation tillage shaped by "good farmer" identity. Agric. Human Values 38, 975–985. doi:https://doi.org/10.1007/s10460-021-10205-1

Lawson, E.T., Alare, R.S., Salifu, A.R.Z., Thompson-Hall, M., 2020. Dealing with climate change in semi-arid Ghana: understanding intersectional perceptions and adaptation strategies of women farmers. Geo Journal 85, 439–452. doi:https://doi.org/10.1007/s10708-019-09974-4

Leong, C., Pan, S.L., Newell, S., Cui, L., 2016. The emergence of self-organizing e-commerce ecosystems in remote villages of China: A tale of digital empowerment for rural development. MIS Q. Manag. Inf. Syst. 40, 475–484. https://doi.org/10.25300/MISQ/2016/40.2.11

Li, F., Gan, Y., 2025. Research on the sustainable development capability of Chinese rural E-Commerce based on multidimensional perspective. Sci. Rep. 15, 1–15. doi:https://doi.org/10.1038/s41598-025-95653-z

Li, H., Liow, G., Yuan, S., 2022. E-commerce adoption among micro agri-business enterprise in Longsheng, China: The moderating role of entrepreneurial orientation. Front. Psychol. 13. doi:https://doi.org/10.3389/fpsyg.2022.972543

Li, J., Ma, W., Botero-R, J.C., Quoc Luu, P., 2023a. Mechanization in land preparation and irrigation water productivity: insights from rice production. Int. J. Water Resour. Dev. 00, 1–22. doi:https://doi.org/10.1080/07900627.2023.2197080

Li, J., Ma, W., Gong, B., 2023b. Market participation and subjective well-being of maize farmers. Econ. Anal. Policy 80, 941–960. doi:https://doi.org/10.1016/j.eap.2023.09.037

Li, J., Vatsa, P., Ma, W., 2025a. Internet use and household debt: insights from rural China. Appl. Econ. 57, 10256–10276. doi:https://doi.org/10.1080/00036846.2024.2427422

Li, J., Vatsa, P., Ma, W., 2024. Flush toilet use and its impact on health and non-health expenditures. J. Int. Dev. 36, 2022–2046. doi:https://doi.org/10.1002/jid.3889

Li, J., Vatsa, P., Ma, W., Luu, P.Q., 2025b. Promoting sustainable agri-food production to achieve food and nutrition security: The role of soil conservation practices. Aust. J. Agric. Resour. Econ. 69, 59–79. doi:https://doi.org/10.1111/1467-8489.12598

Li, S., Dou, Q., Yu, Z., 2023. The influence mechanism of quasi-site creativity stimulation on consumers' impulse buying in e-commerce live streaming. Multimed. Tools Appl. 82, 37407–37430. doi:https://doi.org/10.1007/s11042-023-15101-w

Li, W., He, W., 2024. Revenue-increasing effect of rural e-commerce: A perspective of farmers' market integration and employment growth. Econ. Anal. Policy 81, 482–493. doi:https://doi.org/10.1016/j.eap.2023.12.015

Li, Xiaokang, Guo, H., Jin, S., Ma, W., Zeng, Y., 2021a. Do farmers gain internet dividends from E-commerce adoption? Evidence from China. Food Policy 101, 102024. doi:https://doi.org/10.1016/j.foodpol.2021.102024

Li, Xiaojing, Sarkar, A., Xia, X., Memon, W.H., 2021b. Village environment, capital endowment, and farmers' participation in e-commerce sales behavior: A demand observable bivariate probit model approach. Agric. 11, 1–20. doi:https://doi.org/10.3390/agriculture11090868

Li, Z., Gao, K., Qiao, G., 2025. From Online Markets to Green Fields: Unpacking the Impact of Farmers' E-Commerce Participation on Green Production Technology Adoption. Agric. 15, 1–31. doi:https://doi.org/10.3390/agriculture15141483

Lin, H., Li, R., Hou, S., Li, W., 2021. Influencing factors and empowering mechanism of participation in e-commerce: An empirical analysis on poor households from Inner Mongolia, China. Alexandria Eng. J. 60, 95–105. doi:https://doi.org/10.1016/j.aej.2020.06.010

Liu, C., He, X., Yi, L., 2024a. Determinants of multimodal fake review generation in China's E-commerce platforms. Sci. Rep. 14, 1–28. doi:https://doi.org/10.1038/s41598-024-59236-8

Liu, H., Ding, M., Kan, Y., Dong, Q., 2025. A Study on the Relationship Between Rural E-Commerce Development and Farmers' Income Growth. Sustain. 17. doi:https://doi.org/10.3390/su17093879

Liu, H., Liang, C., 2025. Supply Chain Digitization and Corporate Carbon Disclosure. Int. Financ. doi:https://doi.org/10.1111/infi.70007

Liu, M., Liu, T., Ren, Y., Wu, L., 2024b. How Does the Adoption of e-Commerce Impact the Selling Prices of Agricultural Products? Empirical Evidence From Apple Farmers in China. Rev. Dev. Econ. 1–22. doi:https://doi.org/10.1111/rode.13168

Liu, M., Min, S., Ma, W., Liu, T., 2021. The adoption and impact of E-commerce in rural China: Application of an endogenous switching regression model. J. Rural Stud. 83, 106–116. doi:https://doi.org/10.1016/j.jrurstud.2021.02.021

Liu, M., Zhang, Q., Gao, S., Huang, J., 2020. The spatial aggregation of rural e-commerce in China: An empirical investigation into Taobao Villages. J. Rural Stud. 80, 403–417. doi:https://doi.org/10.1016/j.jrurstud.2020.10.016

Livernois, R., 2024. Externalities and the Limits of Pigovian Policies. Ethics, Policy Environ. 27, 428–450. doi:https://doi.org/10.1080/21550085.2023.2272549

Loo, M.K., Ramachandran, S., Raja Yusof, R.N., 2024. Systematic Review of Factors and Barriers Influencing E-Commerce Adoption among SMEs over the Last Decade: A TOE Framework Perspective. J. Knowl. Econ. 9624–9648. doi:https://doi.org/10.1007/s13132-024-02257-5

Lu, Y.H., Yeh, C.C., Liau, T.W., 2023. Exploring the key factors affecting the usage intention for cross-border e-commerce platforms based on DEMATEL and EDAS method. Electron. Commer. Res. 23, 2517–2539. doi:https://doi.org/10.1007/s10660-022-09548-6

Luo, X., Niu, C., 2019. E-Commerce Participation and Household Income Growth in Taobao Villages (No. 8811), Policy Research Working Paper, Policy Research Working Paper. doi:https://doi.org/10.1596/1813-9450-8811

Lusardi, A., Mitchell, O.S., 2023. The Importance of Financial Literacy: Opening a New Field. J. Econ. Perspect. 37, 137–154. doi:https://doi.org/10.1257/jep.37.4.137

Lyu, D., Zhou, L., Ma, X., 2022. Income-increasing effect of e-commerce of agricultural products based on IT absorptive theory. Wirel. Networks 28, 2337–2344. doi:https://doi.org/10.1007/s11276-022-02904-2

Ma, W., Zhou, X., Liu, M., 2019. What drives farmers' willingness to adopt e-commerce in rural China? The role of Internet use. Agribusiness 36, 159–163. doi:https://doi.org/10.1002/agr.21624

Melkani, A., Mason, N.M., Mather, D.L., Chisanga, B., Jayne, T., 2025. Liquidity constraints for variable inputs at planting time and the maize production and marketing decisions of smallholder farmers in Zambia. Agric. Econ. (United Kingdom) 56, 73–91. doi:https://doi.org/10.1111/agec.12863

Milazzo, A., Goldstein, M., 2019. Governance and Women's Economic and Political Participation: Power Inequalities, Formal Constraints and Norms. World Bank Res. Obs. doi:https://doi.org/10.1596/34344

Misra, P., Pandey, A., 2022. Factors Influencing Customers Loyalty Towards Electronic Commerce. Proc. 2nd Int. Conf. Sustain. Equity 2, 147–154. doi:https://doi.org/10.2991/ahsseh.k.220105.018

Mollick, J., Cutshall, R., Changchit, C., Pham, L., 2023. Contemporary Mobile Commerce: Determinants of Its Adoption. J. Theor. Appl. Electron. Commer. Res. 18, 501–523. doi:https://doi.org/10.3390/jtaer18010026

Natarajan, N., Newsham, A., Rigg, J., Suhardiman, D., 2022. A sustainable livelihoods framework for the twenty-first century. World Dev. 155. doi:https://doi.org/10.1016/j.worlddev.2022.105898

Ndlovu, P.N., Thamaga-Chitja, J.M., Ojo, T.O., 2021. Factors influencing the level of vegetable value chain participation and implications on smallholder farmers in Swayimane KwaZulu-Natal. Land use policy 109. doi:https://doi.org/10.1016/j.landusepol.2021.105611

Nogueira, G.P.M., Silva, S.V., Hasenclever, L., de Assis Rangel, J.J., 2025. Sustainability in B2C e-commerce: a literature review and future research opportunities in last-mile deliveries. Environ. Dev. Sustain. 27, 12415–12436. doi:https://doi.org/10.1007/s10668-024-04471-2

Onjewu, A.K.E., Hussain, S., Haddoud, M.Y., 2022. The Interplay of E-commerce, Resilience and Exports in the Context of COVID-19. Inf. Syst. Front. 24, 1209–1221. doi:https://doi.org/10.1007/s10796-022-10342-w

Paniagua, P., Rayamajhee, V., 2024. On the nature and structure of externalities. Public Choice 201, 387–408. doi:https://doi.org/10.1007/s11127-023-01098-1

Penagos, P., Encarnación, T., Jaramillo-ríos, J., Gonzalez-calderon, C.A., Posada-henao, J.J., 2025. Impact of the COVID-19 pandemic on e-commerce adoption in emerging economies. Lat. Am. Transp. Stud. 3, 100037. doi:https://doi.org/10.1016/j.latran.2025.100037

Phiri, A., 2019. Adoption of E-Commerce by the Small Scale Famers in Zimbabwe: An Empirical Analysis. Int. J. Acad. Res. Bus. Soc. Sci. 9. doi:https://doi.org/10.6007/ijarbss/v9-i4/5815

Qin, Y., Fang, Y., 2022. The Effects of E-Commerce on Regional Poverty Reduction: Evidence from China's Rural E-Commerce Demonstration County Program. China World Econ. 30, 161–186. doi:https://doi.org/10.1111/cwe.12422

Qiu, H., Tang, W., Huang, Y., Deng, H., Liao, W., Ye, F., 2024. E-commerce operations and technology perceptions in promoting farmers' adoption of green production technologies: Evidence from rural China. J. Environ. Manage. 370, 122628. doi:https://doi.org/10.1016/j.jenvman.2024.122628

Quang Doan, H., Truong Tuan, L., Khanh Doanh, N., 2024. The influence of neighborhood dynamics on farmers' intention to adopt e-commerce platforms for organic tea sales: a study in Thai Nguyen province of Northern Vietnam. Org. Agric. 14, 213–230. doi:https://doi.org/10.1007/s13165-024-00459-4

Rahayu, R., Day, J., 2015. Determinant Factors of E-commerce Adoption by SMEs in Developing Country: Evidence from Indonesia. Procedia- Soc. Behav. Sci. 195, 142–150. doi:https://doi.org/10.1016/j.sbspro.2015.06.423

Ramesh, S. &, 2025. Digital Inclusion of Women Entrepreneurs in The Unorganized Sector—A Systematic Review. Adv. Consum. Res.

Saiful, M., Samreth, S., Hayat, A., Islam, S., 2022. Climate change, climatic extremes, and households' food consumption in Bangladesh : A longitudinal data analysis. Environ. Challenges 7, 100495. doi:https://doi.org/10.1016/j.envc.2022.100495

Sevigny, C., Caviglia-Harris, J., Santiago, T.O., Mullan, K., 2025. The new frontier: Social media's influence on farming practices in the Brazilian Amazon. Agric. Resour. Econ. Rev. 1–23. doi:https://doi.org/10.1017/age.2025.18

Shen, B., Ma, W., Li, J., 2025. Role of gender in determining energy poverty, clean energy access, and energy expenditure: Insights from rural China. Energy Econ. 144, 108369. doi:https://doi.org/10.1016/j.eneco.2025.108369

Shiu, J.Y., Liao, S.T., Tzeng, S.Y., 2023. How does online streaming reform e-commerce? An empirical assessment of immersive experience and social interaction in China. Humanit. Soc. Sci. Commun. 10, 1–8. doi:https://doi.org/10.1057/s41599-023-01731-w

Smith, R., Ehrenberg, R., 2016. Modern Labor Economics, Modern Labor Economics. Pearson Education Asia LTD. doi:https://doi.org/10.4324/9781315510651

Soleimani, M., 2022. Buyers' trust and mistrust in e-commerce platforms: a synthesizing literature review. Inf. Syst. E-bus. Manag. 20, 57–78. doi:https://doi.org/10.1007/s10257-021-00545-0

Song, Y., Li, L., Sindakis, S., Aggarwal, S., Chen, C., Showkat, S., 2024a. Examining E-Commerce Adoption in Farmer Entrepreneurship and the Role of Social Networks: Data from China. J. Knowl. Econ. 15, 8290–8326. doi:https://doi.org/10.1007/s13132-023-01379-6

Song, Y., Yang, L., Li, L., 2024b. A study on the impact mechanism of internet embedding on rural E-commerce entrepreneurship. Res. Int. Bus. Financ. 68. doi:https://doi.org/10.1016/j.ribaf.2023.102196

Sundermeier, J., Kummer, T.F., 2022. Does personality still matter in e-commerce? How perceived hubris influences the assessment of founders' trustworthiness using the example of reward-based crowdfunding. Electron. Mark. 32, 1127–1144. doi:https://doi.org/10.1007/s12525-022-00584-6

Sundjaja, A.M., Arisanto, G.V., Fatimah, S., 2020. The Determinant Factors of E-Commerce Usage Behavior During Flash Sale Program. Comm IT J. 14, 65–72. https://doi.org/10.21512/commit.v14i2.6582

Tang, L., 2016. Problems in Development of Rural E-commerce and Logistics and Recommendations. Asian Agric. Res. 8, 41–47.

Thenoz, E., Juteau, S., Rowe, F., 2024. E-commerce transformation: A literature review from an institutional and organizational perspective. Electron. Mark. 34, 1–20. doi:https://doi.org/10.1007/s12525-024-00740-0

UNDP, 2021. Global Assessment of Soil Pollution.

Ünver, Ş., Alkan, Ö., 2021. Determinants of e-Commerce Use at Different Educational Levels: Empirical Evidence from Turkey e-Commerce Use at Different Educational Levels. Int. J. Adv. Comput. Sci. Appl. 12, 40–49. https://doi.org/10.14569/IJACSA.2021.0120305

Utami, H.N., Alamanda, D.T., 2022. Key Factors Determining Relationship Marketing in the Food E-Commerce Network: a Business-To-Business Service Perspective. Agricore J. Agribisnis dan Sos. Ekon. Pertan. Unpad 6. https://doi.org/10.24198/agricore.v6i2.37354

Vavekanand, R., Kumar, S., 2024. Rural Agricultural Development Through E-Commerce Platforms. Authorea Prepr. https://doi.org/10.13140/RG.2.2.35572.97927

Wang, C., Wu, X., Chen, T., 2025. Neighborhood effect, virtual social networks, and farmers' social e-commerce participation behavior. Agribusiness 41, 238–259. doi:https://doi.org/10.1002/agr.21885

Wang, H., Li, Y., Lin, W., Wei, W., 2023a. How does digital technology promote carbon emission reduction? Empirical evidence based on e-commerce pilot city policy in China. J. Environ. Manage. 325. doi:https://doi.org/10.1016/j.jenvman.2022.116524

Wang, L., 2015. The analysis of several realistic problems of rural e-commerce 248–252. doi:https://doi.org/10.2991/icemit-15.2015.53

Wang, M., Ding, X., Cheng, P., 2024a. Exploring the income impact of rural e-commerce comprehensive demonstration project and determinants of county selection. Humanit. Soc. Sci. Commun. 11. doi:https://doi.org/10.1057/s41599-024-03785-w

Wang, Y., Tian, Y., Nasrullah, M., Zhang, R., 2024b. Does social capital influence farmers' e-commerce entrepreneurship? China's regional evidence. Electron. Commer. Res. doi:https://doi.org/10.1007/s10660-023-09794-2

Wang, Y., Yang, A., Li, Y., Yang, Q., 2023b. Effect of e-commerce popularization on farmland abandonment in rural China: Evidence from a large-scale household survey. Land use policy 135, 106958. doi:https://doi.org/10.1016/j.landusepol.2023.106958

Wang, Y., Zhang, Z., 2023. A Study on the Willingness and Factors Influencing the Digital Upgrade of Rural E-Commerce. Behav. Sci. (Basel). 13. doi:https://doi.org/10.3390/bs13020095

Xiang, H., Chau, K.Y., Iqbal, W., Irfan, M., Dagar, V., 2022. Determinants of Social Commerce Usage and Online Impulse Purchase: Implications for Business and Digital Revolution. Front. Psychol. 13, 1–13. doi:https://doi.org/10.3389/fpsyg.2022.837042

Xie, G., 2026. The impact of generative AI shopping assistants on E-commerce consumer motivation and behavior: Consumer-AI interaction design. Int. J. Inf. Manage. 86. doi:https://doi.org/10.1016/j.ijinfomgt.2025.102983

Yang, S., Wang, H., Wang, Z., Koondhar, M.A., Ji, L., Kong, R., 2021. The nexus between formal credit and E-commerce utilization of entrepreneurial farmers in rural China: A mediation analysis. J. Theor. Appl. Electron. Commer. Res. 16, 900–921. doi:https://doi.org/10.3390/jtaer16040051

Yang, W., Wang, L., Zhang, X., 2025. Online or not online: the impact of business owner's risk preference on the adoption of e-business. Electron. Commer. Res. 25, 1375–1394. doi:https://doi.org/10.1007/s10660-023-09755-9

Yang, X., Chen, X., Jiang, Y., Jia, F., 2020. Adoption of e-commerce by the agri-food sector in China: The case of Minyu e-commerce company. Int. Food Agribus. Manag. Rev. 23, 1–16. https://doi.org/10.22434/IFAMR2019.0049

Yildirim, T.M., 2022. Rethinking Women's Interests: An Inductive and Intersectional Approach to Defining Women's Policy Priorities. Br. J. Polit. Sci. 52, 1240–1257. doi:https://doi.org/10.1017/S0007123421000235

Yongdi, L., 2025. Analysis of the Role of Commercialization of Agricultural Markets in the Development of the Pending Special Agricultural Economy. Agric. For. Econ. Manag. 8, 78–84. https://doi.org/10.23977/agrfem.2025.080111

Yu, Z., Zhang, K., 2022. The Determinants of Purchase Intention on Agricultural Products via Public-Interest Live Streaming for Farmers during COVID-19 Pandemic. Sustain. 14. doi:https://doi.org/10.3390/su142113921

Zeng, X.L.H.G.S.J.W.M.Y., 2015. The broadband digital divide and the benefits of mobile broadband for minorities 373–400. doi:10.1007/s10888-015-9296-0

Zhang, Q., 2021. Legal Issues about Online Sales of Agricultural Products in the Development of Rural E-commerce in China. Int. J. Front. Sociol. 3, 31–34. https://doi.org/10.25236/ijfs.2021.031605

Zhang, Y., Wu, X., Cai, R., 2025. The effects of rural e-commerce on income inequality: evidence from the National Rural E-Commerce Comprehensive Demonstration policy in China. Econ. Anal. Policy 87, 221–234. doi:https://doi.org/10.1016/j.eap.2025.05.052

Zhang, Yonghu, Zhang, Yifeng, 2024. The Influence of Digital Literacy on the Phenomenon of Deviation between Farmers' E-Commerce Sales Willingness and Behavior: Evidence from Rural China. Sustain. 16. doi:https://doi.org/10.3390/su16073000

Zhong, Y., Lai, I.K.W., Guo, F., Tang, H., 2021. Research on government subsidy strategies for the development of agricultural products e-commerce. Agric. 11, 1–27. doi:https://doi.org/10.3390/agriculture11111152

Zhu, J.H., Abdul Hanan, S., Chong, K.L., 2024. Bridging the digital financial divide: The relationship between chinese farmers' e-commerce adoption intentions and financial literacy. Multidiscip. Sci. J. 7, 2025243. https://doi.org/10.31893/multiscience.2025243

Žukovskis, J., Raupelienė, A., Pypłacz, P., 2023. Factors Affecting the Need for a Specialized E-Commerce Platform for Managing Agricultural Entities. Polish J. Manag. Stud. 28, 414–432. https://doi.org/10.17512/pjms.2023.28.1.24

Chapter 3
Unequal Access, Uneven Gains: Demographic and Structural Barriers to Rural E-Commerce Adoption in India

Avik Ghosh

3.1 Introduction

The global e-commerce landscape has undergone a significant transformation over the last two decades, reshaping the way consumers and producers interact. With the proliferation of digital infrastructure, e-commerce has become more than a commercial tool—it now serves as a mechanism for social and economic inclusion, particularly in rural areas (Kong 2019; OECD 2019). Across developed and developing countries, digital marketplaces are transforming consumption patterns, enhancing access to goods and services, and reconfiguring production systems. In the Asia-Pacific region, e-commerce platforms are being increasingly integrated into public service delivery, agricultural supply chains, and rural entrepreneurship, thereby decentralizing opportunities and reducing geographic exclusion (UNESCAP 2021; ADB 2022). Countries such as Indonesia, Vietnam, and the Philippines have expanded rural agri-commerce through mobile payments and public-private platforms (GSMA 2022). While e-commerce supports Sustainable Development Goals, such as poverty reduction and inclusive growth, its benefits remain unequally distributed (Bergantino et al. 2026; Pajuste 2025), with rural areas often structurally disadvantaged in both access and the ability to fully participate (World Bank 2021; Hilbert 2011).

India represents a strategic case for examining rural e-commerce due to its rapid digital expansion and socio-economic diversity. Initiatives such as BharatNet, UPI, and Digital India have significantly improved digital infrastructure, internet access, and mobile payment systems. Yet, these gains have produced uneven outcomes (Rupasingha et al. 2026), with rural regions continuing to lag in digital adoption due to informal labour dominance, gendered asset ownership, and educational

A. Ghosh (✉)
Reserve Bank of India, Kanpur, India
e-mail: avikghosh@rbi.org.in

W. Ma et al. (eds.), *E-Commerce for Inclusive Rural and Agricultural Development*, Contributions to Economics,
https://doi.org/10.1007/978-981-92-5237-4_3

disparities (Richa et al. 2025). This rural-urban divide in digital participation is mirrored across Asia-Pacific nations, such as Bangladesh, Nepal, and Sri Lanka, positioning India as a relevant proxy for broader regional trends. Empirical evidence shows persistent gaps in digital expenditure, device access, and trust in e-commerce (Ragnedda 2020). Rural users face multiple barriers, including infrastructure deficits, affordability constraints, and limited digital literacy, which can create a cycle of digital exclusion (Pajuste 2025; Bergantino et al. 2026). Unlike their urban counterparts, rural consumers often rely on low-functionality or shared devices, which exacerbates underutilization (Cámara and Tuesta 2014). These divides are further shaped by demographic dimensions such as occupation, education, gender, and household size, emphasizing the need to move beyond access metrics toward understanding cognitive and behavioral constraints (van Deursen and Helsper 2015). A disaggregated analytical approach is thus essential for inclusive e-commerce development.

India is not only a large emerging economy but also analytically representative of broader challenges in digitalisation across lower- and middle-income countries. It is home to the world's largest rural population—approximately 893 million people—while simultaneously hosting one of the world's largest online populations, with more than 750 million internet users and internet penetration above 50% (UN DESA 2018; DataReportal 2024). This combination of scale and internal diversity, spanning advanced and lagging states, makes India a microcosm of the global rural–urban digital divide. Mobile broadband coverage now reaches the vast majority of the population. Yet, a sizeable "usage gap" persists (Rupasingha et al. 2026), in which households with infrastructure remain offline due to affordability, skills, and relevance constraints (GSMA 2023). In global indices of e-commerce readiness, such as the UNCTAD B2C E-commerce Index, India occupies a mid-range position—ahead of many low-income economies but still behind digital frontrunners in East and Southeast Asia—indicating that it is neither an extreme laggard nor a fully mature digital market (UNCTAD 2021). Insights from the Indian case are therefore informative for a wide range of emerging economies that confront similar tensions between rapid digital infrastructure expansion and persistent socio-economic barriers to rural e-commerce adoption.

Recent evidence confirms that India's 'Digital India' story remains sharply uneven across space. Sub-national analysis shows persistent rural–urban gaps in both digital infrastructure and digital skills across Indian states (Arora and Sapre 2025), while micro-level survey work on the Digital India Programme documents heterogeneous adoption patterns by age, education, and gender in rural districts (Sindakis and Showkat 2024). These findings underscore the importance of analysing rural households' digital spending behaviour using nationally representative microdata.

This paper addresses this analytical gap through a novel contribution that focuses on the demographic and structural underpinnings of the rural-urban divide in digital expenditure, used here as a proxy for e-commerce adoption and digital integration. While prior studies have highlighted infrastructural and policy-level drivers, this study drills deeper into household-level dynamics, leveraging a detailed dataset to uncover how demographic attributes influence digital behavior differently across space. The central research question this study explores is not only whether a rural-urban divide exists, but, more importantly, why and how it persists, even among seemingly similar households. Further, this paper introduces a multi-pronged empirical framework: first, using descriptive analysis to map the heterogeneity across key demographic variables; second, deploying state fixed-effects OLS regressions to identify predictors of digital expenditure; third, utilizing Oaxaca-Blinder decomposition to differentiate between explained and unexplained gaps; and finally, implementing quantile regression to capture distributive heterogeneity across expenditure levels. Together, these techniques enable a comprehensive assessment of both average and distributional differences in digital participation. The focus on demographic categories, such as age, gender composition, education level, occupational group, and household size, enhances the precision of findings, revealing structural inequalities that are often masked in aggregate statistics. The paper thus offers theoretical and empirical value by bridging the literatures on digital inequality, rural transformation, and household economics.

A notable feature of this study is the use of the Consumer Pyramids Household Survey (CPHS), a nationally representative dataset compiled by the Centre for Monitoring Indian Economy (CMIE). With over 100,000 households across India, the CPHS provides granular data on monthly digital expenses, household demographics, income, and consumption. CPHS's design, spanning multiple waves, states, and rural-urban classifications, enables a level of temporal and spatial robustness[1] seldom seen in household panel data. The empirical strategy adopted in this study capitalizes on the dataset's richness, offering novel insights into how household-level characteristics correlate with digital expenditure. The analysis reveals that education has a significantly higher return in urban areas, while household size contributes positively to digital usage only up to a point. Interestingly, gender composition and occupational structure also display asymmetric effects, reflecting both cultural norms and access-related frictions. By embedding these findings within a solid econometric framework, the paper delivers actionable policy insights, particularly for designing inclusive digital infrastructure, targeted digital literacy programs, and scalable e-commerce platforms for rural users (Wang et al. 2024). Furthermore, the combination of decomposition and quantile approaches allows for a simultaneous understanding of macro-structural gaps and micro-distributional inequities, positioning this research at the intersection of data innovation and policy relevance.

In doing so, the study aligns itself with an emerging body of literature that sees digital inclusion not merely as access to the internet, but as meaningful and equitable participation in digital life (Rallet and Rochelandet 2007). The findings presented here are expected to contribute to broader debates on digital development,

[1] Temporal robustness refers to the ability of the dataset to capture changes in household behavior over time. This is enabled by CPHS's high-frequency, longitudinal design that tracks the same households across multiple survey waves. Spatial robustness reflects the dataset's comprehensive geographic coverage across all Indian states, including detailed rural and urban classifications.

particularly in the context of developing economies seeking to leapfrog traditional barriers through technology. As e-commerce continues to redefine economic landscapes, such granular empirical inquiries become indispensable for ensuring that the rural poor are not left behind in this transition. The subsequent section of this paper engages with the academic literature that frames these debates, highlighting the theoretical and empirical foundations upon which this study builds.

The paper is organised as follows. Section 3.2 reviews the theoretical and empirical literature on digital inclusion, rural e-commerce, and demographic barriers. Section 3.3 describes the CPHS data used in this study and the construction of the digital expenditure measures and covariates. Section 3.4 outlines the empirical framework, including OLS with state indicator variables, Oaxaca-Blinder decomposition, and quantile regression. Section 3.5 presents and discusses the results, and Sect. 3.6 concludes with policy implications.

3.2 Literature Review

This literature review is structured in three interlinked parts. The first subsection explores foundational theoretical frameworks and global perspectives on digital inclusion and rural e-commerce development. The second focuses on emerging economies in the Asia-Pacific, highlighting region-specific insights. The third narrows the focus to the Indian context. Each subsection identifies prevailing research gaps, culminating in a discussion of how the present study seeks to address these through specific research questions.

3.2.1 Theoretical Perspectives and Global Context

The concept of digital inclusion has undergone a significant transformation in the global development discourse, evolving from a narrow focus on technological access to a broader concern with equity in usage, skills, and digital outcomes. Early literature emphasized the "first-level digital divide,[2]" centered on access to devices and internet infrastructure. However, scholars quickly recognized that mere connectivity does not equate to meaningful participation. Van Dijk (2006) introduced the concept of a "successive digital divide,[3]" arguing that disparities exist not only in access but also in skills, usage patterns, and ultimately, social and economic outcomes derived from digital engagement. Warschauer (2003) similarly underscored

[2] The first-level digital divide refers to disparities in physical access to digital infrastructure such as internet connectivity and devices (van Dijk 2006).

[3] The successive digital divide conceptualizes digital inequality as a multi-stage process, encompassing disparities in material access, digital skill acquisition, differentiated usage intensity, and the stratified social and economic returns to digital engagement (van Dijk 2006).

that access alone is insufficient without accompanying social capital, education, and institutional frameworks that enable transformative use. Theoretical developments, such as the Capability Approach (Sen 1999), have further expanded this understanding, positioning digital inclusion as a question of individual freedom and agency. This perspective emphasizes that the ability to use technology effectively is conditioned by socio-economic and institutional capabilities, not just technical infrastructure. Accordingly, the global literature increasingly conceptualizes digital inequality as multidimensional, spanning not only access and skills but also distributional outcomes such as poverty and exclusion (Zhang et al. 2024; Li et al. 2025; Wang et al. 2025).

Empirical studies across high- and middle-income countries show that digital transformation often exacerbates existing inequalities. Pick and Nishida (2015) find that structural divides persist across world regions, even where physical infrastructure is widespread. Robinson et al. (2015) note that usage disparities reflect deeper systemic constraints, particularly in marginalized communities. In rural areas, these challenges are compounded by limited broadband reach, low levels of digital literacy, and reduced institutional support (Sun et al. 2025; Hu and Yin 2026). Recent micro-evidence reinforces this link between household endowments and digital engagement: for example, Rodríguez Ruiz et al. (2024) show that ICT ownership and household assets strongly predict penetration into the digital economy in Mexico, with marked heterogeneity across the distribution of assets. While this global literature has provided critical theoretical tools and diagnostic insight, it often lacks empirical attention to how structural and demographic barriers interact to influence the returns to digital access, especially in rural contexts. There is a need for more granular, disaggregated analysis that captures these dynamics, an area this study seeks to address through its household-level approach and distributional lens.

3.2.2 Asia-Pacific Emerging Economies: Regional Experiences

In emerging Asia-Pacific economies, digital transformation is increasingly seen as a lever for inclusive rural development. A growing empirical literature documents how rural e-commerce affects household incomes and poverty. Using county-level data from China, Hou and Liu (2024) and Xie et al. (2025) find that rural e-commerce significantly contributes to regional poverty alleviation in nationally designated poverty-stricken counties. Micro-level studies indicate that participation in rural e-commerce raises farmers' incomes and can narrow income gaps at lower quantiles, although effects may be heterogeneous across the distribution (Guan et al. 2024; Liu et al. 2025; Qiu 2025). These studies also highlight the complementarity between digital commerce and inclusive financial infrastructure (Zhang and Zhao 2025). Structural constraints, including educational deficits, gender disparities, informal labor systems, and lack of localized content, continue to limit the uptake of digital platforms in rural settings (ADB 2022; Liang and Li 2023). In Indonesia, for example, Sham et al. (2024) demonstrate that access to digital platforms alone does not lead to engagement without supporting digital literacy. Similarly, in Bangladesh and Nepal, digital entrepreneurship programs have been hindered by a lack of institutional credit and a mismatch in skills with rural economies. These experiences highlight that rural digital inclusion depends not only on infrastructure, but also on whether individuals and households can convert access into meaningful and productive use. This insight necessitates a more in-depth, micro-level investigation.

In this context, monthly digital expenditure provides a practical, theoretically grounded proxy for gauging e-commerce participation. Unlike binary access indicators (e.g., internet access or mobile ownership), digital spending captures intensity, frequency, and purposefulness of use—core elements of e-commerce engagement (Cámara and Tuesta 2014; Demirgüç-Kunt et al. 2018). Studies in South Korea and Malaysia have demonstrated that higher digital expenditure is strongly correlated with increased online transaction behavior, platform adoption, and digital payment usage (Lee et al. 2019; Lim et al. 2023). However, few Asia-Pacific studies examine how such expenditures vary across demographic groups or how structural variables shape spending behavior. Most rely on aggregate data, overlooking intra-group variation and the dynamics of distribution. Additionally, little attention has been paid to whether rural populations derive equivalent returns from digital investments compared to their urban counterparts (Pick and Nishida 2015; van Deursen and Helsper 2015). This paper addresses these gaps by analyzing household-level digital expenditure as a measure of rural e-commerce potential, using a distribution-sensitive empirical strategy to examine demographic and structural barriers in the Indian context.

3.2.3 India: Demographic Inequalities and Rural E-Commerce Gaps

India stands at the intersection of massive digital progress and persistent rural inequality. Initiatives such as BharatNet, the Digital India Programme, and the Pradhan Mantri Gramin Digital Saksharta Abhiyan (PMGDISHA) have expanded rural internet access and digital literacy. Recent work on smart villages and digital inclusion underscores that rural connectivity and digital skills can translate into broader rural development gains, including productivity and income growth (Doloi 2025), while village-level digital infrastructure has measurable effects on food security, dietary diversity, and subjective well-being (Qiao et al. 2025; Duan 2024). However, these efforts have not translated into uniform digital participation across socio-economic groups or regions. Studies reveal that while urban India has adopted digital payments and e-commerce on a large scale, rural areas continue to lag due to structural and demographic constraints (Richa et al. 2025). The rural digital divide in India is not merely a matter of infrastructure, but a consequence of deeper socio-economic disparities.

Empirical evidence suggests that disparities in education, occupation, gender composition, and household size significantly affect digital behavior (Correa and Pavez 2016). Rural users, especially women, face barriers to owning and using mobile devices, which limits their engagement with digital commerce (Wang et al. 2024). Age structures also play a role, with elderly-led households or those with dependent children being less likely to allocate resources toward digital services (Haji 2021). The relationship between demographic characteristics and digital spending in India is thus embedded in broader systems of inequality. Moreover, while official statistics often focus on access metrics, such as internet or device ownership, they fail to capture usage intensity, expenditure behaviors, or return on digital investment. As Cámara and Tuesta (2014) emphasize, digital financial expenditure can act as a stronger indicator of e-commerce engagement than access alone. Existing literature also underrepresents the role of demographic heterogeneity in explaining the rural-urban gap in e-commerce penetration. Most macro studies rely on state- or district-level aggregates, ignoring the distributional nuances within households. Furthermore, few studies have examined the economic returns of digital participation among rural users, particularly across categorical groups such as gender, occupation, and education. This overlooks how structural barriers hinder the effectiveness of digital adoption in rural India (van Deursen and Helsper 2015).

This paper addresses these limitations by providing a distribution-sensitive, household-level analysis of digital expenditure as a proxy for e-commerce usage. It leverages the Consumer Pyramids Household Survey (CPHS) dataset, comprising over 100,000 households, to analyze how demographic characteristics influence digital spending in rural versus urban areas. It also employs regression analysis, Oaxaca decomposition, and quantile regression to illustrate how structural and demographic barriers persist despite infrastructural improvements. Accordingly, the research is guided by the following key questions:

(a) What is the nature and extent of the rural-urban divide in household-level digital expenditure in India?
(b) How do demographic categories (age group, gender composition, occupation, education, and household size) influence digital spending?
(c) To what extent do structural barriers explain the observed rural disadvantage in e-commerce adoption?
(d) How do returns to digital participation differ across demographic quantiles and subgroups?

By systematically addressing these questions, the paper fills a significant empirical and methodological void in the Indian and broader Asia-Pacific e-commerce literature.

3.3 Data and Variables

The data for this study were drawn from the Consumer Pyramids Household Survey (CPHS), an extensive and nationally representative dataset maintained by the Centre for Monitoring Indian Economy (CMIE). As one of the largest longitudinal household surveys in India, CPHS captures rich and high-frequency data across several dimensions of household economic behavior, well-being, and demographics. The survey is organized into three primary modules: the Income Pyramids, which track household and individual-level income flows from multiple sources; the Consumption Pyramids, which capture a comprehensive account of monthly and weekly expenditures; and the People of India module, which records demographic, social, and educational characteristics of household members. Together, these modules allow researchers to analyze the multifaceted nature of household decision-making and socio-economic outcomes.

This study uses the CPHS Wave covering January–May 2025, which serves as the common sample for all descriptive, regression, and decomposition analyses. For the present analysis, data were consolidated from all three modules, providing a 360° view of household composition, income, expenditure patterns, and demographic diversity. The original unfiltered dataset comprised 161,178 household observations. A transparent three-step cleaning protocol was then implemented. First, households with missing information on key outcome and control variables used in the econometric analysis—namely, monthly digital expenditure, total household expenditure, and the categorical demographic indicators (age group, education group, occupation group, gender composition, and household size)—were removed. Second, observations reporting internally inconsistent or implausible combinations of income and expenditure (for example, cases where reported digital spending exceeded total consumption, or very high expenditure was reported alongside zero income) were excluded, as these are likely to reflect recording or recall errors rather than genuine behaviour. Third, a small number of extreme statistical outliers in the distributions of income and digital expenditure were dropped to limit the undue leverage of atypical observations on the estimates. In total, these procedures led to the exclusion of 58,620 households, yielding a final analytical sample of 102,558 households. This refined sample retains full national coverage, encompassing both rural and urban households from every Indian state and union territory. The panel design and sampling methodology adopted by CPHS ensure representativeness across space and time, making the dataset highly suitable for understanding structural and systemic issues such as rural-urban digital divides and the demographic roots of digital exclusion.

To construct meaningful proxies for e-commerce penetration at the household level, a composite variable titled Monthly Digital Expenses[4] was computed. This is the sum of four expenditure heads recorded in CPHS: expenditure on mobile phones and accessories, mobile usage and recharge, internet and landline services, and subscriptions to over-the-top (OTT) digital platforms. The underlying logic is grounded

[4] Monthly Digital Expenses is a non-negative, continuous expenditure variable (INR/month), constructed as the sum of spending on mobiles and accessories, mobile usage/recharge, internet and landline services, and OTT subscriptions. Households with no spending on any of these heads in the reference month take a value of zero, so that zeros represent genuine non-users rather than censored or missing observations. In the final analytical sample, roughly 3 per cent of households report zero digital expenditure, with a slightly higher share in rural areas.

in the assumption that households investing regularly in digital connectivity and online services are likely to be active or potential users of e-commerce platforms. This approach is justified by established literature. Hilbert (2011) demonstrates that access to ICTs, measured in part by expenditure, is directly linked to opportunities for economic empowerment, particularly among marginalized groups such as women in rural areas. Similarly, researchers emphasize that differences in internet usage outcomes often stem not only from access but also from variations in digital skills and the frequency and nature of online activities, which are closely linked to actual digital spending behavior. Scheerder et al. (2017) further reinforce the relationship between socio-demographic factors, access costs, and the depth of digital engagement, making expenditure a practical and grounded proxy for e-commerce exposure. To enhance transparency about the construction of this proxy, I also report descriptive statistics for each of the four underlying expenditure components—mobile phones and accessories, mobile usage and recharge, internet and landline services, and OTT subscriptions—alongside the composite Monthly Digital Expenses variable. Annexure Table 3.7 presents the mean, standard deviation, minimum, maximum, and the number of observations for each component, separately for rural and urban households.

In addition to the proxy variable for e-commerce, the study includes several categorical demographic variables that capture distinct facets of household structure and identity. These variables—age group, occupation group, education group, gender group, and size group—comprise various internal demographic categories that influence digital behavior. In addition to analyzing category-specific effects and behavior, these variables have been transformed into binary classifications to better capture heterogeneity in distribution across demographic segments. The age group distinguishes between households dominated by young members or children and those led by seniors or adults. Occupation group separates labour-intensive households (e.g., farmers, daily-wage workers, informal labourers) from white-collar or professional households engaged in managerial, technical, or administrative occupations. Similarly, the education group captures educational disparities by dividing households into those without graduate members and those with a majority of graduates, thereby serving as a proxy for human capital. Gender groups differentiate male-dominated households from those led primarily by women, a crucial factor in digital participation. Lastly, size group categorizes households by the number of members, distinguishing between smaller families (up to four members) and larger households (more than four members), which can influence digital expenditure through economies of scale or differential exposure to technology within multigenerational settings. The demographic factors described above align well with global digital divide literature. van Deursen and Helsper (2015) argue that the benefits of being online are not distributed equally, and are often shaped by third-level digital divides—i.e., differences in how outcomes are derived from online engagement. Their work, alongside that of Scheerder et al. (2017), provides a framework for understanding how education, gender, and occupation influence not only access but also the quality and outcomes of digital use.

The CPHS's geographical breadth and demographic inclusivity make it a unique resource for studying rural-urban inequalities. The survey spans all Indian states and union territories and is stratified across 110 Homogeneous Regions, ensuring representation of both urban agglomerations and rural hinterlands. The urban sample comprises metropolitan cities and medium and small towns, while the rural sample comprises villages stratified by agro-climatic, educational, and infrastructural indicators. Moreover, the repeated-measures structure of CPHS, conducted three times annually per household, supports the development of time-series data, enhancing the robustness of the findings and enabling longitudinal interpretation.

3.4 Empirical Strategy

To examine the demographic and structural barriers to rural digital expenditure and e-commerce adoption, this section outlines the empirical methodologies applied in the study. It proceeds in four stages: starting with diagnostic descriptive statistics, followed by regression modeling, decomposition analysis, and distributional estimation to capture both average and heterogeneous effects.

3.4.1 Descriptive Statistics and Rural-Urban Diagnostic Framework

To establish a foundational understanding of the digital divide, this study begins with a descriptive statistical analysis of household-level digital expenditure using a filtered sample of 102,558 households from the Consumer Pyramids Household Survey (CPHS). The methodology adopts a two-pronged approach. First, a comparative analysis is performed between rural and urban sub-samples using the full dataset. Monthly digital expenditure is compared across demographic variables, and independent-samples t-tests are used to test for statistically significant differences between rural and urban areas. This step identifies statistically significant gaps in digital behavior by region. Following this, sub-sample analyses are conducted independently for rural and urban households to understand internal demographic heterogeneity. Key variables such as household size, gender composition, education level, and occupational structure are evaluated against digital spending patterns to uncover within-group dynamics. This bifurcated approach allows the study to identify not only the average gap between regions but also the nuanced distribution of inequality within each region, a method frequently used in studies on economic disparity (World Bank 2004). This combination of *t*-tests and stratified subsample examination has proven effective in studies of rural inequality and technology, offering both statistical precision and conceptual clarity (Alkire 2013). By doing so, the study establishes a robust empirical base for exploring deeper causal mechanisms through regression and decomposition models in subsequent sections.

3.4.2 Baseline Regression Model and Identification Logic

To quantify the relationship between demographic characteristics and digital expenditure, this study employs a cross-sectional Ordinary Least Squares (OLS) regression model with state-level fixed effects.[5] This modeling framework enables the isolation of within-state variation in household digital expenditure while controlling for unobserved heterogeneity across Indian states, such as infrastructure, market access, and state-level policy environments, which could otherwise bias coefficient estimates. The empirical specification is as follows:

$$DigitalExp_i = \theta + \beta_1\, RegionType_i + \varphi\, X_i + \alpha_s + \varepsilon_i \tag{3.1}$$

where $DigitalExp_i$ is the monthly digital expenditure of household *i*. $RegionType_i$ is a binary variable for rural/urban classification, X_i is a vector of household demographic characteristics (age group, education level, gender composition, occupation group, household size), α_s captures state fixed effects, and ε_i is the idiosyncratic error term. Although the analysis is cross-sectional (CPHS Wave January–May 2025), the term "state fixed effects" refers to including a full set of state indicator variables (state dummies) in the OLS regression to absorb time-invariant state-level heterogeneity. For brevity, the coefficients on the state indicators are not reported in the result table, but they are included in all regression specifications (Wooldridge 2010).

Standard errors are clustered at the state level to account for intra-state correlation in digital behavior. The regression estimates both pooled coefficients for the entire sample and stratified coefficients for rural and urban sub-samples, revealing differential marginal effects across contexts. This methodology aligns with standard practice in development economics, where fixed effects are frequently employed to control for policy-driven or institutional confounding at the administrative level (Wooldridge 2010). Studies like those by Jain and Goyal (2022) have used similar models to understand household consumption behavior in India, and Gelbach (2016) emphasizes the interpretive clarity that fixed effects bring when comparing sub-national units.

[5]Although Monthly Digital Expenses is bounded below at zero, all values (including zeros) are observed and reflect actual non-participation, not censoring by design. I therefore treat it as a continuous outcome rather than a left-censored variable and estimate linear fixed-effects models with heteroskedasticity-robust standard errors, complemented by quantile regressions to capture distributional heterogeneity (see, e.g., Wooldridge 2010).

3.4.3 Oaxaca-Blinder Decomposition Strategy

To assess the structural and demographic underpinnings of rural-urban differences in digital expenditure, this study implements the Oaxaca-Blinder decomposition technique. Originally developed for analyzing wage differentials, this method has since been widely used to examine group-based inequality in economic outcomes. The decomposition separates the observed mean difference in digital expenditure (Δ Y) between rural (R) and urban (U) households into two components:

$$\Delta Y = (X_U - X_R) \bullet \beta_U + X_R \bullet (\beta_U - \beta_R) + (X_U - X_R) \bullet (\beta_U - \beta_R) \tag{3.2}$$

where X denotes the vector of average characteristics, and β represents estimated coefficients from group-specific regressions. $(X_U - X_R)$. β_U captures the explained effect, X_R. $(\beta_U - \beta_R)$ captures the unexplained effect, and $(X_U - X_R)$. $(\beta_U - \beta_R)$ indicates the interaction effect. The explained (endowment) effect captures the portion of the digital gap attributable to observable demographic differences, such as education or occupation, between rural and urban households. The unexplained (coefficient) effect reflects structural disparities in returns to those characteristics, often interpreted as systemic barriers, including access, quality of digital infrastructure, and cultural norms. The interaction term accounts for the compound effect of differing characteristics and returns. This approach is ideal for digital inclusion studies, particularly when average effects may mask structural inequities. For instance, studies in developing countries such as Indonesia and Peru have applied the Oaxaca-Blinder decomposition to quantify similar divides in internet adoption and e-service access (Rallet and Rochelandet 2007). By identifying the magnitude and nature of these components, the decomposition allows this study to isolate and quantify demographic versus systemic barriers to digital participation across regions.

3.4.4 Quantile Regression Strategy

While mean-based models, such as OLS, offer a general understanding of average effects, they often conceal how explanatory variables operate differently across the distribution of digital expenditure. To uncover this distributional heterogeneity, this study uses quantile regression as introduced by Koenker and Bassett (1978). This method estimates conditional quantiles (e.g., 10th, 50th, and 90th percentiles) of the dependent variable, enabling a more granular examination of how demographic attributes influence households with varying levels of digital engagement. The quantile regression model is specified as:

$$Q_\tau (Y_i \mid X_i) = \alpha(\tau) + X_i' \beta(\tau) \tag{3.3}$$

where $Q_\tau(Y_i| X_i)$ is the conditional τth quantile of digital expenditure Y_i, X_i includes household-level demographic controls, and $\beta(\tau)$ is quantile-specific coefficients. This model is estimated separately for rural and urban sub-samples to capture context-specific non-linearities. For instance, educational attainment may significantly influence digital spending in the upper quantiles (higher-spending households) but have negligible effects in the lower tail. Similarly, household size or gender composition may exhibit positive effects in some quantiles and negative or neutral effects in others, highlighting the importance of distribution-sensitive estimation. This methodology has been effectively applied in studies on inequality and digital adoption in developing countries (Demirgüç-Kunt et al. 2018), particularly where access to technology is uneven across population strata (Haji 2021). Quantile regression provides a robust tool for revealing such latent disparities and informing targeted digital inclusion policies.

The next sections present the empirical findings derived from the methodologies outlined above. These include detailed results, an interpretative discussion, and a set of policy recommendations to address the structural barriers to rural e-commerce adoption, grounded in the broader development context.

3.5 Results and Discussion

The Results and Discussion section systematically unveils the demographic barriers influencing rural e-commerce development and adoption. It begins by presenting descriptive statistics to highlight rural-urban disparities and internal heterogeneity across demographic groups. This is followed by regression-based analysis to quantify the effects of demographic categories on digital expenditure, serving as a proxy for e-commerce engagement. The subsequent decomposition and quantile regression approaches delve deeper into the structural and distributive dimensions of the digital divide, offering evidence on both visible and latent demographic constraints to rural digital participation.

3.5.1 Descriptive Statistics: Cross-Regional and Intra-Group Heterogeneity

The descriptive analysis highlights the foundational disparities in digital expenditure between rural and urban households across India. Before turning to demographic categories, Annexure Table 3.7 provides summary statistics for each of the four expenditure heads that constitute Monthly Digital Expenses, demonstrating that the rural-urban gap is evident across all components of digital spending and in the composite indicator. As shown in Table 3.1, urban households consistently outspend rural households on monthly digital expenses, including mobile, internet, and OTT services. This rural-urban differential highlights the persistence of first-level digital divides, reflecting unequal access to the infrastructure and services necessary to participate in the digital economy (Robinson et al. 2015). Beyond the average differences, Table 3.2 introduces categorical demographic segmentation and reveals

Table 3.1 Rural-urban differences in monthly digital expenditure across demographic and household categories

Group/categories	Rural mean	Urban mean	t-stat (p)
Total household income	30246.05	38473.16	−73.73 (0.000)***
Total household expenditure	16819.22	22519.46	−36.92 (0.000)***
Total monthly expenditure on mobile phones, internet, and other accessories	555.44	746.79	−49.98 (0.000)***
Demographic and household category-wise differences in digital expenses			
Household age group			
Balanced households with seniors	596.33	748.33	−2.50 (0.012)**
Balanced households with no seniors	579.49	783.83	−27.71 (0.000)***
Children—dominant	437.28	482.32	−1.57 (0.117)
Grown-up—dominant	557.88	751.7	−35.50 (0.000)***
Other households of the Young	540.18	613.53	−5.57 (0.000)***
Other households of grown-ups	591.17	808.72	−15.60 (0.000)***
Seniors—dominant	333.34	519.92	−11.42 (0.000)***
Youngsters—dominant	551.32	719.09	−17.25 (0.000)***
Household occupation			
Agricultural labourers	486.99	491.87	−0.30 (0.762)
Business and salaried employees	803.99	1028.48	−7.75 (0.000)***
Entrepreneurs	723.97	921.81	−9.39 (0.000)***
Home-based workers	465.63	570.93	−2.91 (0.004)***
Industrial workers	659.69	759.01	−4.82 (0.000)***
Legislators/social workers/activists	632.8	729.44	−0.79 (0.434)
Managers/supervisors	899.69	1127.49	−2.10 (0.041)**
Miscellaneous	325.66	378.76	−4.77 (0.000)***
Non-industrial technical employees	630.01	703.06	−5.98 (0.000)***
Organised farmers	616.68	696.76	−4.61 (0.000)***
Qualified self-employed professionals	701.93	1112.2	−4.59 (0.000)***
Retired/aged	454.89	624.11	−12.34 (0.000)***

(continued)

Table 3.1 (continued)

Group/categories	Rural mean	Urban mean	t-stat (p)
Self-employed entrepreneurs	585.38	655.77	−7.77 (0.000)***
Small Traders/Hawkers	502.96	602.37	−6.65 (0.000)***
Small/marginal farmers	480.71	486.99	−0.43 (0.665)
Support staff	617.94	675.28	−4.10 (0.000)***
Wage labourers	488.01	524.18	−7.37 (0.000)***
White-collar clerical employees	991.58	962.4	0.28 (0.779)
White-collar professional employees	825.19	1103.33	−9.04 (0.000)***
Household education			
All graduates household	716.75	1017.79	−10.22 (0.000)***
All matriculates household	576.08	702.34	−14.09 (0.000)***
Graduates dominated household	1031.3	1434.08	−3.91 (0.000)***
Graduates majority household	697.81	937.52	−12.57 (0.000)***
Graduates minority household	776.37	964.68	−6.88 (0.000)***
Households of all illiterates	408.07	435.9	−0.83 (0.407)
Households of all literates	473.5	539.74	−19.29 (0.000)***
Households of some literates	422.69	545.83	−5.16 (0.000)***
Matriculates dominated household	899.17	984.23	−0.86 (0.392)
Matriculates majority household	590.84	656.45	−9.84 (0.000)***
Matriculates minority household	625.24	739.09	−10.19 (0.000)***
Not applicable	413.89	518.97	−1.98 (0.052)*
Household gender			
Balanced	523.2	707.42	−26.51 (0.000)***
Female dominated	546.82	778.96	−17.69 (0.000)***
Female majority	572.1	786.75	−22.78 (0.000)***
Male dominated	627.92	839.35	−18.47 (0.000)***
Male majority	606.34	796.48	−25.78 (0.000)***
Only females	290.5	371.03	−9.51 (0.000)***

(continued)

Table 3.1 (continued)

Group/categories	Rural mean	Urban mean	t-stat (p)
Only males	354.72	484.78	−8.47 (0.000)***
Household size			
1 member	247	296.63	−8.14 (0.000)***
11–15 members	899.9	1557.85	−2.58 (0.011)**
2 members	407.27	565.4	−29.87 (0.000)***
3 members	548.89	749.79	−32.72 (0.000)***
4 members	605.58	825.79	−26.59 (0.000)***
5 members	609.65	840.61	−20.89 (0.000)***
6 members	637.12	866.98	−12.16 (0.000)***
7 members	667.66	867.72	−8.55 (0.000)***
8–10 members	793.61	1075.69	−6.95 (0.000)***
>15 members	15,750	638.75	0.96 (0.513)

(i) This table presents the mean monthly digital expenditure (INR) on mobile phones, accessories, internet/broadband, and related services across a wide range of household-level demographic categories, separately for rural and urban India. The last column reports the t-statistics and p-values from independent two-sample t-tests comparing rural and urban households within each subgroup
(ii) Significance levels: * $p < 0.10$; ** $p < 0.05$; *** $p < 0.01$
(iii) Categories are grouped under five dimensions: Age Composition, Occupation, Educational Composition, Gender Composition, and Household Size
Source: Authors

Table 3.2 Cross-regional heterogeneity

Total monthly digital expenditure	Rural	Urban	t-stat
Age group: households dominated by youngsters, children	564.68	752.63	−34.52***
Age group: households dominated by seniors, grown-ups	549.17	743.63	−37.67***
Occupation: farmers, labourers, other workers, etc.	521.67	611.37	−21.04***
Occupation: managerial, technical, white-collar, etc.	666.85	841.3	−19.11***
Education: households without graduates	545.93	666.68	−33.92***
Education: graduate majority/dominated households	709.51	983.57	−17.09***
Gender: male majority/dominated households	567.95	770.41	−45.02***
Gender: female majority/dominated households	515.12	640.99	−18.17***
Household size: more than 4 members	580.35	759.8	−26.90***
Household size: up to 4 members	537.51	740.55	−43.26***

Source: Authors; Significance levels: * $p < 0.10$; ** $p < 0.05$; *** $p < 0.01$

Table 3.3 Within-region micro heterogeneity

Variable	Region	Group 1 Mean	Group 2 Mean	Difference	t-stat
Household age group	Rural	564.68	549.17	2.75%	3.04***
Household age group	Urban	752.63	743.63	1.20%	1.63
Household occupation	Rural	521.67	666.85	−27.83%	−17.15***
Household occupation	Urban	611.37	841.3	−37.61%	−42.09***
Household education	Rural	545.93	709.51	−29.96%	−11.75***
Household education	Urban	666.68	983.57	−47.53%	−36.38***
Household gender	Rural	567.95	515.12	9.30%	10.76***
Household gender	Urban	770.41	640.99	16.80%	19.5***
Household size	Rural	580.35	537.51	7.38%	8.21***
Household size	Urban	759.8	740.55	2.53%	3.07***

Source: Authors; Significance levels: * $p < 0.10$; ** $p < 0.05$; *** $p < 0.01$

deep intra-group heterogeneity. Households in Group 1—those dominated by younger members, non-graduate adults, male majority, labour-intensive occupations, or larger household sizes—consistently report lower levels of digital expenditure. For instance, graduate-dominated households spend on average 29% more than their non-graduate counterparts, consistent with the well-established role of human capital in digital engagement. Likewise, female-majority households tend to spend more on digital services than male-majority households, aligning with evidence that gendered access dynamics can influence digital adoption and its returns (Hilbert 2011). The ridge plots presented in Figs. 3.7, 3.8, 3.9, and 3.10 in the Annexure reveal distinct distributional disparities in digital expenditure across rural and urban households, highlighting how educational attainment, age structure, gender composition, and occupational category systematically shape the depth and intensity of digital engagement.

Table 3.3 deepens the analysis by showing that, across rural and urban settings, digital expenditure varies sharply by demographic. In rural areas, households led by professionals and educated individuals report higher digital expenditure than those led by unskilled or non-graduate members. These findings reinforce the idea that the second-level digital divide—differences in skills, usage, and purpose—are strongly tied to demographic and socio-cultural capital (van Deursen and van Dijk 2014; Scheerder et al. 2017). In this light, access is necessary but not sufficient; capability and social context critically mediate digital behavior. Figure 3.1 and Table 3.8 (Annexure) further reveal significant regional heterogeneity across Indian states. While Delhi, Uttarakhand, and Meghalaya exhibit high levels of urban and rural digital expenditure, states like Bihar, Assam, and Tripura show a pronounced lag, particularly in rural digital engagement. These interstate disparities align with broader development indicators and highlight the importance of institutional support and the effectiveness of regional digital policies (Pick and Sarkar 2016; Ragnedda 2017).

The combined evidence affirms that demographic and geographic inequalities work in tandem to shape India's digital terrain. From a policy standpoint, bridging the rural-urban digital divide requires more than infrastructure deployment. It demands targeted investment in digital literacy for undereducated groups,

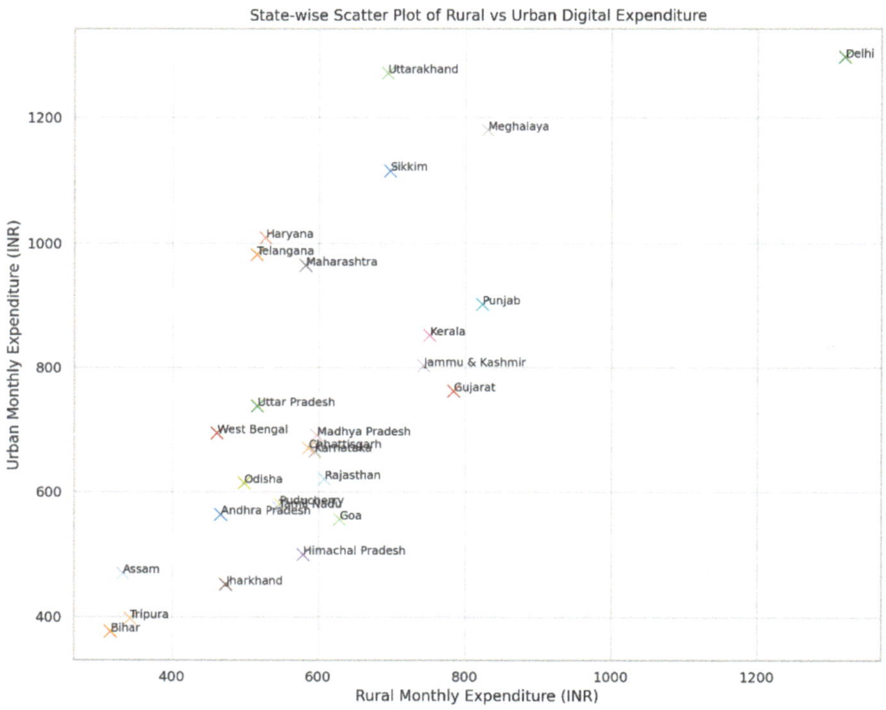

Fig. 3.1 State-wise scatter plot: rural vs urban digital expenditure. Source: Authors. Notes: Each marker represents a state mean of monthly digital expenditure (INR per month) for rural (x-axis) and urban (y-axis) households. Monthly digital expenditure is the composite measure defined in Table 3.1 (mobile phones and accessories, mobile usage/recharge, OTT subscriptions, and internet/landline services). Data source: CMIE Consumer Pyramids Household Survey (CPHS), January–May 2025 wave

gender-inclusive access to mobile technology, and platforms designed for digitally marginalized demographics, especially in larger households and informal employment sectors. As Warschauer (2003) pointed out, digital inclusion must address the interplay of access, capacity, and opportunity, not just device ownership. This section sets the empirical foundation for the econometric analyses that follow by demonstrating both macro-level rural-urban gaps and micro-level demographic disparities in digital access and expenditure. These patterns help frame the demographic barriers that constrain rural e-commerce development and adoption in India.

3.5.2 Regression Analysis of Digital Expenditure: National and Regional Insights

To isolate the effects of household demographics on digital expenditure, Table 3.4 presents OLS regressions that include state indicator variables (state fixed effects) to account for unobserved regional factors, such as infrastructure, pricing, and

Table 3.4 Digital expenditure regression: full and regional samples

	Monthly digital expenditure	Monthly digital expenditure: rural	Monthly digital expenditure: urban
Total household income	0.0043***	0.0012***	0.0067***
	(0.000)	(0.000)	(0.000)
Household age group: balanced households with seniors as reference			
Balanced households with no seniors	29.9087*	30.3705	32.9020
	(17.913)	(19.548)	(26.096)
Children—dominant	−112.2207***	−129.2420***	−89.8650
	(37.294)	(40.026)	(55.138)
Grown-up—dominant	61.7926***	58.1692***	60.8253**
	(17.826)	(19.456)	(25.973)
Other households of the young	−48.5086**	−24.3985	−52.5655*
	(20.004)	(21.419)	(29.580)
Other households of grown-ups	42.1307**	37.4530*	34.1036
	(18.065)	(19.806)	(26.256)
Seniors—dominant	15.6246	−9.2612	15.2897
	(20.377)	(23.245)	(29.051)
Youngsters—dominant	26.6468	38.0226*	27.6982
	(18.492)	(20.045)	(27.065)
Household occupation: organised farmers as reference			
Agricultural labourers	17.9957	−43.3824***	−15.1147
	(13.378)	(10.779)	(43.349)
Business and salaried employees	241.5095***	102.4624***	152.0271***
	(13.548)	(20.584)	(29.286)
Entrepreneurs	250.1443***	71.8015***	166.8034***
	(10.577)	(17.728)	(27.547)
Home-based workers	65.6709**	−14.5611	40.1602
	(31.543)	(34.458)	(51.207)
Industrial workers	138.4194***	42.8556***	95.4324***
	(10.824)	(13.423)	(27.686)
Legislators/social workers/activists	77.4932	1.1284	180.7188
	(70.334)	(63.307)	(128.941)
Managers/supervisors	298.1418***	225.4451***	194.8293***
	(31.044)	(68.881)	(43.469)
Miscellaneous	115.6539***	−14.0431	112.2113***
	(17.482)	(17.363)	(35.785)
Non-industrial technical employees	125.3186***	24.8382*	83.8888***
	(11.448)	(13.700)	(28.149)
Qualified self-employed professionals	315.3643***	44.4821	240.5766***
	(26.731)	(64.139)	(39.224)
Retired/aged	118.6523***	−30.3945***	109.6420***

(continued)

Table 3.4 (continued)

	Monthly digital expenditure	Monthly digital expenditure: rural	Monthly digital expenditure: urban
	(10.729)	(11.564)	(27.950)
Self-employed entrepreneurs	118.0662***	9.7107	85.2374***
	(8.578)	(9.029)	(26.387)
Small traders/hawkers	122.8805***	−36.4237*	92.3837***
	(14.473)	(21.704)	(30.042)
Small/marginal farmers	55.1537***	−21.5058**	77.3759**
	(10.817)	(8.771)	(38.665)
Support staff	114.4970***	16.0062	75.5010***
	(12.073)	(15.090)	(28.561)
Wage labourers	83.3591***	−26.5726***	55.3608**
	(9.323)	(8.926)	(27.127)
White-collar clerical employees	245.1119***	266.5339***	154.4636***
	(13.296)	(21.095)	(29.037)
White-collar professional employees	251.1991***	114.3367***	162.4031***
	(10.932)	(16.794)	(27.621)
Household education: all graduates household as reference			
All matriculates household	−126.9276***	−61.9500**	−72.0521***
	(9.833)	(24.582)	(11.682)
Graduates dominated household	201.9609***	142.9441**	150.8350***
	(25.126)	(63.335)	(29.033)
Graduates majority household	−44.4930***	−26.6666	−13.5238
	(9.445)	(25.287)	(10.899)
Graduates minority household	−60.8500***	5.9270	−13.5418
	(11.234)	(25.610)	(13.702)
Households of all illiterates	−74.1280**	−79.6123*	−18.4572
	(33.666)	(40.841)	(52.144)
Households of all literates	−162.9693***	−94.4692***	−97.6270***
	(9.544)	(23.920)	(11.732)
Households of some literates	−165.2524***	−144.6721***	−84.9511**
	(23.927)	(32.925)	(36.053)
Matriculates dominated household	−40.3067*	64.6122*	−26.0942
	(22.025)	(33.675)	(29.745)
Matriculates majority household	−148.1029***	−58.7737**	−93.1918***
	(9.644)	(24.100)	(11.677)

(continued)

Table 3.4 (continued)

	Monthly digital expenditure	Monthly digital expenditure: rural	Monthly digital expenditure: urban
Matriculates minority household	−160.9923***	−69.3234***	−95.0996***
	(11.954)	(25.093)	(16.156)
Not applicable	−87.3219	−90.9495	13.5404
	(70.371)	(76.317)	(106.207)
Household gender: balanced household as reference			
Female dominated	−29.6822***	−49.8159***	−17.4098
	(9.367)	(11.245)	(12.822)
Female majority	−14.9054	−28.6175**	−4.7930
	(10.036)	(11.203)	(14.426)
Male dominated	18.6708***	16.1882*	21.0188**
	(7.132)	(8.623)	(9.725)
Male majority	1.7283	3.4889	3.1010
	(9.845)	(10.991)	(14.148)
Only females	−12.3134	−33.3805*	1.9556
	(16.217)	(19.165)	(22.406)
Only males	−0.4451	−4.0935	7.2284
	(17.669)	(20.946)	(24.387)
Household size: 1-member household as reference			
11–15 members	863.5749***	577.8139***	962.2112***
	(52.415)	(59.832)	(74.063)
2 members	134.1239***	94.8499***	149.8404***
	(18.218)	(21.483)	(25.354)
3 members	253.5210***	201.8010***	269.7711***
	(19.943)	(23.111)	(28.088)
4 members	336.2360***	271.8250***	355.0129***
	(20.664)	(24.320)	(28.800)
5 members	377.6749***	303.5983***	399.3639***
	(21.222)	(24.619)	(29.821)
6 members	403.7009***	330.2671***	434.9228***
	(21.573)	(24.954)	(30.402)
7 members	435.5827***	367.9201***	466.2500***
	(24.341)	(27.524)	(34.924)
8–10 members	540.5057***	462.5924***	564.5922***
	(26.100)	(29.576)	(37.331)
>15 members	5068.0635***	15124.0275***	197.6587
	(244.903)	(303.625)	(329.521)
Observations	102,558	35,688	66,870
State fixed effects (state dummies)	Yes	Yes	Yes
Standard errors clustered at state level	Yes	Yes	Yes

Source: Authors; Significance levels: * $p < 0.10$; ** $p < 0.05$; *** $p < 0.01$

policy variations. The dependent variable is monthly digital expenditure, capturing spending on internet, mobile, and OTT services. Income remains the strongest predictor of digital engagement across all models. A one-unit increase in total household income is associated with a 0.0043-unit increase in digital expenditure in the full sample, and a 0.0067-unit increase in urban areas, highlighting the disproportionate affordability constraint faced by rural households, where the marginal effect is significantly lower (0.0012). This pattern supports the established role of income inequality in shaping digital divides (Ferreira et al. 2021; Laskar 2023). The age composition of the household strongly influences expenditure. Compared to households with balanced seniority, children-dominated households spend ₹112 less per month ($p < 0.01$), with the rural effect being even larger (₹129 less). In contrast, households with grown-ups spend an additional ₹62 per month. These results imply that younger households may lack the economic decision-making power to invest in digital services, reflecting a capacity-access mismatch.

Occupation is a strong marker of digital inclusion. Using organized farmers as the reference, qualified self-employed professionals spend an average of ₹315 more per month, and managers/supervisors spend ₹298 more, indicating that formal and higher-income occupational groups significantly outpace others in digital engagement. In rural areas, however, many groups, such as agricultural labourers and wage workers, exhibit negative or insignificant coefficients. For instance, agricultural labourers spend ₹43 less, and wage workers ₹26 less than the baseline group ($p < 0.01$), reaffirming the persistent occupational stratification of digital access. Educational attainment shows a steep gradient. Households with graduate-dominated composition spend ₹202 more monthly than all-graduate reference groups, while matriculate-only households spend ₹127 less. The penalty is deeper in rural areas, with illiterate households spending ₹80 less and matriculate minority households spending ₹69 less ($p < 0.01$). These patterns reaffirm the role of education in shaping digital literacy and use, consistent with DiMaggio and Garip (2012).

Gender composition exhibits complex effects. While male-dominated households spend ₹18.7 more ($p < 0.01$), female-dominated households spend ₹29.7 less, particularly in rural India (₹49.8 less). However, households consisting of only females also spend significantly less (₹ 33.40 less), indicating systemic gendered limitations in device access and decision-making, even when women are present (Ragnedda 2020). Household size shows a curvilinear relationship. Compared to one-member households, three- to ten-member families show progressively increasing digital expenditure, peaking at ₹540 for eight- to ten–member households. This suggests shared devices and aggregated household needs, although some of these values may reflect atypical cases or data issues that require robustness checks (van Deursen and van Dijk 2014). These findings suggest that even after controlling for state-level context, demographic asymmetries continue to drive the rural digital gap (Hu and Yin 2026). Education, occupation, household age, and gender composition significantly condition digital engagement. Therefore, rural e-commerce development cannot proceed solely through infrastructure expansion; tailored digital literacy programs, financial access schemes, and community-based models targeting low-skill, low-education, and female-headed households are also essential.

3.5.3 *Oaxaca-Blinder Decomposition: Demographic Barriers behind Digital Divide*

The Oaxaca-Blinder decomposition framework is applied to quantify the contribution of demographic characteristics to the rural-urban gap in monthly digital expenditure. This method partitions the mean difference into three components: the explained part (endowments), the unexplained part (coefficients), and an interaction term that reflects joint differences. As shown in Table 3.5, the total rural-urban digital expenditure gap is ₹191.35. Of this, ₹29.56 (15.4%) is attributed to endowment differences, or demographic disadvantages. However, the major driver is the coefficients component, which accounts for ₹194.62 (101.7%) of the gap. The negative interaction term (₹−32.83) marginally offsets the total difference, indicating a moderation effect between characteristics and their returns. The decomposition clearly highlights that even if rural households had the same characteristics as urban households, they would still spend ₹29.56 less—a direct outcome of demographic disadvantage. Table 3.6 reveals that household education is the largest contributor to the explained component (₹−49.58), indicating that low educational attainment in rural areas significantly depresses digital engagement. In contrast, household size is positively associated (₹21.08), suggesting that larger rural households may exhibit greater shared use or internal demand for digital services.

The coefficients component exposes the deeper issue: educated rural households gain far less from education than their urban counterparts, contributing a striking ₹163.95 to the gap. This implies that beyond access, the returns to digital capital are structurally biased. Similarly, rural households with more members face a penalty of ₹140.06, whereas large urban households benefit from economies of scale or better access. The returns to age, occupation, and gender are not statistically significant, indicating that these attributes do not exhibit systematic differences in value across regions. The interaction effects further amplify educational inequality (₹39.91) and modestly worsen household-size disadvantage (₹−6.85), reinforcing the idea that both differential characteristics and unequal outcomes compound rural disadvantage. The decomposition confirms that demographic variables, especially education and household structure, drive both observable and latent components of

Table 3.5 Oaxaca decomposition components

Component	Value (₹)	Interpretation
Endowments	−29.56***	If rural households had the same characteristics as urban ones, their expenditure would still be ~₹29.56 lower. Demographic disadvantage.
Coefficients	−194.62***	Even with the same characteristics, rural households spend ~₹194 less. Returns to characteristics (structural/systemic barriers).
Interaction	32.83***	Interaction partially offsets the effect. It shows how the joint difference in both characteristics and coefficients moderates the total gap.

Source: Authors; Significance levels: * $p < 0.10$; ** $p < 0.05$; *** $p < 0.01$

Table 3.6 Oaxaca decomposition variable-level interpretation

Endowments effect (explained part: $(X_1 - X_2) \times \beta_2$)		
Variable	Value (₹)	Interpretation
Household age group	−2.08***	Rural areas have less age structure conducive to digital use.
Household occupation	0.77***	Rural occupational mix slightly favours digital usage—minimal.
Household education	−49.58***	Major driver of gap. Rural households are far less educated.
Household gender	0.25***	Slightly favourable gender distribution in rural areas.
Household size	21.08***	Larger rural households could drive higher digital use.
Coefficients effect (unexplained: $X_2 \times (\beta_1 - \beta_2)$)		
Household education	163.95***	Huge urban advantage in returns to education: educated urban users derive far more digital benefit than equally educated rural users.
Household size	−140.06***	Rural large households don't benefit the way urban large families do—maybe due to shared tech or limited access.
Age, occupation, gender	Not significant	No strong differential in return to these characteristics.
Interaction term ($(X_1 - X_2) \times (\beta_1 - \beta_2)$)		
Household education	39.91***	Education gap and returns combine to exacerbate the urban advantage.
Household size	−6.85***	Interaction makes rural disadvantage slightly worse.

Source: Authors; Significance levels: * $p < 0.10$; ** $p < 0.05$; *** $p < 0.01$

the digital divide. Addressing rural e-commerce exclusion thus requires more than infrastructure; targeted interventions in adult education, digital skill-building, and household-level access strategies are critical to overcoming entrenched structural barriers.

The findings on the unequal digital spending profiles of rural households resonate with emerging distribution-sensitive evidence from other contexts. Zhang et al. (2024) and Li et al. (2025) show that digital literacy and social interaction interact with relative poverty across the income distribution, while Wang et al. (2025) and Rodríguez Ruiz et al. (2024) document that rural digital economies and ICT assets can amplify or attenuate inequality depending on local structural conditions. The results in this paper contribute to that literature by providing the first nationally representative, distribution-sensitive assessment of digital spending among rural Indian women.

3.5.4 Distributive Heterogeneity in Digital Spending

Quantile regression is applied to assess how the impact of key demographic factors on digital expenditure varies across the spending distribution. This approach uncovers distributive heterogeneity, highlighting which segments of the population are

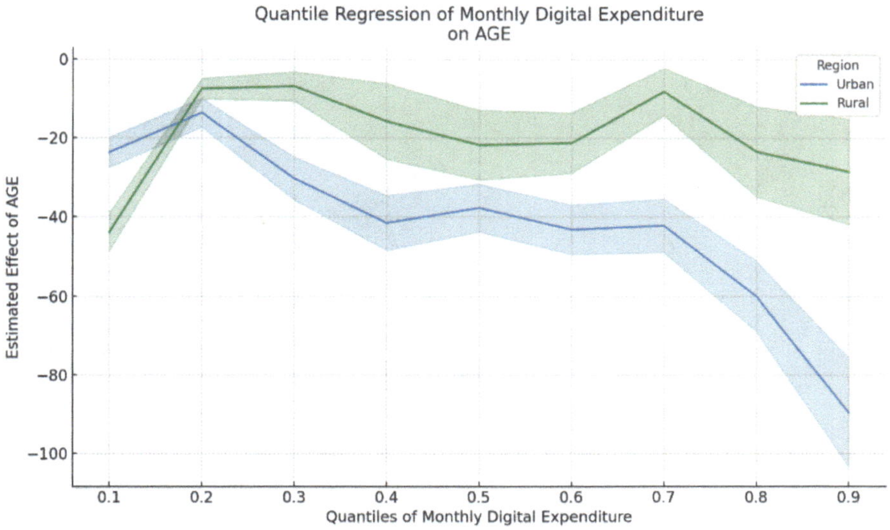

Fig. 3.2 Quantile regression plot—monthly digital expenditure on age. Source: Authors

disproportionately disadvantaged or privileged in digital participation—not just on average, but across the entire expenditure spectrum. Figure 3.2, illustrating the effect of household education, reveals stark stratification. Households with higher educational attainment exhibit increasing marginal influence on digital spending as one moves up the distribution. At lower quantiles, education has a modest impact; however, at the upper end (e.g., the 75th and 90th percentiles), the coefficients become substantially larger. This suggests that educational advantage is more consequential for high-consuming digital households, aligning with findings that education amplifies digital returns and platform engagement (Wei and Hindman 2011; van Deursen and Helsper 2015).

Figure 3.3 shows that occupational structure also exhibits significant heterogeneity. Households engaged in the formal sectors, especially salaried employment and professional services, benefit progressively more across quantiles, while those in agriculture or informal labor see minimal or declining influence. The digital expenditure of rural informal workers thus remains low even at higher quantiles, reinforcing occupation as a persistent barrier to digital inclusion (Pick and Nishida 2015). In Fig. 3.4, the effect of household age composition fluctuates across quantiles. While households dominated by adults and seniors gain moderately across the distribution, those dominated by children or young people consistently trail behind. This suggests that age-based capabilities and digital autonomy are important, especially in lower- and middle-income households, aligning with Correa's (2016) findings.

Figure 3.5 illustrates that the gender composition has asymmetric effects. Female-dominated and all-female households face significant digital disadvantages at lower and middle quantiles, but the effect levels off at the top. This reflects structural gendered constraints, including access to devices and financial control in

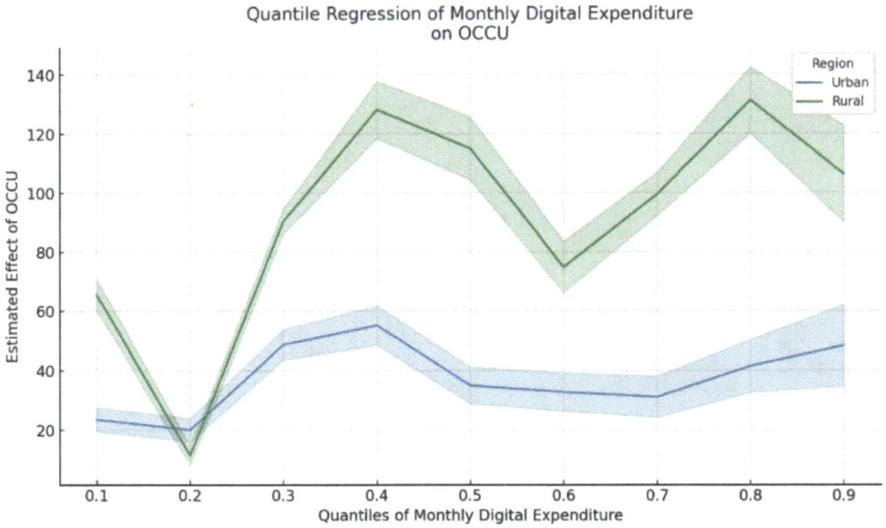

Fig. 3.3 Quantile regression plot—monthly digital expenditure on occupation. Source: Authors

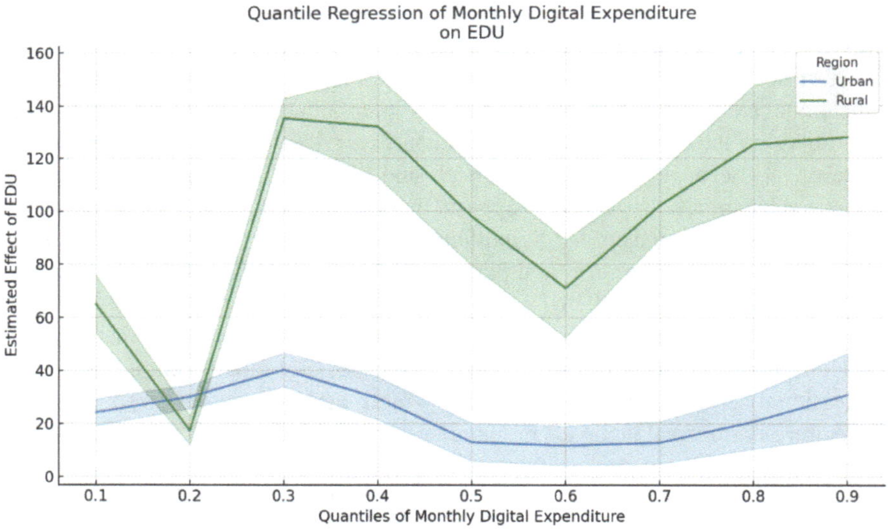

Fig. 3.4 Quantile regression plot—monthly digital expenditure on education. Source: Authors

low-income households (Hilbert 2011), which are somewhat neutralized in digitally affluent households. Figure 3.6 underscores that household size exerts a nonlinear influence. While digital spending increases with size at lower quantiles, likely due to shared consumption, the impact tapers or turns negative at higher quantiles, suggesting access saturation or resource dilution in larger rural families. Together, the findings confirm that demographic inequalities are not uniform but rather quantile-specific, necessitating targeted interventions. It appears that upper-quantile rural

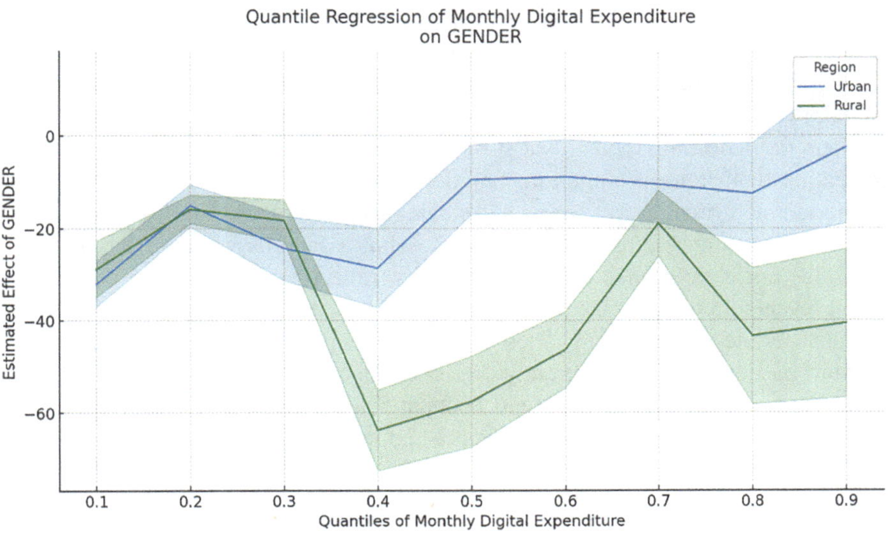

Fig. 3.5 Quantile regression plot—monthly digital expenditure on gender. Source: Authors

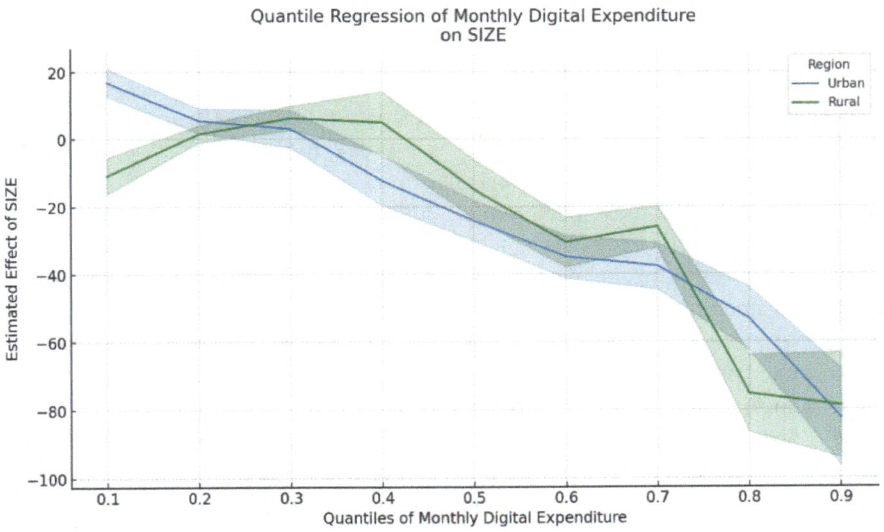

Fig. 3.6 Quantile regression plot—monthly digital expenditure on household size. Source: Authors

households require differentiated support, such as access to credit and infrastructure, to transition from digital access to e-commerce adoption.

The quantile patterns reveal three key mechanisms. First, education exhibits increasing marginal effects across quantiles (near zero at the 10th percentile to substantial at the 90th percentile), reflecting income constraints that prevent poor households from converting educational knowledge into digital engagement, aligning with capability theory perspectives that education's transformative potential requires sufficient financial resources. Second, occupational structure shows starkly different returns: formal-sector occupations (salaried employees, professionals) yield progressively increasing coefficients across quantiles, while informal workers (agricultural laborers, wage workers) display stagnant or negative effects, indicating that digital expenditure functions as productive investment only when supported by formal market access and stable income streams. Third, gender effects are non-monotonic: female-dominated households face larger penalties in lower quantiles but convergence at upper quantiles, reflecting compounded constraints (asset ownership norms, time poverty, household decision-making restrictions) that diminish as income increases. These distributional patterns underscore that demographic barriers operate differently across the income spectrum—lower-quantile policy requires income support and occupational re-skilling. In contrast, upper-quantile policy must address infrastructure and market access constraints.

3.6 Conclusions and Policy Recommendations

3.6.1 Conclusions

This study examines how demographic and structural factors shape inequalities in household digital expenditure, serving as a proxy for e-commerce engagement, across rural and urban India. The analysis shows a clear and persistent rural disadvantage: rural households spend substantially less on digital services even after accounting for income, education, occupation, gender composition, and household size. Decomposition results demonstrate that this gap is driven not only by differences in characteristics, but even more by differences in the returns to those characteristics. In particular, households with similar educational and occupational profiles do not translate these attributes into comparable levels of digital spending when they are located in rural rather than urban areas.

The distribution-sensitive analysis adds further nuance. Quantile regressions reveal that demographic penalties are not uniform across the expenditure distribution. Education, formal-sector occupations, and more favourable age structures yield disproportionately higher digital spending at the upper quantiles, while low-education, informal, and female-majority households remain constrained at the lower and middle quantiles. Household size exhibits a nonlinear pattern, with moderate sizes associated with higher spending but very large households facing diminishing or negative marginal effects. Taken together, these results point to a layered digital divide that combines endowment gaps with structural impediments to converting endowments into effective digital participation.

At the same time, the study has limitations that open avenues for future research. Digital expenditure is an informative but indirect proxy for e-commerce adoption and does not distinguish between different types of online activity. Important determinants such as device quality, local infrastructure, and financial inclusion are not directly observed at the household level. The analysis is essentially associational and cannot fully establish causal pathways from digital engagement to welfare outcomes. Future work could combine these data with complementary sources, exploit panel variation or policy shocks, and investigate how changes in digital behaviour affect income diversification, market access, and resilience among rural households over time.

3.6.2 Policy Recommendations

The empirical evidence establishes that rural digital inequality is fundamentally embedded in demographic structures and structural asymmetries operating simultaneously across multiple dimensions. Effective policy requires targeted, multi-layered intervention rather than generic digital expansion. The following recommendations translate quantified barriers into practical strategies applicable across low- and middle-income countries with similar contexts. First, localized digital literacy must be embedded within adult education frameworks through civil society partnerships that understand micro-level barriers to learning. The finding that education exhibits systematically lower returns in rural areas indicates that formal schooling expansion alone is insufficient. Programs must recognize existing literacy gaps, operate in local languages, and anchor content in agriculture, informal trade, and household management. Critical is the removal of opportunity costs through community institutions such as self-help groups and agricultural cooperatives. Digital literacy should progress from foundational skills like device operation and mobile payments to transaction management and platform navigation, culminating in market-linked applications such as digital vendor registration. Investment in persistent community-embedded facilitation rather than one-off training events is essential, given heterogeneous learning curves across age groups. Government schemes should establish minimum service standards requiring sustained local presence, trained facilitators fluent in regional languages, and performance incentives tied to demonstrated competency rather than completion metrics. Partnerships with financial inclusion initiatives and microenterprise programs leverage established trust networks.

Second, gender-responsive infrastructure must address compounded constraints facing female-headed households. The quantile regression evidence reveals that gender penalties are most severe in lower quantiles, indicating that low-income women face binding affordability constraints and social constraints absent among higher-income women. Policy must move beyond device distribution toward safe, accessible digital access points—community telecenters managed by women—providing physical space, social support, and guidance. Integration with existing women's economic programs, such as microfinance and self-help groups, embeds digital resources within structures that address complementary constraints: credit access, skill development, and social networks. Mobile-based digital financial services, particularly micro-credit accessed through simple interfaces, address payment barriers and income constraints evident at lower quantiles. Policy should mandate gender-disaggregated monitoring of digital participation, establish minimum female participation targets, and provide subsidies to reduce effective adoption costs. Government employment guarantee schemes and welfare programs should prioritize digital payment channels accessible to women, creating transactional familiarity while addressing income poverty. Cultural engagement through local women leaders and community influencers normalizes female digital participation and addresses asymmetries in household decision-making (Table 3.9).

Third, occupation-aligned e-commerce enablement must address the negligible returns to digital expenditure for informal workers. Digital adoption without occupational upgrading yields limited benefit for agricultural workers, informal traders, and home-based producers. Policy requires co-investment by governments, platforms, and development partners in occupation-specific interfaces and supply chain linkages. For smallholder farmers: platforms for collective marketing and real-time pricing integrated with input suppliers and buyers. For artisans: digital storefronts with quality certification and logistics partnerships enabling market reach. Platforms must feature low technical barriers and assisted onboarding. Value-chain integration connecting platforms with credit, consolidation facilities, and buyer institutions converts digital access into income generation. Policy should incentivize private platforms serving lower-income workers by subsidizing fees or offering performance-based grants. Training must be occupation-tailored, delivered through peer networks, emphasizing income-generating applications rather than generic literacy.

Fourth, subnational infrastructure equity and adaptive governance must replace national one-size-fits-all approaches. State fixed effects reveal substantial within-country disparities reflecting differences in state capacity, market conditions, and governance. National broadband plans frequently mask persistent subnational gaps. Effective policy requires state-specific equity mechanisms, such as dedicated rural development funds, with transparent allocation based on distributional diagnostics rather than population criteria. Adaptive local governance ensures digital access designs align with local institutional capacity and demand. Monitoring must track utilization, satisfaction, and demographic penetration—not merely deployment—with incentives tied to equity outcomes.

Fifth, digital financial inclusion must lower payment and credit barriers constraining lower-quantile participation. Strong associations between income and digital expenditure indicate binding affordability constraints. Digital services must feature tiered transaction costs to reduce friction for low-value transactions among informal workers. Digital identity integration with micro-credit enables instant assessment and rapid disbursement for device purchase or transaction collateral. Subsidized fees for rural users and public investment in last-mile payment networks are essential. Finally, equity-focused monitoring must replace aggregate metrics with disaggregated measurement. The decomposition and quantile analyses underscore that average metrics mask substantial demographic variation. Policy implementation requires equity dashboards that track adoption, usage, and participation, disaggregated by gender, occupation, education, and income quantiles. Monitoring should inform regular redesign, triggering targeted reallocation of resources to underperforming segments.

The recommendations illustrate a systems-level alignment between structural barriers and the multidimensional interventions required to activate rural e-commerce ecosystems. Effective rural e-commerce development demands not only access to infrastructure but also the dismantling of structural and demographic barriers. The proposed policy interventions, ranging from targeted digital literacy to occupation-specific enablement, directly address the socio-economic constraints identified in rural India and across the Asia-Pacific. Research indicates that localized digital skills and gender-responsive e-commerce platforms significantly enhance rural digital participation. When embedded in a multi-layered strategy, these measures foster not only adoption but also the sustainable integration of rural users into the digital marketplace, supporting inclusive and resilient rural economies.

Disclaimer *'The views expressed in this paper are purely personal views of the author and not those of the Reserve Bank of India.'*

Annexures

Annexure: Figures

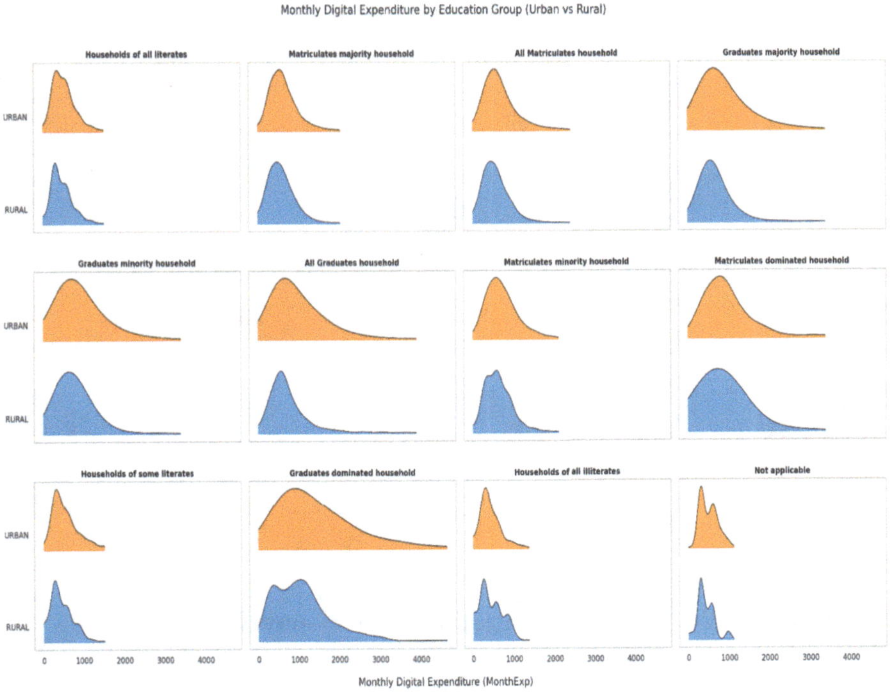

Fig. 3.7 Monthly digital expenditure by education group. Source: Authors

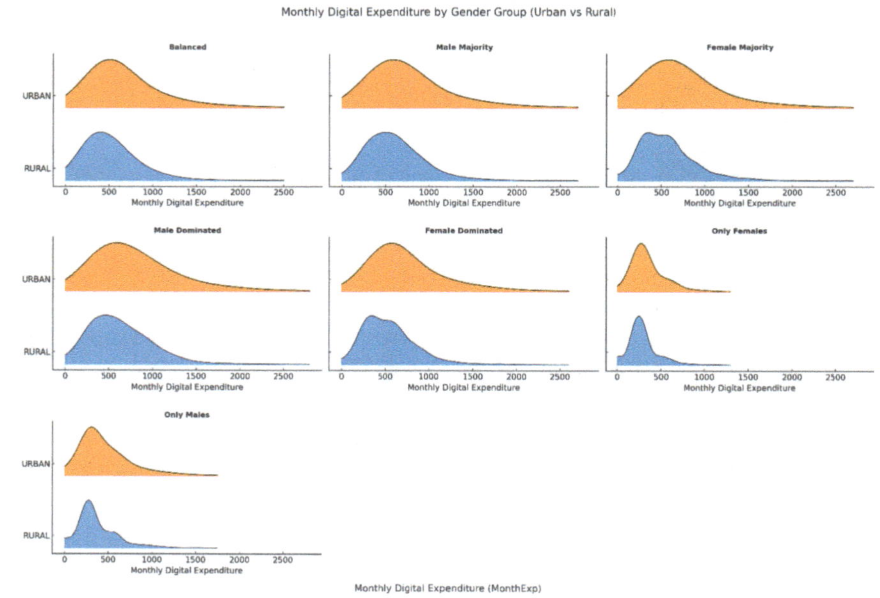

Fig. 3.8 Monthly digital expenditure by gender structure. Source: Authors

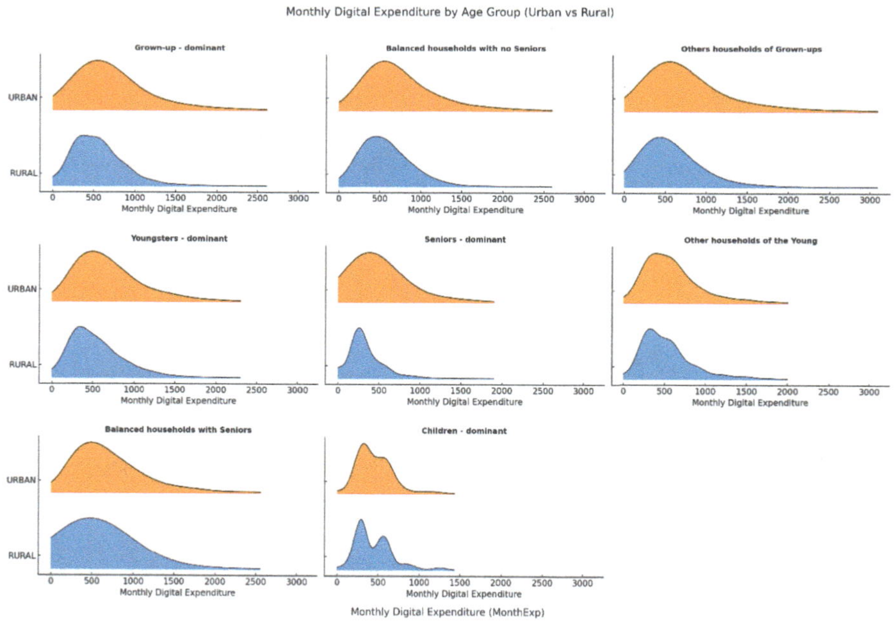

Fig. 3.9 Monthly digital expenditure by age structure. Source: Authors

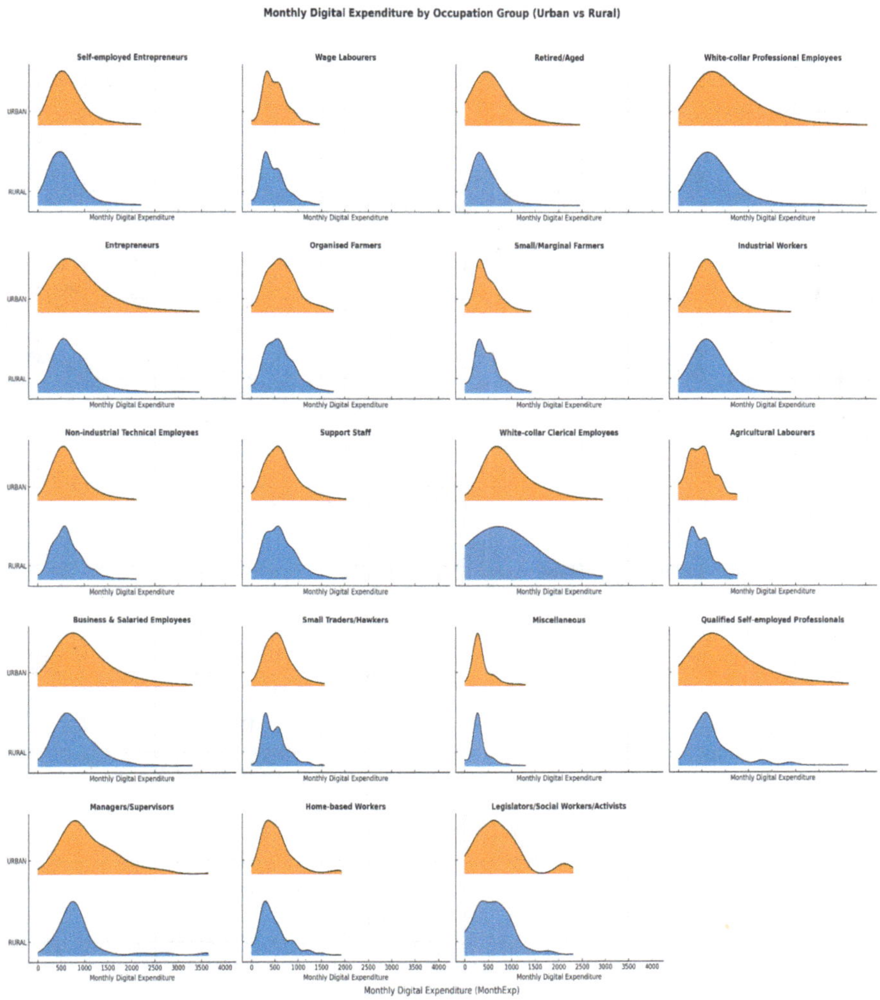

Fig. 3.10 Monthly digital expenditure by occupation structure. Source: Authors

Annexure: Tables

Table 3.7 Descriptive statistics for monthly digital expenses and underlying components (rural vs urban households)

Variable	Rural mean	Rural SD	Rural max	Rural N	Urban Mean	Urban SD	Urban Max	Urban N
Mobile phones and accessories	38.63	348.18	30,000	35,688	60.65	531.87	50,000	66,870
Mobile usage and recharge	506.57	293.81	3500	35,688	597.38	332.05	4730	66,870
OTT subscriptions	3.92	50.45	1560	35,688	24.40	125.50	3060	66,870
Internet and landline services	6.31	67.25	2100	35,688	64.37	212.26	5000	66,870
Monthly Digital Expenses (composite)	555.44	481.91	31,500	35,688	746.79	738.18	50,269	66,870

Source: Authors; all monetary values in INR per month

Table 3.8 Cross-regional heterogeneity in digital expenditure

State	Rural	Urban	t-stat
Andhra Pradesh	466.35	563.69	−9.66***
Assam	332.16	469.44	−4.52***
Bihar	315.86	376.53	−12.35***
Chhattisgarh	586.14	670.35	−3.99***
Delhi	1319.49	1296.03	0.34
Goa	628.55	555.81	0.63
Gujarat	784.25	762.17	1.71*
Haryana	527.14	1008.95	−23.64***
Himachal Pradesh	579.29	499.26	2.47**
Jammu & Kashmir	743.75	802.74	−3.33***
Jharkhand	473.24	451.58	2.27**
Karnataka	594.65	664.59	−5.30***
Kerala	751.75	851.91	−2.11**
Madhya Pradesh	597.55	690.92	−8.33***
Maharashtra	582.27	964.74	−34.32***
Meghalaya	830.8	1179.83	−5.11***
Odisha	497.82	613.81	−14.52***
Puducherry	546.84	580.05	−1.88*
Punjab	823.55	902.56	−3.21***
Rajasthan	608.09	620.95	−1.1
Sikkim	697.38	1115.27	−11.75***
Tamil Nadu	545.62	574.4	−3.86***
Telangana	514.9	981.86	−18.46***
Tripura	342.38	397.42	−3.73***
Uttar Pradesh	515.85	738.3	−16.88***
Uttarakhand	694.09	1270.03	−16.88***
West Bengal	461.2	694.57	−25.12***

Source: Authors; Significance levels: * $p < 0.10$; ** $p < 0.05$; *** $p < 0.01$

Table 3.9 Quantile regression coefficients on monthly digital expenditure—rural households

Variable	τ = 0.10	τ = 0.20	τ = 0.30	τ = 0.40	τ = 0.50	τ = 0.60	τ = 0.70	τ = 0.80	τ = 0.90
Age									
Coef (SE)	−42.5*** (4.2)	−15.3** (3.8)	−4.7 (3.5)	−7.2* (3.2)	−18.9*** (3.8)	−12.6** (3.9)	−5.8 (4.1)	−28.5*** (5.2)	−40.2*** (6.3)
Education									
Coef (SE)	64.3*** (5.1)	18.7** (4.9)	136.5*** (6.2)	133.2*** (7.1)	75.6*** (6.8)	73.4*** (7.2)	127.8*** (8.1)	127.4*** (9.3)	126.7*** (10.5)
Occupation									
Coef (SE)	68.4*** (4.8)	12.5* (4.2)	92.3*** (5.9)	127.8*** (6.7)	77.4*** (6.3)	73.6*** (6.9)	132.5*** (7.8)	128.9*** (8.9)	95.7*** (10.2)
Gender									
Coef (SE)	−23.1*** (3.9)	−18.2*** (3.4)	−62.3*** (4.8)	−64.7*** (5.3)	−45.1*** (4.9)	−20.3*** (5.1)	−41.2*** (5.8)	−42.8*** (6.7)	−38.9*** (7.6)
Household size									
Coef (SE)	−8.2* (3.5)	4.3 (3.1)	5.7 (3.8)	12.6** (4.2)	−23.4*** (3.9)	−26.8*** (4.3)	−28.5*** (4.8)	−75.3*** (6.1)	−78.9*** (7.4)
Total income (TOT_INC)									
Coef (SE)	0.0028** (0.0011)	0.0032*** (0.0010)	0.0043*** (0.0012)	0.0051*** (0.0013)	0.0048*** (0.0012)	0.0045*** (0.0013)	0.0042*** (0.0014)	0.0039*** (0.0015)	0.0031** (0.0017)
Constant									
Coef (SE)	285.4*** (12.3)	198.7*** (11.8)	156.2*** (14.2)	142.8*** (15.6)	198.3*** (14.1)	215.6*** (15.3)	241.9*** (17.2)	318.7*** (21.4)	412.5*** (26.8)
Observations	58,234	58,234	58,234	58,234	58,234	58,234	58,234	58,234	58,234
Pseudo R^2	0.187	0.203	0.218	0.224	0.231	0.228	0.221	0.215	0.198

Source: Authors

Note: Significance levels: * $p < 0.10$; ** $p < 0.05$; *** $p < 0.01$, SE = Standard Error (displayed in parentheses), Observations refer to rural households only in the analytical sample (N = 58,234 out of total 102,558)

References

ADB. (2022). E-commerce in Asia and the Pacific: Case studies and policy recommendations. *Asian Development Bank*. https://www.adb.org/sites/default/files/publication/922086/e--commerce-evolution-asia-pacific-opportunities-challenges.pdf

Alkire, S. (2013). Measuring multidimensional poverty: Insights from around the world. https://www.gov.uk/research-for-development-outputs/measuring-multidimensional-poverty-insights-from-around-the-world

Arora, R., & Sapre, N. (2025). Rural-urban digital divide: Evidence from Indian states. *International Journal of Finance and Economics*. https://doi.org/10.1002/ijfe.70045

Bergantino, A. S., Fusco, G., Intini, M., & Monturano, G. (2026). Digital divide and income inequality: Causal evidence from Italian provinces. *The Annals of Regional Science, 75,*(11). https://doi.org/10.1007/s00168-025-01440-z

Cámara, N., & Tuesta, D. (2014). Measuring financial inclusion: A multidimensional index. BBVA Research Working Paper No. 14/26. https://doi.org/10.2139/ssrn.2634616

Correa, T. (2016). Digital skills and social media use: How Internet skills are related to different types of Facebook use among 'digital natives'. *Information, Communication & Society, 19*(8), 1095–1107. https://doi.org/10.1080/1369118X.2015.1084023

Correa, T., & Pavez, I. (2016). Digital inclusion in rural areas: A qualitative exploration of challenges faced by people from isolated communities. *Journal of Computer-Mediated Communication, 21(3)*, 247–263. https://doi.org/10.1111/jcc4.12154

DataReportal. (2024). *Digital 2024: India.* DataReportal/Kepios. Retrieved from https://datareportal.com/reports/digital-2024-india

Demirgüç-Kunt, A., Klapper, L., Singer, D., Ansar, S., & Hess, J. (2018). *The Global Findex Database 2017: Measuring financial inclusion and the fintech revolution.* World Bank. https://doi.org/10.1596/978-1-4648-1259-0

DiMaggio, P., & Garip, F. (2012). Network effects and social inequality. *Annual Review of Sociology, 38*, 93–118. https://doi.org/10.1146/annurev.soc.012809.102545

Doloi, H. K. (2025). Digital inclusion for rural growth: Internet usage and smart villages development. *Asia-Pacific Journal of Rural Development, 35*(1), 40–57. https://doi.org/10.1177/10185291251343357

Duan, K. (2024). Digital villages construction and subjective well-being of the elderly: Evidence from China Longitudinal Aging Social Survey. *Applied Research in Quality of Life*. Advance online publication. https://doi.org/10.1007/s11482-024-10362-5

Ferreira, D., Vale, M., Carmo, R. M., Encalada-Abarca, L., & Marcolin, C. (2021). The three levels of the urban digital divide: Bridging issues of coverage, usage and its outcomes in VGI platforms. *Geoforum*, 124, 195–206. https://doi.org/10.1016/j.geoforum.2021.05.002

Gelbach, J. B. (2016). When do covariates matter? And which ones, and how much? *Journal of Labor Economics, 34*(2), 509–543. https://doi.org/10.1086/684651

GSMA. (2022). *The Mobile Economy Asia Pacific 2022*. https://www.gsma.com/mobileeconomy/asiapacific/

GSMA. (2023). *The state of mobile internet connectivity 2023*. GSM Association.

Guan, X., He, L., & Hu, Z. (2024). Impact of rural e-commerce on farmers' income and income gap. *Agriculture, 14*(10), 1689. https://doi.org/10.3390/agriculture14101689

Haji, K. (2021). E-commerce development in rural and remote areas of BRICS countries. *Journal of Integrative Agriculture, 20(4)*, 979–997. https://doi.org/10.1016/s2095-3119(20)63451-7

Hilbert, M. (2011). Digital gender divide or technologically empowered women in developing countries? A typical case of lies, damned lies, and statistics. *Women's Studies International Forum, 34*(6), 479–489. https://doi.org/10.1016/j.wsif.2011.07.001

Hou, J., & Liu, Y. (2024). Assessing the impact of rural e-commerce on regional poverty alleviation: Evidence from China's poverty-stricken counties. *International Review of Economics and Finance, 94*, 103399. https://doi.org/10.1016/j.iref.2024.103399

Hu, J., & Yin, G. (2026). Rural E-commerce and air pollution: Evidence of dual mechanisms from prodin expansion. *Frontiers in Environmental Science, 14, 1754204*. https://doi.org/10.3389/fenvs.2026.1754204

Jain, T., & Goyal, A. (2022). Inequality in digital access: Evidence from India. *Journal of Development Economics, 157*, 102881. https://doi.org/10.1016/j.jdeveco.2022.102881

Koenker, R., & Bassett, G. (1978). Regression quantiles. *Econometrica, 46*(1), 33–50. https://doi.org/10.2307/1913643

Kong, S. T. (2019). E-commerce development in rural China. In *ANU Press eBooks* (pp. 129–141). https://doi.org/10.22459/cet.2019.07

Laskar, M. H. (2023). Examining the emergence of digital society and the digital divide in India: A comparative evaluation between urban and rural areas. *Frontiers in Sociology, 8*. https://doi.org/10.3389/fsoc.2023.1145221

Lee, H., Wong, S. F., Oh, J., & Chang, Y. (2019). Information privacy concerns and demographic characteristics: Data from a Korean media panel survey. *Government Information Quarterly, 36(2)*, 294–303. https://doi.org/10.1016/j.giq.2019.01.002

Li, X., Zhang, Y., & Wang, J. (2025). Digital literacy, social interaction, and relative poverty in rural China: Evidence from threshold quantile regression. *Frontiers in Human Dynamics, 7*, 1644928. https://doi.org/10.3389/fhumd.2025.1644928

Liang, W., & Li, W. (2023). Impact of internet usage on the subjective well-being of urban and rural households: Evidence from Vietnam. *Telecommunications Policy, 47(3)*, 102518. https://doi.org/10.1016/j.telpol.2023.102518

Lim, S. C., Kim, J., & Lee, J. Y. (2023). Digital finance and e-commerce participation in rural Southeast Asia: A household-level study. *Information Systems Frontiers, 25*(2), 343–360. https://doi.org/10.1007/s10796-022-10292-2

Liu, H., Ding, M., Kan, Y., & Dong, Q. (2025). A study on the relationship between rural e-commerce development and farmers' income growth. *Sustainability, 17*(9), 3879. https://doi.org/10.3390/su17093879

OECD. (2019). *Measuring the digital transformation: A roadmap for the future*. Organisation for Economic Co-operation and Development. https://doi.org/10.1787/9789264311992-en

Pajuste, T. (2025). The digital divide—Reinforcing vulnerabilities. In Human Rights in the Digital Domain: Core Questions (pp. 361–380). *Cambridge University Press*. https://doi.org/10.1017/9781009606295.025

Pick, J. B., & Nishida, T. (2015). Digital divides in the world and its regions: A spatial and multivariate analysis of ICT usage. *Technological Forecasting and Social Change, 91*, 1–17. https://doi.org/10.1016/j.techfore.2013.12.026

Pick, J. B., & Sarkar, A. (2016). The global digital divide: Explaining change. *Springer Berlin, Heidelberg*. https://doi.org/10.1007/978-3-662-46602-5

Qiao, S., Ouyang, Z., & Jiang, Y. (2025). Digital village development improves household dietary diversity: Evidence from rural China. *Agricultural and Food Economics, 13*, 86. https://doi.org/10.1186/s40100-025-00430-1

Qiu, H. (2025). The impact of rural e-commerce development on farmers' income gap. *Sustainability, 17*(9), 3921. https://doi.org/10.3390/su17093921

Ragnedda, M. (2017). *The third digital divide: A Weberian approach to digital inequalities*. Routledge. https://doi.org/10.4324/9781315606002

Ragnedda, M. (2020). *Enhancing digital equity*. https://doi.org/10.1007/978-3-030-49079-9

Rallet, A., & Rochelandet, F. (2007). ICTs and inequalities: the digital divide. In *Cambridge University Press eBooks* (pp. 693–717). https://doi.org/10.1017/cbo9780511493201.025

Richa, H., Srivastava, A., & Pandey, M. (2025). Exploring e-commerce potential in rural India: opportunities in Northern India. *International Journal of Business and Globalisation*, 40(2), 97–106. https://doi.org/10.1504/ijbg.2025.146216

Robinson, L., Cotten, S. R., Ono, H., Quan-Haase, A., Mesch, G., Chen, W., & Stern, M. J. (2015). Digital inequalities and why they matter. *Information, Communication & Society, 18*(5), 569–582. https://doi.org/10.1080/1369118X.2015.1012532

Rodríguez Ruiz, J. G., Pérez Arellano, D. A., & Murillo Zamorano, L. R. (2024). Influence of ICT and household assets in the penetration of digital economy in Mexico. *Journal of Telecommunications and the Digital Economy, 12*(1), 278–304. https://doi.org/10.18080/jtde.v12n1.876

Rupasingha, A., Partridge, M., & Ali, K. (2026). Broadband initiatives: Impact on employment, teleworking, and rural–urban wage disparities. *Telecommunications Policy, 50(1), 103102.* https://doi.org/10.1016/j.telpol.2025.103102

Scheerder, A., van Deursen, A., & van Dijk, J. (2017). Determinants of Internet skills, uses and outcomes: A systematic review of the second- and third-level digital divide. *Telematics and Informatics, 34*(8), 1607–1624. https://doi.org/10.1016/j.tele.2017.07.007

Sen, A. (1999). *Development as freedom*. New York, NY: Alfred A. Knopf.

Sham, R., Christian, W., Daud, D., & Miraz, M. H. (2024). Sustainable digital economy development for E-Commerce users in Indonesia. *Journal of ASIAN Behavioural Studies*, 9(29), 57–69. https://doi.org/10.21834/jabs.v9i29.455

Sindakis, S., & Showkat, G. (2024). The digital revolution in India: Bridging the gap in rural technology adoption. *Journal of Innovation and Entrepreneurship, 13*, 29. https://doi.org/10.1186/s13731-024-00380-w

Sun, L., Li, F., Zhang, D., Zhang, X., & Hong, K. (2025). Rural E-commerce ecosystem development paths amid digital business enabling agriculture: A crosscase comparative analysis. *SAGE Open, 15(4).* https://doi.org/10.1177/21582440251382573

UNCTAD. (2021). *UNCTAD B2C E-commerce Index 2020: Spotlight on Latin America and the Caribbean (Technical Notes on ICT for Development No. 17).* United Nations Conference on Trade and Development. Retrieved from https://unctad.org/publication/unctad-b2c-e-commerce-index-2020-spotlight-latin-america-and-caribbean

United Nations Department of Economic and Social Affairs (UN DESA). (2018). *World Urbanization Prospects: The 2018 Revision—Highlights.* UN DESA, Population Division. Retrieved from https://population.un.org/wup/assets/WUP2018-Highlights.pdf

UNESCAP. (2021). *Asia-Pacific Digital Transformation Report 2021: Shaping our digital future.* United Nations Economic and Social Commission for Asia and the Pacific. https://www.unescap.org/kp/2021/asia-pacific-digital-transformation-report-2021

van Deursen, A. J. A. M., & Helsper, E. J. (2015). The third-level digital divide: Who benefits most from being online? *Communication and Information Technologies Annual, 10*, 29–52. https://doi.org/10.1108/S2050-206020150000010002

van Deursen, A. J. A. M., & van Dijk, J. A. G. M. (2014). The digital divide shifts to differences in usage. *New Media & Society, 16*(3), 507–526. https://doi.org/10.1177/1461444813487959

van Dijk, J. A. G. M. (2006). Digital divide research, achievements and shortcomings. *Poetics, 34*(4–5), 221–235. https://doi.org/10.1016/j.poetic.2006.05.004

Wang, F., Wang, H., & Xiong, L. (2024). Does the digital economy exhibit multiplier effects? A case study on the optimization of agricultural production structure in the rural digital economy. *International Journal of Agricultural Sustainability, 22*, 2386821. https://doi.org/10.1080/14735903.2024.2386821

Wang, H., Leng, H., & Yuan, M. (2025). From opportunity to inequality: How the rural digital economy shapes intra-rural income distribution. *Humanities and Social Sciences Communications, 12*, 1–14. https://doi.org/10.1057/s41599-025-04848-2

Warschauer, M. (2003). *Technology and social inclusion: Rethinking the digital divide.* MIT Press. https://mitpress.mit.edu/9780262731737/

Wei, L., & Hindman, D. B. (2011). Does the digital divide matter more? Comparing the effects of new media and old media use on the education-based knowledge gap. *Mass Communication and Society, 14*(2), 216–235. https://doi.org/10.1080/15205431003642707

Wooldridge, J. M. (2010). *Econometric analysis of cross section and panel data* (2nd ed.). MIT Press. https://mitpress.mit.edu/9780262232586/

World Bank. (2004). The Microeconomics of income distribution dynamics in East Asia and Latin America. In The *World Bank eBooks*. https://doi.org/10.1596/0-8213-5861-8

World Bank. (2021). *World Development Report 2021: Data for better lives.* World Bank. https://doi.org/10.1596/978-1-4648-1600-0

Xie, X., Luo, Z., & Chen, L. (2025). How can rural e-commerce promote green production on family farms in China? Evidence from Hunan Province. *Journal of Rural Studies, 120, 103843.* https://doi.org/10.1016/j.jrurstud.2025.103843

Zhang, J., Chen, Z., & Yang, F. (2024). Digital literacy, relative poverty, and common prosperity for rural households in China. *International Review of Financial Analysis, 96*, 103739. https://doi.org/10.1016/j.irfa.2024.103739

Zhang, Y.-F., & Zhao, H. (2025). The effect of e-commerce on digital inclusive finance: Evidence from the e-commerce boom in rural China. *Cogent Economics & Finance, 13*(1), 2460082. https://doi.org/10.1080/23322039.2025.2460082

Chapter 4
From Farm to Online Market: Analyzing E-Commerce Adoption Trends and Drivers for Indonesian Farmers

Alan Ray Farandy, Apri Laila Sayekti, and Rika Reviza Rachmawati

4.1 Introduction

The digital revolution has reshaped global trade, consumption patterns, and livelihoods, such as opening new opportunities through e-commerce for traditionally underserved populations, especially in rural areas (Chen and Li 2025). Among these groups, smallholder farmers represent both the most vulnerable to exclusion and the most promising agents of transformation. E-commerce offers farmers more affordable access to agricultural inputs, reduces information asymmetry, and directly connects them to consumers or wholesalers, thereby increasing profit margins by bypassing intermediaries (Chen et al. 2023). Yet in practice, these benefits remain unrealized for most rural farmers due to persistent digital divides (Tang et al. 2024). This divide involves more than infrastructure. As Salemink et al. (2017) argue, digital exclusion stems from a convergence of factors, including limited ICT infrastructure, high costs, low digital literacy, and socio-economic inequalities. For farmers in particular, the relevance of digital platforms to agricultural livelihoods and their capacity to use these tools effectively remain critical constraints.

Indonesia provides a critical context for studying these challenges. As an archipelagic country, Indonesia has over 40% of its population living in rural areas, where agriculture remains the backbone of local economies (World Bank 2023). While the government envisions Southeast Asia's largest digital economy by 2025, the nation continues to exhibit one of the lowest internet penetration rates in the region (Azali 2017). The use of the internet in Indonesia is strongly correlated with education level and is particularly limited in rural areas. In these areas, many

A. R. Farandy (✉) · A. L. Sayekti · R. R. Rachmawati
Research Center for Behavioral and Circular Economics, National Research and Innovation Agency (BRIN), Jakarta, Indonesia
e-mail: alan002@brin.go.id; alan.ray.farandy@brin.go.id; apri020@brin.go.id; rika017@brin.go.id

W. Ma et al. (eds.), *E-Commerce for Inclusive Rural and Agricultural Development*, Contributions to Economics,
https://doi.org/10.1007/978-981-92-5237-4_4

smallholder farmers—often older, less formally educated, and from low-income groups—remain digitally excluded (Azali 2017; Choczyńska 2024; Fahmi and Sari 2020; Hidayat et al. 2023; Kusumawardhani et al. 2023; Simamora and Ningsih 2020; Sugandi et al. 2024).

Although mobile internet coverage has improved nationwide, rural and remote regions continue to experience weak signal strength, limited connectivity, and high access costs (Sugandi et al. 2024). Moreover, digital infrastructure alone is insufficient. Even when connectivity is available, many farmers struggle with affordability, a lack of technical support, and limited awareness of how to leverage e-commerce platforms for agricultural production and marketing (Fahmi and Sari 2020). Their socio-economic profiles further shape digital participation. Research has shown that older adults, those with lower levels of education, and individuals in lower income brackets are significantly less likely to use the internet for commercial purposes (Choi and DiNitto 2013; Luo et al. 2025). These patterns suggest that without targeted policies, e-commerce could exacerbate rather than alleviate rural inequality.

Despite the growing importance of rural e-commerce, most existing literature continues to focus on urban e-commerce trends, consumer behavior in cities, or national-level regulatory frameworks (Jiang and Qin 2024; Salemink et al. 2025; Suseno 2018; Wei et al. 2024). Empirical evidence on e-commerce participation among rural farmers, using nationally representative data, remains scarce. Furthermore, studies integrating behavioral household data with spatial infrastructure indicators, such as mobile signal strength or internet coverage, remain limited. Existing Indonesian studies, available studies often focus on a single province or rely on qualitative case studies (Fahmi and Sari 2020; Hidayat et al. 2023; Simamora and Ningsih 2020), limiting their policy relevance for national-scale digital transformation. However, these provincial or qualitative studies—while informative—cannot capture large-scale spatial disparities or national-level patterns of digital adoption among farmers. As a result, the literature still lacks a comprehensive, multi-regional analysis that links farmers' socio-economic conditions with variations in digital infrastructure across Indonesia. This creates a clear gap in understanding how large-scale infrastructural disparities and farmers' socio-economic characteristics jointly influence e-commerce uptake.

To address these gaps, this study draws on three waves of the National Socio-economic Survey (Susenas) from 2019, 2021, and 2024 combined with village-level infrastructure data from the Village Potential Statistics (Podes). This integration provides a unique opportunity to generate nationally representative evidence on rural e-commerce participation that has not been available in previous studies. Moreover, it enables analysis of both behavioral and spatial determinants of e-commerce adoption among rural farmers, with particular focus on internet infrastructure as a critical enabler. By employing a rare-event logistic model to account for the very low prevalence of farmers selling agricultural products online, this study improves estimation accuracy compared to conventional logistic models used in earlier research. This represents a significant advancement over earlier provincial or qualitative studies.

This study aims to identify trends in e-commerce adoption among rural farming households; analyze spatial disparities in infrastructure and e-commerce adoption; assess how key infrastructural and socio-economic factors, such as signal strength, gender, and education, are associated with e-commerce usage among farmers, and provide actionable, evidence-based policy recommendations for inclusive rural digital transformation in the agricultural sector.

The study makes three key contributions. First, it provides the first multi-wave, nationally representative analysis of e-commerce adoption among rural farmers in Indonesia. Second, it combines behavioral household data with village-level indicators of digital infrastructure, offering a spatially grounded understanding of digital inclusion. Third, it applies rare-event logistic modelling, which improves the accuracy of estimates for behaviors that remain uncommon among rural farmers. Together, these contributions generate new policy-relevant insights into how digital divides shape the transition toward digital agriculture.

The remainder of the paper is structured as follows. Section 4.2 reviews the literature on rural e-commerce and digital inclusion among farmers. Section 4.3 describes the data and methodology. Section 4.4 presents empirical results and discussion. Section 4.5 draws policy implications and concludes.

4.2 Theoretical Framework: Understanding E-Commerce Adoption Among Farmers

4.2.1 E-Commerce as a Catalyst for Rural Agricultural Growth

E-commerce is increasingly recognized as a transformative tool for rural agricultural development, offering new pathways to market access, income generation, and economic inclusion for smallholder farmers. By reducing geographic and transactional barriers, e-commerce enables farmers to engage directly with consumers, bypassing intermediaries and benefiting from greater price transparency and higher margins (Wei and Claire 2022; Ye et al. 2024). Evidence from China and other developing countries indicates that rural e-commerce fosters agricultural modernization by increasing mechanization, enhancing total factor productivity, and improving access to market information and logistics services. These advances contribute not only to farm-level profitability but also to broader rural revitalization and industrial transformation. Among low-income households, participation in digital commerce has been associated with income diversification, reduced transaction costs, and higher earnings (Liu et al. 2021).

However, realizing the full potential of rural e-commerce depends on several enabling conditions—particularly digital infrastructure, logistics, skills, and institutional support. In many rural regions, challenges persist, including underdeveloped delivery systems, limited digital literacy, and shortages of skilled labor (Liu et al.

2021). Thriving e-commerce ecosystems often emerge where these constraints are addressed holistically through policies such as government-backed training, logistics subsidies, and the development of local e-commerce hubs or associations (Wei and Claire 2022; Ye et al. 2024). Examples from China and India illustrate how digital engagement can catalyze rural transformation. In Shi Zhu Mountain Village, China, improved e-commerce access expanded income opportunities and enhanced connectivity with urban markets (Cuiping et al. 2024). In Tamil Nadu, India, local entrepreneurs have increasingly adopted digital platforms due to rising digital awareness and supportive government policies (Lalitha 2022).

Indonesia has also experienced a significant growth in rural digital engagement. The country's e-commerce sector grew from USD 8 billion in 2017 to a projected USD 55–65 billion by 2022, driven by smartphone adoption, improved internet access, and shifts in consumer behavior and retail (Das et al. 2018). By 2022, the sector supported around 26 million jobs, and approximately 35% of sellers were women (Siahaan et al. 2022). E-commerce users outside Java achieved 11–25% cost savings (Martini et al. 2023), suggesting potential for greater spatial economic equity.

Smallholder farmers have begun to engage in e-commerce through both formal platforms, such as Tokopedia and Shopee, and informal channels, including WhatsApp and Facebook, which accounted for nearly 40% of agricultural e-commerce activity in 2019 (Morgan 2019; iPrice 2021). In Kintamani, Bali, farmers utilized these platforms to market their specialty coffee directly to consumers, leveraging digital tools for branding and product storytelling (Fahmi and Savira 2023). Access to real-time market information further empowered farmers to adjust production and pricing strategies (ITA 2022). In addition to reducing transaction costs, digital platforms help rural producers become more responsive to consumer preferences. Ownership of smartphones, support from younger tech-savvy household members, and increased access to e-payment tools have all contributed to this transition (Permani et al. 2023; Morgan 2019). Food-related e-commerce alone reached USD 5 billion in 2022, up from 0.39% of market share in 2017 to 12%, signaling growing consumer demand for agricultural products via digital channels (Statista 2023).

E-commerce also significantly benefits farmers as consumers by fostering more competitive pricing and offering a greater variety of products, ultimately leading to substantial welfare gains. As consumers, farmers can purchase a wide range of items, from agricultural production inputs to various daily necessities unrelated to farming. Spatially, the impact of e-commerce is relatively even, as it facilitates faster price convergence across different locations, thereby enhancing overall consumer well-being, provided farmers have access to it (Jo et al. 2024).

Beyond competitive pricing and a vast product selection, e-commerce offers consumers significant gains in time and energy efficiency, along with access to comprehensive and more accurate product information. Consumers can conveniently shop anytime and anywhere, eliminating the need for physical travel, queuing, or carrying heavy purchases. This digital convenience saves considerable time and physical effort (ADB 2023). Crucially, e-commerce platforms provide detailed product specifications and, perhaps most importantly, abundant prior customer reviews. Understanding consumer behavior and preferences through data analysis can help design more effective marketing strategies and improve the user experience (Guojie et al. 2025). These features enable price comparisons across multiple sellers and provide insights into product quality and performance from real-world users. This, in turn, mitigates information asymmetry and empowers consumers to make well-informed purchasing decisions (Xu et al. 2024).

Despite these gains, rural e-commerce in Indonesia still faces structural challenges—especially unequal access to high-speed internet and logistics infrastructure. Studies have underscored that digital transformation must be accompanied by investments in connectivity, skill development, and cybersecurity (Ariansyah et al. 2021; Chen and Long 2024). Nonetheless, Indonesia's demographic profile, rising internet use (175.4 million users in 2020), and consistent economic growth (5% annually from 2015 to 2020) position it favorably to harness the benefits of rural digitalization (World Bank 2020; Siahaan et al. 2022).

4.2.2 Theoretical Anchors for Technology Adoption

Diffusion of Innovations (DOI) Theory provides a macro-level lens, positing that the spread of a new technology, such as e-commerce, is influenced by its perceived attributes—relative advantage, compatibility, complexity, trialability, and observability (Stoneman 2018). For farmers, the relative advantage of e-commerce (e.g., higher prices, better market access) may be clear, but its compatibility with existing practices and perceived complexity are often major hurdles (Deichmann et al. 2016a, b). This theory helps explain the slow rate of adoption and the socio-economic disparities (e.g., education, age) that characterize early adopters and laggards.

Complementing DOI, the Technology Acceptance Model (TAM) offers a micro-level, behavioral perspective, suggesting that adoption is primarily driven by two beliefs: perceived usefulness (the degree to which a person believes that using a system would enhance their job performance) and perceived ease of use (the degree to which a person believes that using a system would be free from effort) (Davis 1989). For a farmer, perceived usefulness encompasses whether e-commerce can genuinely increase profits or reduce input costs. Perceived ease of use is directly tied to digital literacy and platform user-friendliness. These perceptions are not formed in a vacuum; they are shaped by external variables such as the individual's socio-economic context and the quality of available infrastructure (Caffaro et al. 2020).

Finally, the Digital Divide framework shifts the analysis from individual adoption to systemic inequality. The divide is not a single binary but a cascade of gaps: the first-level divide in physical access to technology and infrastructure; the second-level divide in the digital skills and literacy required to use it effectively; and the third-level divide in the tangible outcomes derived from its use (Coca et al. 2025). This multi-level framework is crucial for differentiating between mere internet connectivity and meaningful economic participation in e-commerce.

4.2.3 *Synthesizing the Literature: A Conceptual Framework for Farmer E-Commerce Adoption*

Guided by these theories, we critically synthesize the literature to build a conceptual framework (see Fig. 4.1) that positions e-commerce adoption as a function of multilevel determinants, while explicitly differentiating the adoption drivers for purchasing (consumer role) and selling (producer role). The literature consistently identifies Information and Communication Technology (ICT) infrastructure as a non-negotiable prerequisite, constituting the first-level digital divide (Aslam 2025). However, as our study emphasizes, it is the quality of infrastructure (e.g., 4G vs. 2.5G signal) that determines the complexity and usefulness of e-commerce. Slow, unreliable connections increase the effort required (perceived ease of use) and limit functionalities such as uploading product images or using digital payments, thereby reducing Perceived Usefulness (Goldfarb and Tucker 2019; Perwangsa et al. 2024). This creates a spatial disparity, whereby farmers in regions with poor infrastructure are excluded at the first hurdle. Even with access, adoption is mediated by individual characteristics that form the second-level digital divide (Lasdun et al. 2025). Education is a powerful proxy for digital literacy, directly reducing the perceived complexity of platforms and enhancing an individual's ability to leverage them strategically (Li 2025). Age and generation align with DOI's adopter categories, with older farmers typically demonstrating greater resistance to innovation due to lower digital literacy and different perceptions of usefulness (Kazunari et al. 2024). Furthermore, gender influences adoption through gendered access to resources, time, and social capital, often limiting women's participation as producers rather than as consumers (Njuki et al. 2022).

A core distinction in our framework separates two types of adoption. The consumer role (purchasing) has a lower barrier to entry, as its relative advantage is clear: access to a wider variety of goods, competitive pricing, and convenience (Bronnenberg 2015). The primary requirements are basic digital literacy, financial access for payment, and a connection sufficient for browsing, which explains why purchasing rates are consistently higher, as observed in Indonesia (Zhang et al. 2024) and China (Liu et al. 2021). In contrast, the producer role (selling) is far more complex and demanding. It requires not only digital skills but also complementary

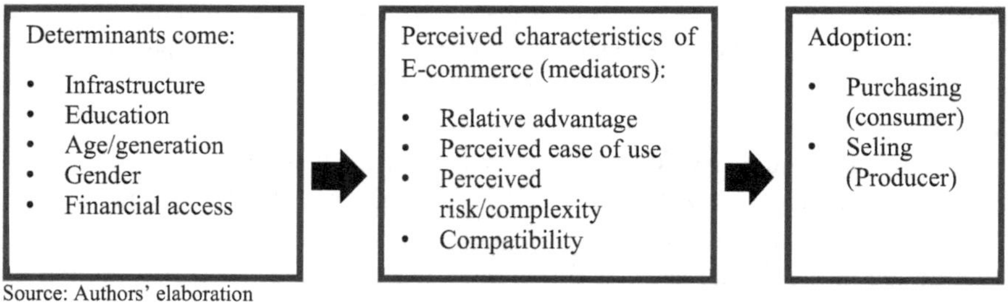

Fig. 4.1 A conceptual framework for farmer e-commerce adoption. Source: Authors' elaboration

assets, such as access to reliable logistics, digital payment gateways or banking services, marketing skills, and the ability to manage customer relationships and trust (Baumüller 2018; Cortes et al. 2024). The perceived risk is higher, and compatibility with existing sales channels must be managed. This is why farmers often start with low-risk, informal channels like WhatsApp (Fahmi and Savira 2023), and why adoption of selling lags significantly behind that of purchasing.

The synthesis leads to a conceptual framework that posits that e-commerce adoption is driven by a combination of external enablers (infrastructure) and individual capacities (socio-economic factors), with the adoption mechanism differing fundamentally between the consumer and producer roles.

Based on the synthesized conceptual framework, we derive a set of testable hypotheses that directly inform the empirical analysis. First, we hypothesize that higher-quality internet infrastructure is positively associated with a greater probability of e-commerce adoption, anticipating a stronger effect on the more complex activity of selling compared to purchasing (H1). Second, we posit that higher levels of education are positively associated with e-commerce adoption, with the effect expected to be more pronounced for selling, given the greater digital and strategic literacy this role demands (H2). Third, we hypothesize that older farmers are less likely to adopt e-commerce, particularly for selling, than their younger counterparts (H3). Finally, we propose that the determinants of e-commerce adoption will differ in both magnitude and significance between the purchasing and selling models, reflecting the distinct barriers and prerequisites for consumers vs. producers (H4). By grounding the analysis in this integrated theoretical framework, the study moves beyond merely describing what factors influence adoption to explaining why and how they do so, thereby providing a robust foundation for interpreting the empirical results and formulating targeted policy recommendations.

4.3 Methodology

4.3.1 Data

This study utilizes a combined dataset constructed from two major sources published by Statistics Indonesia (Badan Pusat Statistik/BPS), namely the National Socio-economic Survey (Susenas) and the Village Potential Statistics (Podes). Susenas is a nationally representative biannual survey that covers more than 300,000 households. It provides comprehensive information at both the individual and household levels, including data on education, health, housing conditions, household consumption, and expenditure patterns. Podes, conversely, offers complete village-level data across Indonesia, encompassing over 80,000 villages. This dataset compiles detailed information on local infrastructure, public service facilities, socio-economic characteristics, and natural resource potential, collected through official village records and structured interviews with local authorities. The integration of Susenas and Podes yields a uniquely rich, multi-level dataset that captures the interplay between household-level behaviors and village-level contextual factors, thereby significantly enhancing the analytical strength and empirical relevance of our study.

We leverage Susenas data from 2019, 2021, and 2024 to assess the evolution of e-commerce adoption among farmers over 5 years. For this study, farmers are broadly defined as individuals primarily engaged in the agricultural sector, encompassing crop cultivation, plantation, fisheries, livestock farming, and forestry. E-commerce participation, as captured in Susenas, includes both the purchase and sale of goods and services, measured through questions posed separately and consistently since 2019. To investigate the determinants of e-commerce adoption, we merge the Susenas data with the corresponding Podes data for each survey year. Given that Susenas is a repeated cross-sectional dataset rather than a panel, we employ a pooled dataset comprising multiple survey years. Selecting these 3 years provides sufficient temporal variation to capture the dynamics influencing digital platform adoption, particularly given that e-commerce engagement among farmers has only recently begun to emerge compared to other occupational sectors. The total sample for this study comprises 688,761 observations from farmers, providing a robust empirical base.

For regression analysis only, village-level data from Podes, including indicators of internet infrastructure and telecommunication service quality, are aggregated to the district level to align with the finest administrative level publicly available in Susenas. This aggregation might introduce bias, as it may not perfectly reflect the specific conditions of individual farmers within a village. However, due to the relative homogeneity of conditions within a single district, with a low standard deviation, we are confident that the variables sufficiently proxy for communication infrastructure at the village level. Our primary indicators for digital infrastructure at the village level within Podes include the number of cellular network operators available and the quality of mobile internet signals. While alternative variables such as the number of Base Transceiver Stations (BTS) and general cellular signal quality per village are also available, we prioritize the number of cellular operators and mobile internet signal quality as more direct and reliable proxies for actual digital infrastructure and service usability. A greater number of cellular operators typically indicates a more extensive network presence, implying a larger number of BTS installations within or near a village, as each operator maintains its own infrastructure. However, BTS counts alone can be misleading due to their non-uniform distribution (e.g., a village might rely on a BTS located in an adjacent area). Conversely, mobile internet signal quality directly reflects the practical usability and accessibility of digital services for residents.

Table 4.1 Summary statistics for all variables included in our analysis

Variables	Obs	Mean	Std. Dev.	Min	Max
Purchasing goods/services on internet	709,548	0.022	0.147	0	1
Selling goods/services on internet	709,548	0.007	0.083	0	1
Sex					
Man	709,548	0.656	0.475	0	1
Woman	709,548	0.344	0.475	0	1
Generation					
Gen Z & Alpha	709,548	0.099	0.299	0	1
Millennials	709,548	0.283	0.450	0	1
Gen X	709,548	0.376	0.484	0	1
Baby Boomers and other	709,548	0.242	0.428	0	1
Education					
Up to Elementary	709,548	0.629	0.483	0	1
Junior	709,548	0.178	0.382	0	1
High	709,548	0.170	0.376	0	1
Diploma to doctoral	709,548	0.023	0.151	0	1
Rural	709,548	0.857	0.350	0	1
Have bank account	709,548	0.307	0.461	0	1
Owns mobile phone/s	709,548	0.538	0.499	0	1
Place to access internet					
Own home	709,548	0.297	0.457	0	1
Public spaces	709,548	0.117	0.321	0	1
Expenditure (million IDR)	709,548	3.760	2.570	0.182	152.763
Average number of cellular providers per district	709,548	2.494	1.387	0.020	7
Average internet quality per district					
5G/4G/LTE	709,548	0.587	0.492	0	1
3G/H/H+/EVDO	709,548	0.305	0.460	0	1
2.5G/E/GPRS	709,548	0.079	0.270	0	1
No internet signal	709,548	0.029	0.169	0	1

Sources: Susenas and Podes, author's calculation

4.3.2 Summary Statistics

In this study, we analyze how e-commerce adoption among farmers is associated with socio-economic factors and internet infrastructure. Table 4.1 presents the summary statistics for all variables included in our analysis, encompassing a robust sample of 809,548 observations from farmers. The data highlights both the limited penetration of e-commerce among rural farmers and key demographic, economic, and infrastructural characteristics relevant to e-commerce access determinants.

The adoption of e-commerce among farmers remains remarkably low: only 2.2% of respondents report online purchases, and a mere 0.7% engage in internet-based selling. These low adoption rates pose a significant challenge for regression modeling, resulting in severe class imbalance and limited variation in the dependent variable. Consequently, this makes it difficult to ascertain statistically significant relationships and can result in unstable coefficient estimates (King and Zeng 2001). However, if the model yields statistically significant results despite these challenges, it would strongly suggest that the identified independent variables are genuinely associated with the probability of e-commerce adoption among farmers.

Regarding demographic composition, the sample is predominantly male (66%), with a skewed generational distribution favoring older cohorts. Generation X and Baby Boomers constitute the majority (37.6% and 24.2%, respectively), while Millennials represent 28.3%, and Generation Z and Alpha account for only 9.9%. Education levels are generally low, with the majority (62.9%) having attained only elementary education. While 17% completed junior or senior high school, only a small fraction (2.4%) holds a diploma or higher, underscoring the generally low human capital among farmers.

Geographic and financial inclusion aspects are also notable. A substantial 85.7% of the farmers in our sample reside in rural areas, confirming the focus of our study on the rural agricultural landscape. Financial inclusion, proxied by having a bank account, stands at 30.7%, suggesting that a significant portion of farmers still rely on informal financial channels, which could impede e-commerce participation. Mobile phone ownership is more widespread at 53.8%, highlighting the potential for mobile-based e-commerce. Farmers primarily access the internet from their own homes (29.7%), while a smaller proportion (11.7%) uses public spaces. The average monthly household expenditure is approximately IDR 3.76 million, with considerable variation (standard deviation of IDR 2.57 million), indicating diverse economic capacities within the farming population.

On the infrastructural dimension, districts have an average of more than two cellular network providers per village, with a maximum of seven providers in some districts, suggesting varying degrees of market competition and network coverage. Regarding internet quality, 58.7% of farmers are in districts with predominantly 5G/4G/LTE signal quality, while 30.5% are in 3G/H/H+/EVDO areas, 7.9% are constrained to slower 2.5G networks (EDGE/GPRS), and the rest have no internet signal at all. These differences in connectivity are expected to be critical in shaping digital adoption patterns among rural agricultural communities.

4.3.3 Empirical Strategy

This study employed Global Moran's I to assess spatial autocorrelation in internet signal quality across Indonesian villages during the study period. The analysis was conducted using a spatial weights matrix that reflects geographic relationships between administrative village units, enabling assessment of clustering patterns in digital infrastructure access. The dependent variable represents internet signal quality, measured ordinally on a scale from 1 to 4, with lower values indicating better connectivity. Category 1 is 5G/4G/LTE, 2 is 3G/H+/EVDO, 3 is 2.5G/GPRS, and 4 is a village with no internet signal. The signal variable was treated as ordinal for the Moran's I analysis to reflect the directional degradation of quality across categories.

Given Indonesia's archipelagic geography, a k-nearest neighbors (k-NN) spatial weights matrix was used, with k = 6, to ensure that all spatial units had meaningful neighbors regardless of land contiguity. The spatial weights file was constructed using centroid coordinates of each village polygon. This method avoids the limitations of rook or queen contiguity in non-contiguous island regions. Global Moran's I was calculated for each year using the following standard formula (Eq. 4.1) where z_i is the deviation of an attribute for feature i from its mean $\left(x_i - \overline{X}\right)$, $w_{i,j}$ is the spatial weight between feature i and j, n is equal to the total number of features, and S_0 is the aggregate of all the spatial weights. In additional, Local Indicator of Spatial Association (LISA) using Local Moran's I was used to identify spatial clusters and outliers of internet signal quality across Indonesian villages. LISA statistics were computed to detect significant High–High (strong connectivity clusters), Low–Low (low-connectivity exclusion clusters), and High–Low/Low–High spatial outliers.

$$I = \frac{N}{S_0} \frac{\sum_{i=1}^{n} \sum_{j=1}^{n} w_{i,j} z_i z_j}{\sum_{i=1}^{n} z_i^2} \tag{4.1}$$

This study also investigates the determinants of e-commerce adoption among farmers using a logistic regression analysis of pooled cross-sectional data. The event is rare in the sample of this study: only 2.2% and 0.7% of observations take the value 1 for reporting purchase and selling online, respectively, while the remaining are 0. According to King and Zeng (2001), such settings are characterized as rare-event data, i.e., binary dependent variables with dozens to thousands of zeros for everyone. Given that this setting can bias standard logistic regression and may lead to underestimation of event probabilities. Therefore, this study employed the rare-events logistic (ReLogit) model with the dependent variable Y_i is defined as:

$$Y_i = \begin{cases} 1 \text{ if farmer } i \text{ participates in e?commerce} \\ 0 \text{ otherwise} \end{cases}$$

Under the standard logit model,

$$\Pr\left(Y_i = 1 \middle| x_i, \beta\right) = \pi_i = \frac{1}{1 + e^{x_i \beta}} \tag{4.2}$$

where β is a $k \times 1$ vector of parameters to be estimated. However, when the fraction of ones in the data is very small, the mean of the binary outcome contains limited information, and standard maximum-likelihood (ML) logit estimates can be substantially biased even in samples of several thousand observations. In particular, King and Zeng (2001) show that ML logit tends to underestimate event probabilities and produce downward-biased intercepts in rare-events applications.

The rare events logistic model introduces two key improvements relative to the conventional logit. First, this approach derives an analytical approximation to the small-sample bias of the ML estimator β, based on the information matrix and the predicted probabilities, and then constructs an adjusted estimator $\tilde{\beta} = \hat{\beta} - bias\left(\hat{\beta}\right)$. This correction primarily affects the intercept but also adjusts the slope coefficients, yielding estimates that are closer to the true parameters and that no longer systematically underestimate the probability of rare events.

Second, if coefficient bias is corrected, the usual plug-in estimator in $\pi_i = 1/\left(1+e^{-x_i\beta}\right)$ ignores uncertainty in $\hat{\beta}$ and remains sub-optimal in finite samples of rare events. King and Zeng propose an approximate Bayesian estimator that integrates over the sampling distribution of leading to adjusted probabilities $\Pr\left(Y_i = 1\right) \approx \pi_i + C_i$, where $\pi_i = 1/\left(1+e^{-x_i\tilde{\beta}}\right)$ and C_i is a correction term depending on π_i, the variance–covariance matrix $V\left(\tilde{\beta}\right)$, and the covariate vector x_i. This correction moves very small probabilities closer to 0.5 when warranted by parameter uncertainty, thereby reducing mean squared error relative to the standard ML predictions.

Then, the model estimates the probability of participation $P(Y_i = 1)$, which is specified as follows in Eq. (4.3):

$$Y_i = \beta_0 + X_i\beta_1 + \delta_j\beta_2 + \gamma_p + \theta_t + \varepsilon_i \tag{4.3}$$

where X_i is a vector of individual- and household-level variables hypothesized to influence technology adoption, including crucial demographics such as sex, generational age group, and education level. It also incorporates socio-economic status indicators, such as rural or urban classification and expenditure levels, alongside access variables, including bank account ownership, mobile phone ownership, and household internet access. Complementing these individual-level variables is the vector δ_j, which represents district-level infrastructure variables. This vector includes measures that quantify the quality and reach of local internet connectivity, specifically the average number of cellular network operators and signal quality per village. The ε represents the error term, the coefficients β_1 and β_2 measure the effects of the respective explanatory variables on the dependent variable, while α denotes the constant term in the model.

The model includes province fixed effects (γ_p) and year-fixed effects (θ_t) to capture time-invariant characteristics and broader temporal shocks not directly observed in the model. The province-fixed effects account for time-invariant, province-specific characteristics that might systematically influence e-commerce adoption across the sample, such as consistent local cultural norms or unmeasured geographical differences. Concurrently, the year fixed effects capture common, nationwide temporal shocks, such as major shifts in national policy, general macroeconomic trends, or technology adoption milestones (like a major network upgrade) that affect all provinces equally but change over time.

4.4 Result and Discussion

4.4.1 Digital Engagement Among Indonesian Farmers: Patterns of Internet Use

Between 2019 and 2024, Indonesian farmers demonstrated modest progress in adopting digital technology, primarily reflected in increased mobile phone ownership. As detailed in Table 4.2, ownership rose from 51.3% in 2019 to 55.5% in 2024. However, these figures remain relatively low when compared to farmer mobile phone adoption rates in other developing nations, such as Sudan, Nigeria, and Bangladesh (Ibitunde et al. 2024; Rahman et al. 2024). For instance, in North Kordofan, Sudan, 90% of farmers reported using mobile phones, highlighting the untapped potential and the persistent structural barriers that hinder more widespread digital integration among Indonesian farmers.

However, when utilized effectively, mobile phones serve as critical tools for Indonesian farmers, enabling access to timely information such as weather forecasts, market prices, pest alerts, and government support services (Santoso et al. 2025). Meta-analyses confirm that digital tools, such as mobile phones, can improve agricultural productivity and profitability by up to 2% in yields and 5% in income (Erlangga et al. 2023; Gouroubera et al. 2024). Moreover, mobile phones strengthen coordination along the agricultural value chain, enhancing decision-making and reducing risk (Furuholt and Matotay 2011).

The more significant transformation lies in internet adoption, which rose sharply from 18.8 to 50.2% over the same period. This growth underscores the positive impact of rural digital infrastructure development and national inclusion initiatives. The majority of these users access the internet via their mobile phones, indicating that mobile phones are the primary driver of internet adoption among farmers, often serving as their first—and sometimes only—gateway to digital services.

The place of internet access also reflects broader shifts in connectivity. In 2024, nearly half (48.6%) of internet-using farmers accessed the web from their own homes, up from 17.6% in 2019. This increase indicates improved domestic connectivity, potentially driven by programs such as the Palapa Ring Project (Eschachasthi et al. 2022) and Desa Pintar (Smart Villages), which aim to provide internet access to all rural villages by 2025 (Susilowati et al. 2025). Nevertheless, disparities persist—many farmers still rely on public spaces (24.6%) or workplaces (12.6%) for internet access. As Piabuo et al. (2020) note, public access points remain essential in regions with limited household connectivity.

Regarding digital behavior, the most common online activities among farmers in 2024 were obtaining information or news (39.6%), entertainment (39.6%), and using social media (39.1%). These patterns suggest growing digital awareness and point to untapped potential for agricultural extension through online platforms. Social media provides farmers with direct channels to connect with agricultural professionals, peers, and market actors, thereby enhancing knowledge exchange, market intelligence, and technical learning (Riley and Robertson 2022).

Table 4.2 Penetration of internet use among farmers

	2019		2021		2024	
	Mean	Std. Dev.	Mean	Std. Dev.	Mean	Std. Dev.
Owns mobile phone/s	0.513	0.500	0.529	0.499	0.555	0.497
Accesses the internet	0.188	0.391	0.326	0.469	0.502	0.500
Devices used to access the internet						
Computer/Desktop	0.003	0.056	0.002	0.044	0.002	0.043
Laptop/Notebook	0.006	0.078	0.007	0.081	0.006	0.079
Tablet	0.003	0.053	0.002	0.042	0.001	0.029
Mobile phone	0.183	0.387	0.323	0.468	0.500	0.500
Other	0.001	0.036	0.001	0.025	0.001	0.030
Place to access the internet						
Own home	0.176	0.381	0.310	0.463	0.486	0.500
Not own home	0.068	0.252	0.107	0.308	0.202	0.402
Workplace/office	0.036	0.186	0.056	0.231	0.126	0.332
School/campus	0.005	0.071	0.006	0.078	0.012	0.109
Public spaces	0.048	0.213	0.073	0.259	0.246	0.431
While on the move	0.034	0.182	0.078	0.268	0.148	0.355
Uses of the internet						
Obtaining information/news	0.122	0.328	0.220	0.414	0.396	0.489
Online learning	0.015	0.123	0.029	0.167	0.009	0.097
Sending/receiving emails	0.008	0.091	0.014	0.116	0.020	0.140
Social media/social networks	0.166	0.372	0.299	0.458	0.391	0.488
Purchasing goods/services	0.009	0.096	0.022	0.146	0.054	0.225
Selling goods/services	0.004	0.066	0.010	0.097	0.014	0.119
Entertainment	0.102	0.303	0.183	0.387	0.396	0.489
Financial services (e-banking)	0.004	0.060	0.008	0.092	0.015	0.123
Obtaining information about goods/services	0.013	0.113	0.025	0.156	0.090	0.286
Other	0.006	0.076	0.013	0.112	0.027	0.163

Sources: Susenas and Podes, author's calculation

However, the use of the internet for online learning declined from 2.9% in 2021 to just 0.9% in 2024, after peaking during the COVID-19 pandemic when e-learning temporarily became the primary method of knowledge dissemination (Rizvi and Nabi 2021). This decline suggests a return to traditional, in-person learning methods. Yet this trend also underscores a broader challenge in rural digital engagement: online learning platforms remain insufficiently localized, insufficiently interactive, and often disconnected from farmers' everyday information needs. Strengthening digital agricultural extensions will require not only expanding access but also investing in content quality, ensuring that learning materials are culturally relevant, available in local languages, and tailored to specific commodity systems.

In the context of our research, the share of farmers using the internet to participate in e-commerce, such as purchasing goods and services, rose from 0.9% in 2019 to 5.4% in 2024—a sixfold increase. Although the base rate was low, the growth is significant, signaling the gradual adoption of digital marketplaces. This uptake may be driven, as Deichmann et al. (2016a, b) argue, by digital platforms that can reduce transaction costs and expand access to affordable inputs. In contrast, the proportion of farmers selling goods and services online grew more slowly—from 0.4% in 2019 to 1.4% in 2024. This discrepancy between buying and selling reflects the structural challenges faced by farmers, including logistical constraints, limited digital marketing skills, and competition from better-resourced agribusinesses. While the data indicates incremental adoption of e-commerce for sales, more targeted support is needed to engage farmers in digital markets fully (Cortes et al. 2024). Barriers, including delivery infrastructure, familiarity with online platforms, and trust in payment systems, limit their ability to engage effectively in e-commerce and connect directly with consumers (Vijayshena et al. 2025).

The higher uptake in purchasing than in selling suggests that farmers are currently more engaged as digital consumers than producers in e-commerce, which can be attributed to several underlying factors. Engaging as a consumer generally requires fewer skills, lower technological literacy, and minimal upfront investment. Farmers can browse, compare prices, and purchase inputs with relative ease. By contrast, selling requires navigating complex tasks such as product branding, quality assurance, packaging, and managing logistics—activities that demand both digital and entrepreneurial competencies.

Further, the dominance of cash-based transactions in rural areas limits farmers' ability to engage fully in digital selling. Many online platforms require digital payments, yet a considerable share of farmers remain unbanked or digitally inexperienced. Although innovations such as Cash on Delivery (COD) offer interim solutions that enhance purchasing access, they do not fully resolve barriers for sellers, who must still manage returns, verification, and shipping risks.

This dynamic aligns with previous research indicating that consumers generally adopt online services more readily due to perceived ease and tangible benefits. In contrast, producers face higher hurdles related to infrastructural limitations, trust issues, and capacity constraints. The relatively lagging engagement in digital selling also reflects infrastructural disparities and the limited availability of supportive policies or training programs for farmers as digital entrepreneurs.

These findings both correspond with and diverge from earlier studies; while the potential for e-commerce to significantly boost farmer incomes is well documented, our results highlight that adoption remains highly uneven, with farmers' participation shaped by digital literacy, access to payment systems, and the maturity of last-mile logistics in rural regions. Limited digital literacy is a significant barrier to the adoption of e-commerce in agriculture. Farmers' willingness to adopt digital technologies is influenced by factors such as age, education, and experience (Jusoh et al. 2025). Addressing this requires strategic interventions—such as e-commerce training, improved rural logistics, mobile-based payment systems, and access to cooperative selling platforms. As Baumüller (2018) highlights, targeted support in digital capacity and infrastructure is essential for realizing the developmental benefits of rural e-commerce. Furthermore, building consumer trust is essential for the success of e-commerce in agriculture. Factors such as advertising credibility, influencer marketing, and customer reviews play a significant role in influencing purchasing decisions (Nurhayati and Madjid 2025).

For the rest, internet utilization for other purposes remains notably low. Financial services, specifically e-banking, account for a mere 1.5% of usage. Similarly, sending or receiving electronic mail stands at 1.5%. Obtaining information about goods or services (excluding social media) is used by 9% of users, with the "other" category comprising the remaining 2.7%.

4.4.2 Rural Connectivity Landscape: Internet Infrastructure in Agricultural Villages

The adoption of e-commerce among farmers in rural areas relies heavily on the internet infrastructure, including in Indonesia. Graph 1 vividly illustrates the evolving landscape of internet signal quality across Indonesia from 2019 to 2024, disaggregated by agricultural village areas. The map is crucial because it visually identifies critical spatial disparities in internet infrastructure, providing the geographic evidence necessary for targeted policy intervention to enhance e-commerce adoption among rural Indonesian farmers. Each map uses a color-coded legend to categorize signal strength: dark green representing 5G/4G/LTE, light green for 3G/H+/EVDO, yellow for 2.5G/GPRS, and red indicating no internet signal. A clear trend emerges over the 5 years. There is a notable expansion of higher-quality internet coverage (dark and light green) across the archipelago, particularly in areas previously dominated by 2.5G/GPRS or lacking internet altogether. Conversely, the prevalence of "no internet signal" (red areas) appears to diminish, suggesting improvements in infrastructure accessibility. However, significant disparities persist, with certain remote or less developed regions, particularly in parts of Kalimantan, Sulawesi, and Papua, continuing to exhibit limited or no internet access.

This visual evidence of the highly varied and improving, yet still incomplete, internet infrastructure across Indonesian agricultural villages is crucial for understanding farmers' adoption of e-commerce. As various studies have consistently highlighted, robust internet infrastructure is a foundational prerequisite for digital engagement and economic participation (OECD 2017; World Bank 2016). The quality and availability of internet connectivity directly influence a farmer's ability to access online marketplaces, conduct transactions, gather market information, and utilize digital financial services. For instance, the shift from 2.5G/GPRS to 3G/H+/EVDO or, more significantly, to 5G/4G/LTE, implies a substantial increase in bandwidth and reliability. Such improvements reduce transaction costs associated with slow or intermittent connections, enhance the user experience, and enable more complex e-commerce activities, such as uploading high-resolution product images/video or participating in live online selling. Research by Koutroumpis (2019) and Vélez-Muñoz et al. (2024) emphasizes that the quality of ICT infrastructure, beyond mere presence, has a significant impact on economic growth and adoption (Fig. 4.2).

Furthermore, the Global Moran's I values indicate a consistently strong and statistically significant spatial autocorrelation in internet signal quality across Indonesian villages. In 2019, the Moran's I value was 0.630, suggesting a pronounced spatial clustering of similar signal conditions—villages with high or low signal quality tended to be near others with comparable conditions. In 2021, the value slightly declined to 0.562, possibly reflecting temporary dispersion due to sporadic infrastructure expansion or policy interventions reaching previously unconnected areas. By 2024, the index rose again to 0.603, indicating a return to more consolidated spatial patterns. This trend suggests that while access may have improved overall, spatial inequality persists, with strong digital infrastructure concentrated in specific regions and areas with limited or no signal continuing to form geographic clusters. These findings highlight the spatially uneven nature of Indonesia's digital development and the need for geographically targeted connectivity policies.

These findings carry critical policy implications. A stable, high Moran's I value signals that market-driven infrastructure expansion may reinforce existing inequalities rather than reduce them. Regions with already strong digital connectivity continue to benefit from incremental upgrades, while underserved regions remain trapped in weak-signal clusters. Such spatial persistence indicates that without targeted intervention, the digital divide will not resolve organically.

The graph over the year showed that regions transitioning from "no internet signal" to even 2.5G/GPRS might see initial, basic e-commerce engagement. Still, such connectivity only supports lightweight digital activities—typically browsing, messaging, and basic communication. This low bandwidth severely limits farmers' ability to upload product photos, use integrated payment systems, or engage in intensive e-commerce transactions. In contrast, areas gaining 4G/LTE or 5G connectivity are poised for more sophisticated and frequent online commercial activities.

The persistent "red zones" on the maps, however, underscore the continued digital divide, creating significant barriers for farmers in these areas to participate in the burgeoning digital economy. This uneven infrastructure landscape thus contributes

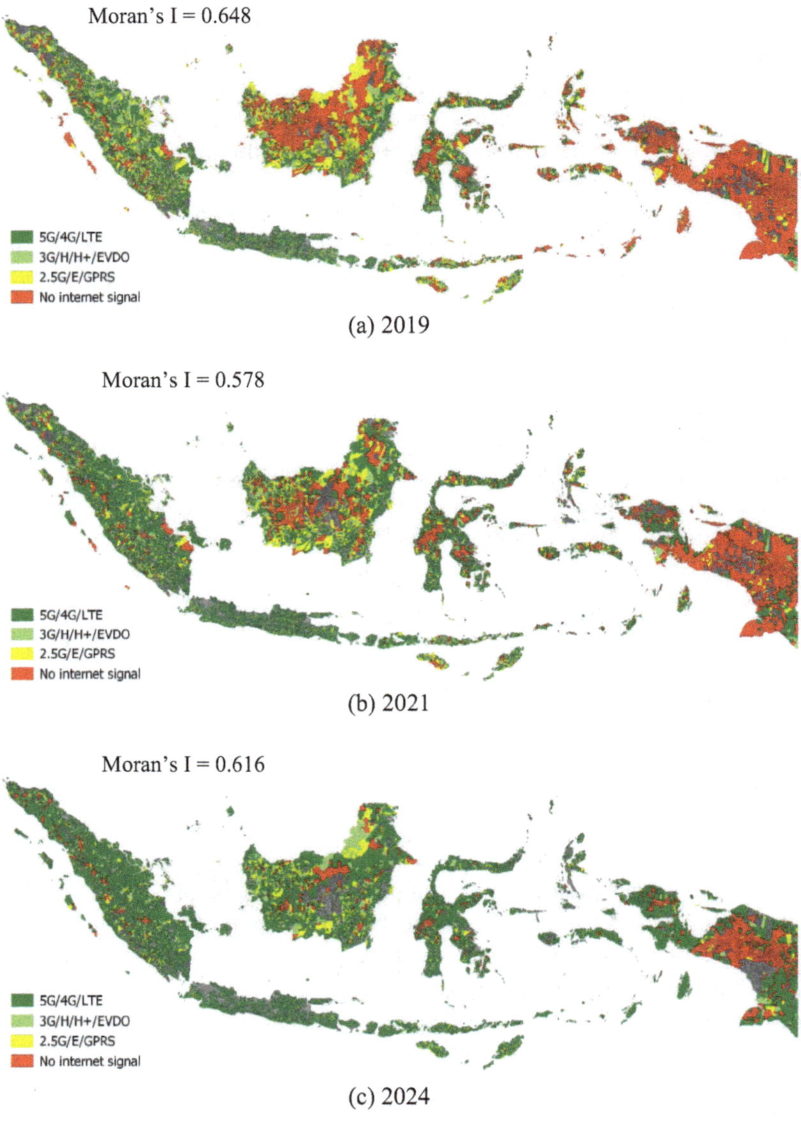

Sources: Podes, author's calculation.

Fig. 4.2 Map of internet signal quality of agriculture village and spatial autocorrelation. (**a**) 2019. (**b**) 2021. (**c**) 2024. Sources: Podes, author's calculation

directly to disparities in e-commerce adoption rates among farmers, with those in well-connected regions having a distinct advantage (Goldfarb and Tucker 2019). In remote locations—especially eastern Indonesia—the combination of weak signals and high logistical costs creates a dual disadvantage, limiting both digital participation and market access.

Policy interventions need to prioritize the targeted expansion and upgrading of internet infrastructure in underserved agricultural regions, especially in eastern Indonesia. The LISA results (see Fig. 4.3) show persistent High–High clusters of weak or absent internet signal in areas such as the central of Papua, West Sulawesi, and North Kalimantan, indicating that villages with poor connectivity are spatially concentrated and mutually reinforcing. This spatial clustering suggests that connectivity challenges are not isolated phenomena but structural regional issues requiring bundled interventions—combining infrastructure expansion, electricity reliability, digital literacy programs, and support for agricultural e-commerce. Addressing the structural disadvantages faced by these clusters is essential to ensure that farmers in remote regions can meaningfully exercise their equal rights to participate in digital markets and benefit from emerging e-commerce opportunities.

4.4.3 Estimation Results of Farmers' Adoption of E-Commerce

The findings of this study highlight the complex interplay between demographic characteristics, socio-economic conditions, and digital infrastructure in shaping e-commerce participation among rural households in Indonesia. Using marginal effects from a logistic model derived from a nationally representative dataset, we find that the probability of engaging in e-commerce, both as consumers and producers, is unevenly distributed across gender, age, education, access to digital tools, and infrastructural quality (Table 4.3).

Gender differences emerge as an important dimension of digital inclusion. Women are significantly more likely to use e-commerce to purchase goods and services, with a 1.3% marginal effect compared to men. However, there is no statistically significant difference in their likelihood of selling agricultural products online. This suggests that, while women are active consumers of e-commerce, their participation as producers remains limited, reflecting a broader gendered division in digital economies and agricultural commercialization (Cebekhulu-Msomi and Singh 2025; Kusumawardhani et al. 2023). In the Indonesian rural context, this pattern echoes long-standing gender norms in agricultural households, where women tend to shoulder domestic responsibilities, manage household consumption, and engage in small non-farm activities, while men handle market-facing tasks such as marketing crops, negotiating prices, and interacting with traders. These structural constraints help explain why women exhibit high participation as buyers but remain underrepresented among online sellers—a dynamic also observed in studies of women's roles in agricultural value chains and household decision-making in Indonesia (Sugandi et al. 2024). Barriers such as limited time, mobility constraints, and restricted access to capital and markets may constrain women's ability to leverage e-commerce for income-generating purposes in rural areas (Djurfeldt 2018).

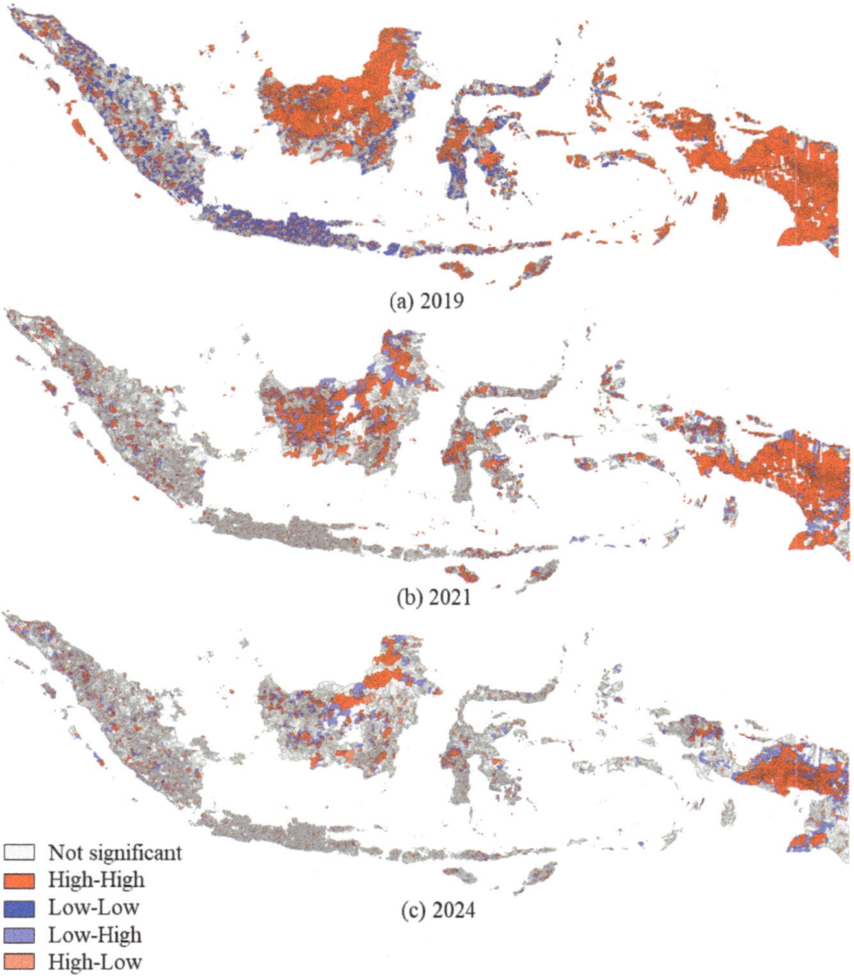

Sources: Podes, author's calculation.

Fig. 4.3 Map of identification of Spatial Hotspots and Coldspots using Local Moran's I (LISA) Analysis. (**a**) 2019. (**b**) 2021. (**c**) 2024. Sources: Podes, author's calculation

Generational divides are also pronounced. Compared to Gen Z and Alpha (the reference group), older farmers—Millennials, Gen X, and Baby Boomers—are significantly less likely to purchase online, with a decrease from 1 to 4.3%. However, Millennials show a slight positive effect (0.3%) on selling, while Baby Boomers are significantly less likely to engage in both purchasing and selling. These findings align with existing studies that emphasize a decline in digital engagement with age, attributed to reduced digital literacy and decreased familiarity with online platforms (Choi and DiNitto 2013; Luo et al. 2025). The generational gaps underscore the

Table 4.3 Marginal effects of determinants on farmers' adoption of e-commerce

Variables	Purchasing (1)	Selling (2)
Woman	0.013***	−0.001
	(0.001)	(0.000)
Generation		
Millennials	−0.010***	0.003***
	(0.001)	(0.001)
Gen X	−0.026***	(0.000)
	(0.001)	(0.001)
Baby Boomers and other	−0.043***	−0.003***
	(0.002)	(0.001)
Education		
Junior	0.007***	0.002***
	(0.001)	(0.001)
High	0.013***	0.005***
	(0.001)	(0.001)
Diploma to doctoral	0.026***	0.007***
	(0.001)	(0.001)
Rural	−0.005***	−0.002***
	(0.001)	(0.000)
Have bank account	0.013***	0.006***
	(0.001)	(0.000)
Owns mobile phone/s	0.025***	0.013***
	(0.002)	(0.001)
Place to access internet		
Own home	0.058***	0.027***
	(0.002)	(0.001)
Public spaces	0.021***	0.006***
	(0.001)	(0.000)
Expenditure (million IDR)	0.002***	0.000***
	(0.000)	(0.000)
Average number of cellular providers per district	0.002***	0.002***
	(0.000)	(0.000)
Average internet quality per district		
3G/H/H+/EVDO	−0.003**	−0.001
	(0.001)	(0.001)
2.5G/E/GPRS	−0.006*	−0.007***
	(0.003)	(0.002)
No internet signal	−0.025	0.000
	−0.017	(0.000)

(continued)

Table 4.3 (continued)

Variables	Purchasing (1)	Selling (2)
Province dummy	Yes	Yes
Year dummy	Yes	Yes
N	709,548	688,761

Note: The baseline category for the generation variable is Generation Z and Alpha. The baseline for education is up to elementary school, and the baseline for average internet quality per district is 5G/4G/LTE. Standard errors in the parentheses. *, **, and *** indicate statistical significance at the 10%, 5%, and 1% levels, respectively
Sources: Susenas and Podes, author's calculation

need for targeted digital literacy programs that include older farmers, who are often overlooked in technology adoption efforts.

Education, as a proxy for digital literacy, is among the strongest and most consistent predictors of e-commerce participation. Compared to individuals with elementary education, those with junior high, senior high, and tertiary education (diploma to doctoral level) are significantly more likely to engage in both purchasing and selling through e-commerce platforms. The marginal effects reveal a clear gradient: tertiary-educated individuals are 2.6% more likely to buy and 0.7% more likely to sell online. This pattern supports the view that education serves as a foundational enabler of digital literacy, not just in operating digital devices, but also in evaluating information, managing transactions, and utilizing platforms for commercial purposes (Chen et al. 2023; Chen 2020; Chen and Li 2025; Jiang and Qin 2024; Luo et al. 2025; Tang et al. 2024; Wei and Claire 2022).

While our dataset does not directly measure digital literacy, educational attainment is widely recognized as a robust proxy for digital skills in rural information and communication technology (ICT) research (Azali 2017; Luo et al. 2025; Tang et al. 2024). Formal education fosters operational, evaluative, and strategic competencies essential for e-commerce usage (Luo et al. 2025; Tang et al. 2024). Recent studies in Indonesia also confirm that higher digital literacy, which is often correlated with education, is positively associated with e-commerce engagement among SMEs (Azali 2017; Choczyńska 2024). Therefore, enhancing education and digital skills in rural areas is crucial to bridging the digital divide and promoting broader participation in the digital economy.

To reduce the digital divide, targeted digital literacy interventions are needed. Programs that combine basic ICT training, agricultural extension, and e-commerce awareness, which are delivered through trusted channels such as farmer groups, cooperatives, or local extension agents, can lower barriers to adoption. Community-based digital learning hubs or mobile-based tutorials in local languages may also be effective, particularly for low-income and low-education segments (Chen et al. 2023; Choi and DiNitto 2013; Luo et al. 2025). Furthermore, the adoption of ecological agricultural technologies increases significantly when rural households engage with digital production, digital finance, and digital sales simultaneously. Consequently, governments and local authorities must integrate financial empowerment with the expansion of digital platforms and production services. In addition to alleviating financial constraints, subsidies for e-commerce training, credit packaging, and logistics will enable households to increase their returns on agricultural products. Such efforts are especially crucial in areas where connectivity has already improved, but usage remains low due to skill gaps (Yu et al. 2026).

Digital access and ownership of tools are also significant predictors of e-commerce use. Households with bank accounts are 1.3% more likely to buy, and 0.6% more likely to sell online. Similarly, those who own mobile phones show a strong positive effect, with 2.6% for purchasing and 1.3% for selling. These results reaffirm that digital and financial inclusion are interlinked prerequisites for online engagement (Chen and Li 2025; Wei et al. 2024; Zhang and Zhang 2024). However, as rural areas continue to experience low financial inclusion—particularly among women, older people, and low-income farmers—policy responses must consider the trade-offs between strengthening digital financial services (e.g., mobile banking, e-wallets) and expanding transitional mechanisms such as COD.

COD plays a dual role. On one hand, it reduces entry barriers by allowing unbanked farmers to transact without digital accounts, thereby accelerating early-stage adoption and building trust. On the other hand, excessive reliance on COD may slow the transition toward formal digital finance ecosystems, as it shifts logistical risks and higher operational costs to sellers and platforms. For policymakers, the challenge lies in balancing these approaches: expanding COD to onboard new users while simultaneously investing in financial literacy and rural fintech infrastructure to ensure long-term digital financial inclusion.

Likewise, having access to the internet from one's own home significantly boosts e-commerce engagement (by 5.8% for buying and 2.7% for selling), while public access (e.g., public office or shared facilities) also provides a positive, though smaller, effect. This suggests that private and consistent digital access is more conducive to habitual e-commerce use (Kusumawardhani et al. 2023; Luo et al. 2025).

Geographic disadvantages, which encompass both infrastructural and spatial exclusion, continue to be a significant barrier to e-commerce participation. Households located in rural areas are significantly less likely to engage in e-commerce, even after controlling for income and assets. Specifically, living in a rural area reduces the likelihood of purchasing by 0.5% and the likelihood of selling by 0.2%, respectively. This disadvantage is not merely spatial but structural, as rural areas tend to have weaker digital infrastructure, fewer cellular providers, and slower internet speeds.

As confirmed by the results, lower internet quality (e.g., 2.5G or 3G networks) significantly reduces the likelihood of both buying and selling online. Compared to those in areas with 5G coverage, households in 3G areas are 0.3% less likely to buy, while those in 2.5G areas are 0.6% less likely to buy and 0.7% less likely to sell. These findings are consistent with the visual evidence presented in Fig. 4.1, which maps the changes in internet signal quality in agricultural villages across Indonesia from 2019 to 2024. The maps show a steady improvement in coverage, with 4G/5G access expanding into many previously underserved regions. However, persistent "red zones" in parts of Kalimantan, Sulawesi, and Papua highlight areas where farmers still face severe connectivity constraints or no access at all. This reinforces the need to address place-based disparities in digital access and infrastructure quality, which underpin broader patterns of rural digital exclusion (Chen et al. 2024; Luo et al. 2025; Zhang and Zhang 2024). Internet speed and bandwidth are essential for supporting meaningful digital engagement, particularly for activities such as uploading agricultural product listings, managing transactions, or participating in live selling. The movement from basic 2.5G to higher-speed infrastructure not only improves technical performance but also expands the scope of possible economic behaviors. Thus, while Indonesia's overall digital infrastructure has improved, rural farmers' unequal access to high-quality internet remains a structural barrier to inclusive e-commerce participation. Targeted investments in upgrading connectivity, particularly in lagging agricultural regions, are crucial for closing the rural digital divide and enabling farmers to fully participate in the digital economy.

Moreover, the number of cellular providers in a district, serving as a proxy for market competition and service availability, is positively associated with both e-commerce outcomes. Each additional provider increases the likelihood of participation by 0.2%. This finding highlights the role of competitive infrastructure markets in reducing prices and enhancing service quality for rural populations. Finally, economic capacity, measured by household expenditure, has a small but significant impact on digital participation. While the effect size is modest, it highlights the importance of the affordability of both devices and data packages as a threshold factor in accessing e-commerce. In sum, e-commerce participation is not merely a function of connectivity, but also of education, digital capability, financial access, and infrastructure quality, especially in geographically disadvantaged regions.

4.5 Conclusion and Policy Recommendation

4.5.1 Conclusion

This study provides the first national-level empirical analysis of e-commerce adoption among Indonesian farmers by integrating multi-wave Susenas data with village-level infrastructure information from Podes and applying rare-event logistic modeling to capture relatively infrequent digital market participation. The findings reveal that e-commerce adoption in rural agricultural settings is shaped not only by improvements in digital infrastructure but also by socio-demographic characteristics such as gender and education, highlighting the multidimensional nature of farmers' engagement with digital markets. While internet connectivity has improved steadily between 2019 and 2024, the digital landscape remains spatially uneven, with persistent clusters of low or absent signal quality in eastern Indonesia. These structural disparities directly influence the likelihood of e-commerce uptake, reinforcing the digital divide between farmers in well-connected and underserved regions.

A nuanced examination of gender-related patterns indicates that male farmers remain significantly more likely to adopt e-commerce than women, reflecting long-standing gendered roles in Indonesian agricultural households and digital economies. Women's participation in farm decision-making and market-facing activities remains constrained by domestic workload, limited access to digital tools, and lower involvement in marketing channels. This gender gap mirrors broader findings in the literature on rural digital inclusion, which emphasizes asymmetrical access to mobile devices, digital payments, and information networks. Likewise, education plays a critical role in facilitating e-commerce adoption, as farmers with higher educational attainment are more likely to possess the digital literacy and confidence needed to navigate online platforms, verify information, and manage digital financial transactions.

The results also reveal important policy trade-offs. Expanding COD (Cash on Delivery) services can reduce entry barriers for farmers in low-connectivity regions or those with limited familiarity with digital finance, offering an accessible transitional mechanism for participating in online markets. However, relying solely on COD cannot sustain long-term digital transformation. Strengthening digital financial infrastructure—including mobile banking, e-wallet interoperability, and agent banking—will be essential for enabling farmers to access credit, savings, and trusted payment systems. Thus, policies must strike a balance between meeting farmers where they are and building an inclusive digital ecosystem that supports deeper and more secure engagement over time. Infrastructure expansion, particularly in regions identified as persistent low-signal clusters, is a critical foundation for ensuring that digital opportunities do not exacerbate regional inequalities.

Despite its contributions, this study has limitations. The dataset does not fully capture the complex marketing pathways farmers use when selling online. Many farmers participate indirectly through cooperatives, farmers' groups, or intermediaries who manage e-commerce transactions on their behalf. As a result, some digitally engaged farmers may appear as non-adopters in the data, suggesting that our estimates likely represent a conservative lower bound of true participation. Future research could benefit from survey data that distinguishes between direct and indirect forms of online selling and explores platform-level dynamics, including the roles of digital cooperatives and community-based digital facilitators.

Overall, this study underscores the importance of addressing structural constraints—digital, social, and institutional—to accelerate e-commerce adoption among Indonesian farmers. Effective policy must integrate infrastructure development, financial inclusion, digital capacity-building, and gender-responsive strategies to ensure that the benefits of the digital economy extend equitably across regions and population groups. As Indonesia continues to invest in rural digitalization, bridging these interconnected gaps will be essential to unlocking the transformative potential of e-commerce for agricultural livelihoods.

4.5.2 Policy Recommendations

The findings from this study provide several policy implications that, if implemented strategically, can enhance the inclusiveness of e-commerce participation among rural farmers in Indonesia. First, given the substantial gaps in age and education, digital literacy programs must be specifically tailored for older and less educated farmers, who remain the least engaged in online commerce. The most feasible approach is to integrate hands-on digital training into existing agricultural extension activities, enabling extension officers to deliver modules on basic smartphone use, navigating e-commerce platforms, online safety, and product marketing. Because older farmers often learn more effectively through social interaction, peer-learning models within farmer groups—such as assigning digitally skilled "champions" to guide their peers—offer a low-cost and scalable solution. Complementary offline learning tools, such as printed guides or video tutorials distributed through local extension offices, are particularly important in low-connectivity areas where online learning may be impractical.

Second, the gendered patterns observed in this study underscore the need for gender-responsive digital inclusion strategies. While women participate actively as e-commerce consumers, they remain underrepresented as sellers due to mobility constraints, limited access to capital, and weaker market networks. Addressing this requires embedding e-commerce training within women's farming groups, strengthening women-focused cooperatives, and developing community-based micro-fulfillment hubs that reduce the logistical burden of selling products online. Such interventions not only improve women's access to digital markets but also align with broader evidence on gendered roles within Indonesian agriculture and digital economies.

Third, infrastructure development must prioritize regions where connectivity deficits remain most severe. Despite improvements in recent years, substantial "red zones" and high-high-low or no-internet clusters persist in parts of Indonesia—including the clustered areas of Central Papua, West Sulawesi, and North Kalimantan—where 2G/3G or no networks dominate. Upgrading these areas to reliable 4G service is essential for enabling meaningful participation in e-commerce, particularly given the strong association between internet quality and both purchasing and selling behaviors. However, acknowledging the high infrastructure costs in sparsely populated areas, public-private partnerships and infrastructure-sharing mandates will be necessary to support equitable expansion. Strengthening competition in the telecommunications sector also remains crucial, as the presence of additional cellular providers significantly increases adoption rates by improving service quality and lowering consumer costs.

Fourth, the results reveal an important trade-off between expanding Cash-on-Delivery (COD) options and promoting digital financial inclusion. COD serves as a critical entry point for unbanked and financially excluded populations, particularly in rural areas where trust in online payments remains low. Maintaining COD as a transitional mechanism is therefore essential. At the same time, policymakers should promote simplified digital wallet systems with streamlined registration processes and develop hybrid payment models—such as partial COD—to gradually shift users into digital finance ecosystems while managing risks for sellers. These approaches offer a balanced path toward expanding financial inclusion without undermining early engagement in e-commerce.

Finally, strengthening rural logistics systems is a complementary priority. Investments in village-level logistics hubs, courier pick-up points, and integrated cooperative-based distribution systems can reduce transaction costs, support small-scale producers, and enable both women and older farmers to participate more easily in online markets. Taken together, these targeted interventions—centered on demographic-specific digital training, gender-responsive programming, geographically prioritized infrastructure development, balanced payment innovations, and improved logistics ecosystems—provide a practical and actionable policy roadmap for enhancing inclusive e-commerce participation among Indonesia's rural farming communities.

Acknowledgements This paper was presented in the session "E-commerce for Rural and Agricultural Development" at the International Conference on "Innovations for Sustainable Agriculture and Rural Development", held at the Asian Development Bank Institute (ADBI), Tokyo, Japan, on 22–24 September 2025. ADBI and Lincoln University, New Zealand jointly organized the conference. The authors gratefully acknowledge the valuable comments and suggestions from the participants, as well as travel support from ADBI.

Declaration

Competing Interests The author(s) declared no potential conflicts of interest with respect to the research, authorship, and/or publication of this article.

Funding Statement The author(s) received no financial support for the research, authorship, and/or publication of this article.

References

ADB (Asian Development Bank). (2023). *E-Commerce Evolution in Asia and the Pacific Opportunities and Challenges*. https://doi.org/10.22617/TCS230473-2

Ariansyah, K., Sirait, E. R. E., Nugroho, B. A., & Suryanegara, M. (2021). Drivers of and barriers to e-commerce adoption in Indonesia: Individuals' perspectives and the implications. Telecommunications Policy, 45(8), 1–15. https://doi.org/10.1016/j.telpol.2021.102219

Aslam, S. (2025). Social Sciences & Humanities Open Digital exclusion in agricultural communication: Exploring socio-economic and infrastructural barriers to ICT use in rural Pakistan. 12(November).

Azali, K. (2017). Indonesia's divided digital economy. *ISEAS, 70*(2017).

Baumüller, H. (2018). The Little We Know: An Exploratory Literature Review on the Utility of Mobile Phone-Enabled Services for Smallholder Farmers. *Journal of International Development*, *30*(1), 134–154. https://doi.org/10.1002/jid.3314

Bronnenberg, B. J. (2015). The provision of convenience and variety by the market. The RAND Journal of Economics, 46(3), 480–498. http://www.jstor.org/stable/43895602

Caffaro, F., Micheletti Cremasco, M., Roccato, M., & Cavallo, E. (2020). Drivers of farmers' intention to adopt technological innovations in Italy: The role of information sources, perceived usefulness, and perceived ease of use. Journal of Rural Studies, 76, 264–271. https://doi.org/10.1016/j.jrurstud.2020.04.028

Cebekhulu-Msomi, P., & Singh, S. (2025). The Impact of Industry 4.0 on Women-Owned Agribusinesses in South Africa- Gauteng Province. *Sustainability Science and Resources, 8*, 15–37. doi:https://doi.org/10.55168/ssr2809-6029.2025.8002

Chen, L. (2020). *Improving digital connectivity for e-commerce: A policy framework and empirical note for ASEAN*. Retrieved from https://www.eria.org/research/improving-digital-connectivity-for-e-commerce-a-policy-framework-and-empirical-note-for-asean

Chen, W., & Li, J. (2025). Digital finance, rural E-commerce development and consumption upgrading. *International Review of Financial Analysis, 104*, 104351. doi:https://doi.org/10.1016/j.irfa.2025.104351

Chen, M., & Long, Y. (2024). Empowering Rural Revitalization: Unleashing the Potential of E-commerce for Sustainable Industrial Integration. *Journal of the Knowledge Economy, 15*, 18813–18831. https://doi.org/10.1007/s13132-024-01813-3

Chen, C., Gan, C., Li, J., Lu, Y., & Rahut, D. (2023). Linking farmers to markets: Does cooperative membership facilitate e-commerce adoption and income growth in rural China? *Economic Analysis and Policy, 80*, 1155–1170. doi:https://doi.org/10.1016/j.eap.2023.09.040

Chen, J., Hou, H., Liao, Z., & Wang, L. (2024). Digital Environment, Digital Literacy, and Farmers' Entrepreneurial Behavior: A Discussion on Bridging the Digital Divide. *Sustainability, 16*(23).

Choczyńska, A. (2024). Intersectional digital inequality in Indonesia. *Insights into Regional Development, 6*(3), 11–22.

Choi, N. G., & DiNitto, D. M. (2013). The Digital Divide Among Low-Income Homebound Older Adults: Internet Use Patterns, eHealth Literacy, and Attitudes Toward Computer/Internet Use. *Journal of Medical Internet Research, 15*(5). doi:https://doi.org/10.2196/jmir.2645

Coca, E., Pereira, A., & Giacopini, R. (2025). Imagining agri-food futures across digital divides: Agribusiness and family farmers in Minas Gerais, Brazil. Digital Geography and Society, 9(April), 100139. https://doi.org/10.1016/j.diggeo.2025.100139

Cortes, J. D., Jackson, J. E., & Cortes, A. F. (2024). Farmers' markets or the supermarket? Channel selection in small farming businesses. *New England Journal of Entrepreneurship, 27*(1), 40–62. https://doi.org/10.1108/NEJE-07-2022-0045

Cuiping, H., Yu, X., & Junyao, Z. (2024). Seeds of Change: Cultivating Prosperity in Rural China through E-Commerce. Current Journal of Applied Science and Technology, 43(6), 173–177. https://doi.org/10.9734/cjast/2024/v43i64398

Das, K., Tamhane, T., Vatterott, B., Wibowo, P., & Wintels, S. (2018). The digital archipelago: How online commerce is driving Indonesia's economic development. McKinsey & Company, August, 1–72. www.mckinsey.com/featured-insights/asia-pacific/the-digital-archipelago-how-online-

Davis, F. D. (1989). Perceived Usefulness, Perceived Ease of Use, and User Acceptance of Information Technology. MIS Quarterly, 13(3), 319–340. https://doi.org/10.2307/249008

Deichmann, U., Goyal, A., & Mishra, D. (2016a). Will digital technologies transform agriculture in developing countries? *Agricultural Economics (United Kingdom), 47*, 21–33. https://doi.org/10.1111/agec.12300

Deichmann, U., Goyal, A., & Mishra, D. (2016b). Will digital technologies transform agriculture in developing countries? 47. https://doi.org/10.1111/agec.12300

Djurfeldt, A. A. (2018). Gender and rural livelihoods: Agricultural commercialization and farm/non-farm diversification. In A. A. Djurfeldt, F. Mawunyo Dzanku, & A. Cuthbert Isinika (Eds.), *Agriculture, Diversification, and Gender in Rural Africa: Longitudinal Perspectives from Six Countries* (pp. 81–112).

Erlangga, E., Machuku, O., & Jun Dahino, C. (2023). A review article on the impact and challenges of mobile phone usage on agricultural production in Africa. *Cogent Food and Agriculture*, *9*(2). https://doi.org/10.1080/23311932.2023.2273634

Eschachasthi, R., Purwa, T., & Cendekia, D. G. (2022). Does Palapa Ring Project Infrastructure Bridging Connectivity and Economic Activity? *Proceedings of The International Conference on Data Science and Official Statistics*, *2021*(1), 418–435. https://doi.org/10.34123/icdsos.v2021i1.99

Fahmi, F. Z., & Sari, I. D. (2020). Rural transformation, digitalisation and subjective wellbeing: A case study from Indonesia. *Habitat International, 98*, 102150. doi:https://doi.org/10.1016/j.habitatint.2020.102150

Fahmi, F. Z., & Savira, M. (2023). Digitalization and rural entrepreneurial attitude in Indonesia: a capability approach. *Journal of Enterprising Communities*, *17*(2), 454–478. https://doi.org/10.1108/JEC-06-2021-0082

Furuholt, B., & Matotay, E. (2011). The Developmental Contribution From Mobile Phones Across the Agricultural Value Chain in Rural Africa. *Electronic Journal of Information Systems in Developing Countries*, *48*(1), 1–16. https://doi.org/10.1002/j.1681-4835.2011.tb00343.x

Goldfarb, A., & Tucker, C. (2019). Digital Economics. *Journal of Economic Literature*, *57*(1), 3–43. https://doi.org/10.1257/jel.20171452

Gouroubera, M. W., Adechian, S. A., Segnon, A. C., Moumouni-Moussa, I., & Zougmoré, R. B. (2024). Drivers and impacts of mobile phone-mediated scaling of agricultural technologies: a meta-analysis. *Frontiers in Sustainable Food Systems*, *8*(January), 1–13. https://doi.org/10.3389/fsufs.2024.1514546

Guojie X, Haiquan C, Wenjuan W, Jebbouri A, Weiwei C, (2025). Sustainable Development of Rural E-Commerce: Exploring the Cognitive Themes and Emotional Expressions of Consumers When Purchasing Agricultural and Sideline Foodstuffs Online. *IEEE Access*, *13*(July), 135652–135668. https://doi.org/10.1109/ACCESS.2025.3589869

Hidayat, A. R. T., Onitsuka, K., Sianipar, C. P. M., Basu, M., & Hoshino, S. (2023). To migrate or not to migrate: Internet use and migration intention among rural youth in developing countries (case of Malang, Indonesia). *Digital Geography and Society, 4*, 100052. doi:https://doi.org/10.1016/j.diggeo.2023.100052

Ibitunde I O, Ojo T F and Bello O D. (2024). Level of Utilisation of Mobile Phones Among Maize Farmers in Osogbo Agricultural Development Programme Zone of Osun State, Nigeria. *Proceedings of the Annual Conference of the Agricultural Extension Society of Nigeria*, *2020*, 23–30.

iPrice (2021), "The map of e-commerce in Indonesia", available at: https://iprice.co.id/insights/mapofecommerce/en/.

ITA (2022), Market Intelligence: Indonesia E-commerce Sectors, The International Trade Administration, U.S. Department of Commerce, Washington, D.C.

Jiang, P.-C., & Qin, S. (2024). E-commerce empowers urban entrepreneurial activity—Empirical evidence from the construction of national e-commerce demonstration cities. *Cities, 150*, 105092. doi:https://doi.org/10.1016/j.cities.2024.105092

Jo, Y., Matsumura, M., & Weinstein, D. E. (2024). The Impact of Retail E-Commerce on Relative Prices and Consumer Welfare. *The Review of Economics and Statistics*, *106*(6), 1675–1689. https://doi.org/10.1162/rest_a_01272

Jusoh, A., Abbas, A. F., Haider, M., Yazid, A., Latip, A., Razak, A., & Hussin, C. (2025). Cultivating Digital Pathways: A Systematic Review of e-Commerce Adoption in Asian Agriculture Cultivating Digital Pathways: A Systematic Review of e-Commerce Adoption in Asian Agriculture. *Journal of Agricultural & Food Information*, *0*(0), 1–37. https://doi.org/10.1080/10496505.2025.2553282

Kazunari, C., Júlio, C., Figueiredo, D., & Scornavacca, E. (2024). Technological Forecasting & Social Change Investigating the diffusion of innovation: A comprehensive study of successive diffusion processes through analysis of search trends, patent records, and academic publications. 198(October 2023).

King, G., & Zeng, L. (2001). Logistic Regression in Rare Events Data. *Political Analysis*, *9*(2), 137–163. https://doi.org/10.1093/oxfordjournals.pan.a004868

Koutroumpis, P. (2019). The economic impact of broadband: Evidence from OECD countries. *Technological Forecasting and Social Change*, *148*, 119719. https://doi.org/10.1016/j.techfore.2019.119719

Kusumawardhani, N., Pramana, R., Saputri, N. S., & Suryadarma, D. (2023). Heterogeneous impact of internet availability on female labor market outcomes in an emerging economy: Evidence from Indonesia. *World Development, 164*, 106182. doi:https://doi.org/10.1016/j.worlddev.2022.106182

Lalitha, T M. (2022). Magnitude of E-Commerce in Rural Areas—A Review. International Journal of Research Publication and Reviews, 3(4), 114–121. https://doi.org/10.55248/gengpi.2022.3.4.7

Lasdun, V., Harou, A. P., Magomba, C., & Guereña, D. (2025). Peer learning and technology adoption in a digital farmer-to-farmer. Journal of Development Economics, 176(November 2022), 103496. https://doi.org/10.1016/j.jdeveco.2025.103496

Li, S. (2025). Digital literacy and farmers ' non-farm employment-an empirical study based on CFPS. Sustainable Futures, 10(November 2024), 100999. https://doi.org/10.1016/j.sftr.2025.100999

Liu, M., Min, S., Ma, W., & Liu, T. (2021). The adoption and impact of E-commerce in rural China: Application of an endogenous switching regression model. Journal of Rural Studies, 83(3), 106–116. https://doi.org/10.1016/j.jrurstud.2021.02.021

Luo, Y., Zhou, L., & Zhang, W. (2025). Can e-commerce bring dividends to rural households? New evidence from the income inequality perspective. *Economic Analysis and Policy, 86*, 363–379. doi:https://doi.org/10.1016/j.eap.2025.03.036

Martini, Setiawan, D., Adhariani, D., Harymawan, I., & Widodo, M. (2023). E-commerce and micro and small industries performance: The role of firm size as a moderator. *Journal of Open Innovation: Technology, Market, and Complexity*, *9*(3), 100142. https://doi.org/10.1016/j.joitmc.2023.100142

Morgan JP. (2019). "E-commerce payment trends: Indonesia", January, available at: https://www.jpmorgan.com/merchant-services/insights/reports/indonesia

Njuki, J., Eissler, S., Malapit, H., Meinzen-dick, R., Bryan, E., & Quisumbing, A. (2022). A review of evidence on gender equality, women's empowerment, and food systems. 33(June).

Nurhayati, A., & Madjid, R. (2025). Innovations in Agricultural E-Commerce: Analyzing Purchase Decisions and the Role of Consumer Credibility. *J. Glob. Innov. Agric. Sci*, *13*(2), 607–616. doi: https://doi.org/10.22194/JGIAS/25.1637

OECD. (2017). *OECD Digital Economy Outlook 2017*. OECD Publishing. https://doi.org/10.1787/9789264276284-en. Available at: https://www.oecd.org/content/dam/oecd/en/publications/reports/2017/10/oecd-digital-economy-outlook-2017_g1g7aa8d/9789264276284-en.pdf.

Permani, R., Sahara, S., Satria, D., Suprehatin, S., & Nuryartono, N. (2023). The impacts of food certificate adoption on e-commerce income among small online agri-food sellers. *Journal of Agribusiness in Developing and Emerging Economies*, *15*(3), 579–600. https://doi.org/10.1108/JADEE-10-2022-0231

Perwangsa, N. I., Nur, Y., Muhamad, F., Alil, R., Sandy, Y. E., & Taufic, H. (2024). Perceived ease of use, perceived usefulness, and customer satisfaction as driving factors on repurchase intention: the perspective of the e-commerce market in Indonesia. Cogent Business & Management, 11(1). https://doi.org/10.1080/23311975.2024.2413376

Piabuo, S. M., Yakan, H. B., Puatwoe, J. T., Nonzienwo, V. Y., & Mamboh, T. R. (2020). Effect of rural farmers' access to information on price and profits in Cameroon. *Cogent Food and Agriculture*, *6*(1). https://doi.org/10.1080/23311932.2020.1799530

Rahman, M. S., Haque, M. E., Afrad, M. S. I., Hasan, S. S., Rahman, M. A., & Noman, M. R. A. F. (2024). Usage of the mobile phone on agricultural farm enterprise development by women in rural Bangladesh. *Cogent Social Sciences, 10*(1). https://doi.org/10.1080/23311886.2024.2383393

Riley, M., & Robertson, B. (2022). The virtual good farmer: Farmers' use of social media and the (re)presentation of "good farming." *Sociologia Ruralis, 62*(3), 437–458. https://doi.org/10.1111/soru.12390

Rizvi, Y. S., & Nabi, A. (2021). Transformation of learning from real to virtual: an exploratory-descriptive analysis of issues and challenges. *Journal of Research in Innovative Teaching and Learning, 14*(1), 5–17. https://doi.org/10.1108/JRIT-10-2020-0052

Salemink, K., Strijker, D., & Bosworth, G. (2017). Rural development in the digital age: A systematic literature review on unequal ICT availability, adoption, and use in rural areas. *Journal of Rural Studies, 54*, 360–371. doi:https://doi.org/10.1016/j.jrurstud.2015.09.001

Salemink, K., Townsend, L., & Chapman, P. (2025). The remapping of rural digitalisation: A just-rural narrative review. *Journal of Rural Studies, 113*, 103499. doi:https://doi.org/10.1016/j.jrurstud.2024.103499

Siswanto Imam Santoso, Hery Setiyawan, Pramesti Megayana, A. Setiadi. (2025). Impact of Mobile Phone Usage and Credit Access on the Revenue of Duck Farmers in Brebes, Indonesia. *Journal of Animal Health and Production, 13*(2), 387–392. https://doi.org/10.17582/journal.jahp/2025/13.2.387.392 ISSN

Siahaan, M. N., Handayani, P. W., & Azzahro, F. (2022). Self-disclosure of social media users in Indonesia: the influence of personal and social media factors. *Information Technology and People, 35*(7), 1931–1954. https://doi.org/10.1108/ITP-06-2020-0389

Simamora, C. M., & Ningsih, R. (2020). Inklusivitas Ekonomi Digital di Indonesia: Perspektif Gender dan Penciptaan Lapangan Kerja: (Studi Kasus Kampung Marketer). *Cendekia Niaga, 4*(2), 39–53.

Statista (2023), "E-commerce: Indonesia", available at: https://www.statista.com/outlook/dmo/ecommerce/indonesia.

Stoneman, P. (2018). The Diffusion of Innovations: Some Reflections The Diffusion of Innovations: Some Reflections. International Journal of the Economics of Business, 25(1), 85–95. https://doi.org/10.1080/13571516.2017.1390834

Sugandi, E. A., Putri, T. E., & Vermonte, P. (2024). *Bright Prospect, Lingering Shadows: Toward an Inclusive Digital Transformation in Indonesia* (N. Shimomura & J. A. Sopacua Eds.).

Suseno, Y. (2018). Disruptive innovation and the creation of social capital in Indonesia's urban communities. *Asia Pacific Business Review, 24*(2), 174–195. doi:https://doi.org/10.1080/13602381.2018.1431251

Susilowati, A. P. E., Rachmawati, R., & Rijanta, R. (2025). Smart village concept in Indonesia: ICT as determining factor. *Heliyon, 11*(1), e41657. https://doi.org/10.1016/j.heliyon.2025.e41657

Tang, L., Chen, M., Tang, Y., & Xiong, Y. (2024). Can E-commerce development alleviate farm household poverty vulnerability: Evidence from rural China. *Cities, 153*, 105297. doi:https://doi.org/10.1016/j.cities.2024.105297

Vélez-Muñoz, J. A., Sebastián, F.-C., Silvana, C.-H., & and Valencia-Arias, A. (2024). Exploring the determinants of electronic commerce adoption in a municipality with limited internet access. *Cogent Business & Management, 11*(1), 2308090. https://doi.org/10.1080/23311975.2024.2308090

Vijayshena, P. M., Lokeshwaran, N., & Dhanasekar, S. (2025). A Digital Farmer Marketplace Connecting Rural Farmer and Consumer without Middle Person. *International Journal for Research in Applied Science and Engineering Technology, 13*(July). https://doi.org/10.22214/ijraset.2025.73255

Wei, G., and Claire, K. (2022). The promise of the internet for rural economic development in China: a study of agricultural e-commerce. *Peking University Law Journal, 10*(2), 151–172. doi:https://doi.org/10.1080/20517483.2023.2171595

Wei, X., Yang, Z., Yan, Y., & Sun, J. (2024). Rural E-commerce, Digital finance, and urban–rural common prosperity: A Quasi-natural Experiment Based on China's Comprehensive

Demonstration of E-commerce Entering Rural Areas Policy. *Finance Research Letters, 69*, 106237. doi:https://doi.org/10.1016/j.frl.2024.106237

World Bank. (2016). *World Development Report 2016: Digital Dividends*. World Bank. https://doi.org/10.1596/978-1-4648-0671-1

World Bank. (2023). *Rural population (percent of total population)—Indonesia*. Retrieved from: https://data.worldbank.org/indicator/SP.RUR.TOTL.ZS?end=2023&locations=ID&start=1960&view=chart

World Bank Group. (2020). Commodity markets Outlook, January. *Commodity Market Outlook Implications of Covid 19 for Commodities, 1*(April), 1689–1699. https://doi.org/10.1017/CBO9781107415324.004

Xu, X., Fan, R., Wang, D., Wang, Y., & Wang, Y. (2024). The role of consumer reviews in e-commerce platform credit supervision: A signaling game model based on complex network. *Electronic Commerce Research and Applications, 63*, 101347. https://doi.org/10.1016/j.elerap.2023.101347

Ye Y, Fang J, Ye J. (2024). Does E-Commerce Construction Boost Farmers' Incomes? Evidence from China. Sustain. 16(11). https://doi.org/10.3390/su16114595

Yu, P., Deng, X., Chen, Y., & Chen, Y. (2026). Digital economy—driven empowerment of ecological agricultural technologies in rural China: Implications for sustainable agricultural transformation. *Journal of Rural Studies, 123*(December 2025). https://doi.org/10.1016/j.jrurstud.2026.104032

Zhang, Y., & Zhang, Y. (2024). The Influence of Digital Literacy on the Phenomenon of Deviation between Farmers' E-Commerce Sales Willingness and Behavior: Evidence from Rural China. *Sustainability, 16*(7).

Zhang, H., Zheng, S., & Zhu, P. (2024). Why are Indonesian consumers buying on live streaming platforms? Research on consumer perceived value theory. Heliyon, 10(13), e33518. https://doi.org/10.1016/j.heliyon.2024.e33518.

Chapter 5
Digital Inclusion and Rural Earnings in Indonesia: Evidence from E-Commerce Adoption Across Sectors

Kadir Ruslan and Weni Lidya Sukma

5.1 Introduction

Digital transformation is rapidly reshaping economic landscapes, with e-commerce emerging as a key driver of productivity, market access, and income generation (World Bank 2016). Yet, the diffusion of such digital innovations remains highly uneven, particularly in developing countries where structural barriers to technology adoption persist (ITU 2022; OECD 2018). In Indonesia, this digital divide is most pronounced in rural areas, where infrastructure constraints, limited digital skills, and labor informality intersect to constrain inclusive economic development (Akbar and Wijaya 2024; Amalia et al. 2025; BPS 2023b; Hadi 2018; Onitsuka et al. 2018).

Rural Indonesia is home to the majority of the nation's poor. Almost 60% of the people with low incomes reside in rural areas, and many are employed in low-productivity sectors such as agriculture and informal services (BPS 2023a, c). Improving the livelihood of rural workers remains a central challenge for poverty alleviation and rural development (Zhang et al. 2025a, b). In this context, expanding the digital economy in rural areas through digital inclusion offers a promising and sustainable development pathway.

Digital inclusion can enhance rural incomes through multiple pathways, notably by expanding access to financial services and extending market reach via e-commerce adoption. Evidence from prior studies reinforces these relationships. Fernandes et al. (2021) showed that digital financial services significantly improved financial access for the underserved population, including rural residents, in Mozambique, while Ma et al. (2020) found that internet use is a primary driver of e-commerce adoption in rural China. These findings collectively suggest that digitalization in rural areas can promote both digital financial inclusion and e-commerce

K. Ruslan (✉) · W. L. Sukma
BPS-Statistics Indonesia, Jakarta, Indonesia
e-mail: kadirsst@bps.go.id; wenilidya@bps.go.id

W. Ma et al. (eds.), *E-Commerce for Inclusive Rural and Agricultural Development*, Contributions to Economics,
https://doi.org/10.1007/978-981-92-5237-4_5

participation, both of which may positively affect rural income (Wu 2025; Yin et al. 2025). Beyond these direct channels, digital inclusive finance has also been shown to influence rural earnings through entrepreneurship, financial investment, non-agricultural employment, and mechanized production (Lian et al. 2023). A growing body of empirical evidence further indicates that digital inclusive finance and rural e-commerce operate jointly to stimulate rural income growth. Wu (2025) reported that digital inclusive finance contributed to narrowing China's urban–rural income gap, with rural e-commerce serving as a key mediating mechanism, while Wang et al. (2024), similarly, found that digital inclusive finance facilitates rural e-commerce development in China, thereby promoting sustained increases in rural income.

Rural e-commerce provides rural residents with new channels for selling and buying goods, accessing services, and engaging with broader markets that transcend geographic limitations (Chen et al. 2022; Goldfarb and Tucker 2019). Therefore, e-commerce adoption improves rural incomes by expanding market access, reducing transaction costs, enhancing the availability of timely market information, and increasing access to digital payment systems and financial services (Ma et al. 2023; Zhang and Zhao 2025). These mechanisms collectively raise productivity, lower operational barriers, and strengthen producers' ability to secure better prices and manage cash flows more efficiently, ultimately leading to higher earnings for rural workers.

Many studies have also confirmed its potential to reduce income inequality among rural households by empowering traditionally excluded groups, such as small-scale farmers, informal workers, and rural women (Chen et al. 2022; Guan et al. 2024; Li and He 2024; Qiu et al. 2025; Zhang et al. 2025a, b). For rural women, particularly those employed in agriculture, e-commerce adoption represents an important opportunity to narrow Indonesia's gender income gap, as highlighted by several studies (e.g., Akbar 2022; Ruslan and Sukma 2025a). This potential is reinforced by the rapid rise in women's participation in digital commerce. Wihardja and Wibisana (2021) report that the share of female entrepreneurs engaging in e-commerce increased from 2.7% in 2017 to 7.5% in 2020, and that women accounted for approximately 56% of digital merchants in Indonesia.

E-commerce in rural contexts encompasses a range of activities linked to agriculture and rural populations. This includes the distribution of industrial goods to rural areas, the sale of agricultural products to urban markets, online transactions involving agricultural inputs, and the provision of e-commerce services aimed at poverty alleviation and rural development (Li and Zhao 2020; Wang et al. 2024). E-commerce adoption refers to the adoption of processes for purchasing, selling, transferring, or exchanging products, services, and information through a network, including the internet (Rainer and Cegielski 2011). At the individual level, it is a decision that can be influenced by many factors, including individual characteristics (gender, age, education, marital status, and employment status), household characteristics (number of household members), geographic location, digital skill, technology experience, physical infrastructure, and industrial specialization (Ariansyah et al. 2021; Astuti et al. 2023; He et al. 2024; Purevkhuu and Munkhbold 2021; Rogers 2003; Selorm et al. 2022; Valarezo et al. 2020).

While the macroeconomic potential of digital inclusion through rural e-commerce is well recognized, the adoption rate of e-commerce in rural Indonesia is relatively low: only 20% of small and medium-sized enterprises (SMEs) adopt e-commerce, compared to 52% in urban areas (Market Research Indonesia 2025). Therefore, understanding the determinants of rural workers' decisions to adopt e-commerce and how this adoption affects rural earnings can provide significant insights into rural development in Indonesia, particularly by promoting digital inclusion.

Although numerous studies have documented the positive economic effects of e-commerce adoption among micro, small, and medium-sized enterprises (MSMEs) in Indonesia (e.g., Abdullah 2025; Kilay et al. 2022; Priyatna 2022; Rolando 2025; Wirdiyanti et al. 2023; Yacob et al. 2021), micro-level evidence on the determinants and income implications of e-commerce adoption within rural labor markets remains limited. Moreover, recent studies have examined the heterogeneous income effects of broader digital transformation and internet diffusion in Indonesia (e.g., Fointuna et al. 2025; Wihardja et al. 2024). However, evidence on the distributional heterogeneity of income associated with e-commerce participation—particularly within rural labor markets—remains limited and underexplored.

Specifically, while women's participation in digital commerce has grown rapidly, a substantial gender earnings gap persists in Indonesian rural labor markets (Ruslan and Sukma 2025a; World Bank 2021). Determining whether unequal access to e-commerce drives these disparities is critical to formulating inclusive digital policies. Therefore, it is essential to quantify the extent to which gender-specific differences in e-commerce adoption account for observed income gaps. By decomposing rural gender-earning gaps, our study seeks to isolate the 'endowment effect'—differences in adoption rates and skills—from the 'structural effect,' which captures systemic barriers and unequal returns to digital tools. This distinction is vital in the Indonesian context, where women often face a 'double burden' of domestic responsibilities that may limit their ability to translate e-commerce access into equivalent financial gains compared to their male counterparts.

More broadly, the current literature exhibits several gaps regarding the income effects of e-commerce adoption, particularly in isolating rural-specific dynamics, applying rigorous causal identification strategies, differentiating effects across sectors (agriculture vs. non-agriculture) and employment statuses (employers vs. employees), and its potential contribution to reducing the income gap in rural areas. Consequently, little is known about who adopts e-commerce in rural areas, what factors drive such adoption, and whether it improves incomes for different categories of rural workers or contributes to narrowing rural income disparities in Indonesia.

This study aims to fill these gaps by analyzing the determinants of e-commerce adoption and the income effects of adoption among rural employers and employees in Indonesia across agricultural and non-agricultural sectors. By disaggregating the rural workforce by employment type and sector, this study provides nuanced insights into the heterogeneous pathways by which digital inclusion through e-commerce adoption affects rural earnings. We investigate three key research questions: (1) What are the demographic and structural determinants of e-commerce adoption in rural labor markets? (2) Does e-commerce adoption enhance income, and if so, for whom? (3) Does it help to close income gaps in rural Indonesia?

This study makes several key contributions to the literature on digital inclusion and rural development. First, it provides one of the few micro-level examinations of e-commerce adoption among rural workers in Indonesia, a context where digital transformation remains uneven, and evidence on individual-level determinants is scarce. Second, by disaggregating rural workers into employers and employees across agricultural and non-agricultural sectors, the study offers a nuanced assessment of the heterogeneous income effects of e-commerce, an area largely overlooked in prior research that has focused primarily on MSMEs or economy-wide indicators of digitalization. Third, the paper advances the literature methodologically by applying a quantitative method that isolates rural-specific effects and identifies income gains attributable to e-commerce adoption. Finally, the study provides new empirical insights into whether e-commerce adoption can help reduce income disparities within rural labor markets, particularly in low-productivity agricultural settings. Together, these contributions deepen our understanding of how digital inclusion unfolds in rural Indonesia and highlight the conditions under which e-commerce can serve as an equitable and sustainable pathway for improving rural livelihoods.

The rest of the paper proceeds as follows. Section 5.2 describes the study's methodology. Section 5.3 reports and discusses the empirical results, and Sect. 5.4 offers concluding remarks, policy recommendations, and the limitations of this study.

5.2 Methodology

5.2.1 Data

This study utilized microdata from the National Labour Force Survey (SAKERNAS), a household survey conducted twice a year in February and August by BPS-Statistics Indonesia. The survey collects information on sociodemographic characteristics, employment, and earnings. It used the 2010 Population Census for the period 2018–2021 and the 2020 Population Census for the period 2022–2024 as its master sampling frames and employed a stratified two-stage sampling design. In the first stage, census blocks were systematically selected with explicit stratification by urban and rural areas within each municipality. In the second stage, households were systematically chosen from updated household listings within each selected census block, with the listing implicitly stratified by the educational attainment of the household head.

We used official microdata obtained from BPS through its website (www.silastik.bps.go.id). No additional cleaning, editing, or imputation was applied, as BPS had already conducted these procedures during data processing. We used the August survey rounds data from 2018 to 2024, focusing on rural areas across 514 municipalities in 38 provinces. The dataset is cross-sectional, and the pooled sample contains 1,940,207 individuals. Of these, we analysed 1,322,452 individuals for whom main-job earnings information was available, comprising 693,874 employers and 628,578 employees. Most of the individuals excluded from the analysis were unpaid family workers, while the remaining excluded cases were employers without earnings information, such as farmers who experienced crop failure during the survey period. Therefore, the earnings variable analyzed contains no zero values, and transforming it to logarithmic terms to allow for percentage-change interpretations poses no issues.

To distinguish between employers and employees, we refer to the International Classification of Status in Employment, stated by the International Labour Organization (ILO) in the Fifteenth International Conference of Labour Statisticians (ICLS) report (ILO 1993). In the report, the definitions for employers and employees are formulated based on the fundamental distinction between 'paid employment' jobs and 'self-employment' jobs. Therefore, in this study, the term 'employer' refers to workers who are self-employed, assisted by unpaid/temporary labour, or assisted by paid/permanent labour. In contrast, the term 'employee' refers to wage earners, whether they are labourers or freelancers. As the classification reflects the job from which an individual earns the most, a person cannot be considered both an employer and an employee at the same time.

We construct a binary e-commerce adoption variable based on respondents' reported internet activities related to buying or selling goods and services in the workplace/main job (not for personal purposes). The indicator is coded as 1 (adopters) if a respondent engages in any of the following: selling via email, social media, or instant messaging apps; selling through websites or marketplace platforms; purchasing via email, social media, or instant messaging apps; or purchasing through websites or marketplace platforms. Respondents who report none of these activities are coded as 0 (non-adopters). While e-commerce adoption is consistently defined as the use of digital platforms for economic activity, its functional role and subsequent impact on earnings differ fundamentally by employment status. For employers, adoption represents a strategic business transaction—encompassing the digital sale of outputs or procurement of inputs—which influences earnings primarily through expanded market reach, reduced transaction costs, and improved profit margins. Conversely, for employees, adoption captures engagement in digitally mediated work activities within their primary job. In this context, the income effect is driven by enhanced labor productivity, more efficient task allocation, or a wage premium associated with higher firm-level digital integration. Distinguishing between these two groups is essential to isolate the specific economic mechanisms at play and to ensure that the impact estimates are not biased by grouping disparate forms of economic agency. The descriptions of the remaining variables used in this study are presented in Table 5.1.

Table 5.1 Description of research variables

Variable	Definition	Mean	S.D.
Earning	Log of monthly real earnings of the main job adjusted for rural inflation (in Rupiahs)	14.044	0.904
E-commerce	E-commerce adoption in the workplace/main job: 0—non-adopters (reference category) 1—adopters	0.055	0.227
Female	Gender of an individual: 0—male (reference category) 1—female	0.325	0.468
Household members	Number of household members to which an individual belongs (person)	3.902	1.637
Married	Marital status: 0—unmarried (reference category) 1—married	0.764	0.424
Education completed	The highest education level completed by an individual: 1—no education/elementary school (reference category) 2—junior high school 3—senior high school 4—vocational 5—diploma 1/2/3 6—university	2.236	1.552
Years of schooling	Years of schooling are approached with the highest educational attainment converted into years of schooling	9.282	3.961
Age	Age of an individual in years	42.796	13.485
Experience	Working experience of an individual (years). It is a potential experience in years calculated by the formula: age minus years of schooling minus 6 years	27.445	15.250
Working hours	Average working hours per week in the main job	35.376	17.243
Tenure	The length of time an individual has been employed at their current job (years)	17.520	19.010
Trained	Participation of an individual in work training (not specific to e-commerce): 0—untrained (reference category) 1—trained	0.124	0.330
Employer	Employment status of employers based on the kind of work: 1—self-employed (reference category) 2—assisted by unpaid/temporary labor 3—assisted by paid/permanent labor	1.439	0.572
Employee	Employment status of employees based on the kind of work: 0—freelance (reference category) 1—labour/employee	2.724	0.447
Formal	Formality status of employment: 0—informal (reference category) 1—formal	0.341	0.474
Agriculture	Participation in the agricultural sector: 0—non-agriculture (reference category) 1—agriculture	0.446	0.497

(continued)

Table 5.1 (continued)

Variable	Definition	Mean	S.D.
Pandemic (temporal dummy)	Pandemic periods: 1—pre-pandemic (2018–2019) (reference category) 2—pandemic (2020–2022) 3—post-pandemic (2023–2024)	2.129	0.713
Peer proportion	The proportion of e-commerce adopters within an individual's village, computed as a leave-one-out measure that excludes the individual from the calculation	0.053	0.039
Regional dummy	Provincial dummy of provinces	–	–

Note: Sampling weight was not used. S.D. refers to standard deviation.
Source: Author calculation

5.2.2 *Empirical Model*

We employed a set of econometric models to examine the determinants of e-commerce adoption across employment types (employers and employees) and sectors (agriculture and non-agriculture), and to estimate its impact on real earnings, including its contribution to income inequality and the gender earnings gap among rural agricultural workers. To strengthen the causal interpretation of our findings, we adopted a triangulation strategy that combines Endogenous Switching Regression (ESR), Propensity Score Matching (PSM), and Inverse Probability Weighting with Regression Adjustment (IPWRA). Within this strategy, ESR served as the primary empirical approach because of its capacity to correct for selection bias arising from both observable and unobservable characteristics, and to address endogeneity stemming from potential reverse causality. The PSM and IPWRA methods were used as robustness checks for the ESR estimates. To assess heterogeneity in the relationship between e-commerce adoption and earnings, and to evaluate its potential role in narrowing the gender income gap among rural agricultural workers, we additionally applied conditional quantile regression and a Blinder–Oaxaca decomposition.

5.2.2.1 Rural Workers' E-Commerce Adoption

The decision to adopt e-commerce is treated as binary, with rural workers deciding whether to adopt based on observable characteristics. In this regard, we assume that the propensity of workers to adopt e-commerce in their work is represented by a latent variable that is a function of observable characteristics and can be denoted as follows:

$$P_i^* = Z_i^{'}\gamma + \mu_i, P_i = \begin{cases} 1 \text{if } P_i^* > 0 \\ 0 \text{ otherwise} \end{cases} \tag{5.1}$$

where P_i^* is an unobserved variable representing the propensity to adopt e-commerce and μ_i is a normally distributed error term. Following the random utility maximization model of Marschak (1959), Eq. (5.1) assumes that the decision to adopt e-commerce arises when the latent utility P_i^* exceeds a threshold (normalized to zero), and the observed binary outcome P_i reflects that decision. A rural worker's probability of adopting e-commerce is specified as follows:

$$pr\left(P_i = 1 | Z_i\right) = pr\left(P_i^* > 0\right) = pr\left(\mu_i > -Z_i'\gamma\right) = 1 - F\left(-Z_i'\gamma\right) \quad (5.2)$$

where $P_i \in \{0, 1\}$ denotes a dummy variable indicating whether the individual i adopts e-commerce in their work or not, Z_i denotes observable characteristics influencing the decision of an individual to adopt e-commerce, consisting of individual characteristics, household characteristics, employment characteristics, and temporal and spatial dummy variables; F is the cumulative distribution function (CDF) of the standard normal distribution; and γ is a vector of coefficients to be estimated.

We estimated Eq. (5.2) separately by employment status and sector. This disaggregated approach enables the identification of heterogeneous patterns of digital uptake across different segments of the rural labor market. We assume that employment status and sectoral affiliation are likely to influence both the incentives and the constraints individuals face when deciding to engage with e-commerce. For instance, structural differences in access to technology, digital skills, and market integration may condition the likelihood of adoption (Ariansyah et al. 2021; Valarezo et al. 2020). Analyzing these groups separately allows us to capture context-specific dynamics and highlight where targeted interventions may be most effective in promoting inclusive digital participation in rural Indonesia.

5.2.2.2 Earnings Effect of E-Commerce Adoption

To gauge the magnitude of e-commerce adoption's impact on rural workers' earnings, we assume that our outcome variable is a linear function of a set of observable rural workers' characteristics and the e-commerce adoption dummy. Therefore, we specify the linear equation as follows:

$$Y_i = \vartheta P_i + X_i'\beta + \varepsilon_i \quad (5.3)$$

where Y_i denotes the real earnings adjusted for rural inflation of the i-th individual in logarithmic term, P_i denotes the e-commerce adoption dummy variable, X_i' denotes the vector of control variables (socio-demographic characteristics, employment characteristics, and temporal and spatial dummy variables) of the ith individual, ϑ is the regression coefficient of the e-commerce adoption denoting the magnitude of the earnings impact, β is a vector of parameters corresponding to control variables, and ε_i denotes the error term that follows a normal distribution. Since the dependent variable in the logarithmic term, ϑ can be interpreted as the percentage change of real earnings due to participating as an adopter. Following Halvorsen and Palmquist (1980), the average treatment effect was corrected using $(e^{\vartheta} - 1) \times 100\%$.

We also estimated Eq. (5.3) separately by employment status and sector to disaggregate the impact of e-commerce adoption on rural income by employment role and sector. It is essential for understanding the differentiated ways in which e-commerce adoption shapes economic opportunities in rural areas. Employers, particularly those operating small rural enterprises or farms, may leverage e-commerce to expand market reach, improve supply chain efficiency, and increase revenues, effects that may not translate similarly to employees, whose earnings are mediated by wage structures and firm-level dynamics. Likewise, the agricultural and non-agricultural sectors may differ in their production processes, market access, and exposure to digital tools. E-commerce may provide substantial benefits to agricultural employers through direct-to-consumer sales or online input sourcing, while non-agricultural activities, such as retail, services, or manufacturing, may engage with digital platforms in entirely different ways.

The causality impact (ϑ) estimation in Eq. (5.3) may be affected by a selection bias associated with observable and unobservable characteristics (e.g., digital skill, motivation, and risk preference) that simultaneously impact adoption and earnings, particularly using the ordinary least squares (OLS). Individuals who adopt e-commerce may differ systematically from non-adopters in terms of these characteristics that also influence income. Without accounting for these differences, estimates of the effect of e-commerce adoption may be biased (Ma et al. 2023; Lin et al. 2022; Liu et al. 2021; Yang et al. 2022). In such a case, the error terms in Eqs. (5.2) and (5.3) may be correlated $[(corr(\mu_i, \varepsilon_i) \neq 0]$. Moreover, potential endogeneity, such as reverse causality, where individuals with higher earnings are more likely to adopt digital tools, could compromise causal inference. To address this issue, we applied a triangulation approach combining ESR, PSM, and IPWRA.

5.2.2.3 Endogenous Switching Regression (ESR) method

As mentioned before, the earning impact estimation can be biased by selectivity bias arising from observable and unobservable factors. The ESR method can address this issue as well as the issue of endogeneity due to the presence of reverse causality between e-commerce adoption and earnings, given that a valid instrument exists. The ESR model is specified as two regimes of equations for e-commerce adopters and non-adopters, with a criterion function P_i determining which regime a rural worker faces.

$$\text{Regime 1}: Y_{1i} = X'_{1i}\beta_1 + \varepsilon_{1i} \text{ if } P_i = 1 \tag{5.4}$$

$$\text{Regime 2}: Y_{0i} = X'_{0i}\beta_0 + \varepsilon_{0i} \text{ if } P_i = 0 \tag{5.5}$$

where Y_{1i} and Y_{0i} are real earnings (in log form) for the adopters and non-adopters groups, respectively, $X_{1i}^{'}$ and $X_{0i}^{'}$ are vectors of observed rural workers' characteristics. β_1 and β_0 are vectors of parameters representing the direction and magnitude of the effect of each characteristic on real earnings. ε_{1i} and ε_{0i} are error components that are assumed to have a trivariate normal distribution with a mean vector of zero and a variance matrix of

$$\Omega = \text{cov}\left(\mu, \varepsilon_1, \varepsilon_0\right) = \begin{bmatrix} \sigma_{\mu}^2 & \sigma_{\mu 1} & \sigma_{\mu 0} \\ \sigma_{1\mu} & \sigma_1^2 & . \\ \sigma_{0\mu} & . & \sigma_0^2 \end{bmatrix} \tag{5.6}$$

where $\sigma\mu^2 = \text{var}(\mu), \sigma_1^{\ 2} = \text{var}(\varepsilon_1), \sigma_0^{\ 2} = \text{var}\ (\varepsilon_0), \sigma_{\mu 1} = \sigma_{1\mu} = \text{cov}(\varepsilon_1, \mu), \sigma_{\mu 0} = \sigma_{0\mu} = \text{cov}\ (\varepsilon_0, \mu)$. Furthermore, the expected values of ε_1 and ε_0 conditional on the results of the criterion function can be formulated as follows:

$$E\left(\varepsilon_{1i} \mid P = 1\right) = \sigma_{1\mu} \frac{\phi\left(Z_i^{'}\gamma\right)}{\Phi\left(Z_i^{'}\gamma\right)} \equiv \sigma_{1\mu}\lambda_{1i} \tag{5.7}$$

$$E\left(\varepsilon_{0i} \mid P = 0\right) = \sigma_{0\mu} \frac{-\phi\left(Z_i^{'}\gamma\right)}{1 - \Phi\left(Z_i^{'}\gamma\right)} \equiv \sigma_{0\mu}\lambda_{0i} \tag{5.8}$$

where is ϕ the standard normal distribution density function, and Φ is the standard normal cumulative distribution function. λ_{1i} and λ_{0i} are the inverse Mills ratios calculated from the selection model and will be included in the estimation of the outcome equation. Therefore, we have:

$$Y_{1i} = X_{1i}^{'}\beta_1 + \sigma_{1\mu}\lambda_{1i} + \varepsilon_{1i} \text{ if } P_i = 1 \tag{5.9}$$

$$Y_{0i} = X_{0i}^{'}\beta_0 + \sigma_{0\mu}\lambda_{0i} + \varepsilon_{0i} \text{ if } P_i = 0 \tag{5.10}$$

The selectivity bias arising from unobservable factors will be accounted for by the inverse Mills ratios in Eqs. (5.9) and (5.10) (Greene 2012). Following Lokshin and Sajaia (2004), the ESR model will be estimated using the full information maximum likelihood (FIML) method. Besides estimating the selection and outcome equations jointly, the method also generates correlation coefficients $\rho_{1\mu}$ and $\rho_{2\mu}$ associated with the error terms in the selection and outcome equations. The significance of the two components will confirm the presence of selection bias issues (Lokshin and Sajaia 2004).

This two-stage estimation requires exclusive variables. In this case, at least one of the variables in $Z_i^{'}$ is not present in $X_{1i}^{'}$ and $X_{0i}^{'}$ (Li et al. 2024). This variable is called the instrument variable (IV), and in our study, we used the leave-one-out proportion of adopters in the same village as the instrument. We argue that this measure is relevant because local peers facing similar market conditions influence each other's adoption decisions, making neighboring adoption rates predictive of individual adoption. Constructing the proportion in a leave-one-out manner removes mechanical correlation with the individual's own choice and avoids the reflection problem. Conditional on sub-district fixed effects and controls, the adoption behavior of other households affects the outcome only through its impact on the individual's adoption decision, supporting the exclusion restriction. Empirically, the instrument is strongly and positively correlated with e-commerce adoption, and it shows no statistically significant association with earnings in the falsification test, providing further support for its validity.

5.2.2.4 Estimating the Treatment Effects of E-Commerce Adoption

The impact of e-commerce adoption on real earnings was estimated by computing Treatment Effects on the Treated (ATT), measuring the average difference in real earnings in the adopter group with or without e-commerce adoption, using this formula:

$$ATT = E\left(Y_{1i} \mid P_i = 1, p\left(X_i\right)\right) - E\left(Y_{0i} \mid P_i = 1, p\left(X_i\right)\right) \tag{5.11}$$

and using the ESR method, Eq. (5.11) can be expressed as follows:

$$ATT = \left(X_{1i}^{'}\beta_1 + \sigma_{1\mu}\lambda_{1i}\right) - \left(X_{1i}^{'}\beta_0 + \sigma_{0\mu}\lambda_{1i}\right) \tag{5.12}$$

To assess the robustness of the treatment effect estimation, we also estimated the ATT using the PSM and IPWRA methods. Unlike the ESR method, which addresses selectivity bias arising from both observable and unobservable factors (Ma et al. 2023), PSM mitigates selectivity bias associated with observable factors by constructing a comparison group of non-adopters who are statistically similar to adopters in terms of their propensity to participate in e-commerce. Technically, to pair adopters with non-adopters based on similar observable characteristics, we used propensity scores estimated via a probit model in Eq. (5.2) (Rosenbaum and Rubin 1983). For robust pairing outcomes, we also employed two matching algorithms: Nearest-neighbour matching (n = 5) combined with Calliper or radius matching (threshold = 0.005) and Kernel matching.

Given the substantial imbalance in the sample, where e-commerce adopters are notably fewer than non-adopters, we also applied IPWRA to address selectivity bias arising from observable factors. Unlike PSM, which may exclude unmatched units and thus reduce statistical power, IPWRA retains the full sample by reweighting observations based on treatment probabilities (Wooldridge 2002). The method integrates inverse probability weights into a regression framework to account for non-random selection into treatment when modeling the outcome, provided that either the propensity score model or the outcome regression model is correctly specified, a property known as double robustness.

Although PSM and IPWRA help mitigate selectivity bias associated with observable characteristics, these methods rely on the assumption of selection on observables. They therefore cannot address endogeneity stemming from unobserved factors or reverse causality. As a result, unlike the ESR method, they improve comparability between adopters and non-adopters but do not correct for the possibility that higher earnings may influence e-commerce adoption decisions, leaving the estimates vulnerable to bias when treatment is endogenous.

5.2.2.5 Examining Distributional Heterogeneity in the Adoption-Earnings Association

To complement the ESR, PSM, and IPWRA estimates, particularly to assess the role of e-commerce adoption in addressing income inequality among rural workers, we also examined how the association between e-commerce adoption and earnings varies across the income distribution using quantile regression. Unlike ESR, PSM, and IPWRA, which estimate the conditional mean of the dependent variable, quantile regression describes the conditional distribution of earnings. It allows the coefficient on adoption to differ at various quantiles. This approach is useful for identifying whether the association is stronger among low-, middle-, or high-income rural workers.

Quantile regression is not intended to identify causal effects in this context, as it does not account for endogeneity arising from selection on unobservable factors or reverse causality. Instead, it provides a descriptive distributional perspective that complements the ESR estimates. We specifically use quantile regression to examine whether the income gap between adopters and non-adopters is more pronounced at the lower tail of the distribution, which may indicate the potential equalizing role of digital participation.

The conditional quantile regression for the τ-th quantile of log earnings Y_i given a vector of covariates X_i is specified as:

$$Q_{Y_i}\left(\tau \mid X_i, P_i\right) = \gamma_0\left(\tau\right) + \gamma_1\left(\tau\right) P_i + X_i^{'} \gamma\left(\tau\right) \tag{5.13}$$

where $Q_{Y_i}\left(\tau \mid X_i\right)$ is the conditional quantile of the log earnings given X_i; $\tau \in (0, 1)$ represents the quantile level ($\tau = 0.1, 0.3, 0.5, 0.7, 0.9$); $\gamma_0(\tau)$ is the model intercept at each quantile; $\gamma_1(\tau)$ denotes the magnitude of the association between e-commerce adoption and earnings at each quantile level; X_i includes independent control variables, and $\boldsymbol{\gamma}(\tau)$ is the vector of quantile-specific parameters of control variables to be estimated. Equation (5.13) allows the association to vary across the earnings distribution, capturing whether the gains are concentrated among lower-, median-, or higher-earners.

5.2.2.6 Examining the Contribution of Adoption in Explaining Gender Earnings Gaps

The gender earning gaps in the rural agricultural sector may be attributed to unequal access to e-commerce. In examining it, we also applied the Blinder-Oaxaca decomposition (Blinder 1973; Oaxaca 1973) to analyze the contribution of e-commerce adoption in explaining the gender earnings gap among agricultural rural workers, as captured in the outcome equation. Specifically, this method separates the observed earnings gap into two components: the explained portion, which is attributable to differences in observable characteristics such as education, training, work experience, and e-commerce adoption; and the unexplained portion, which reflects differences in the returns to these characteristics, potentially capturing discrimination, structural barriers, or unobserved factors such as social norms or access to networks. This approach is particularly relevant for rural agricultural contexts, where women often face compounded disadvantages, not only in access to productive resources and digital tools but also in how those resources translate into economic outcomes (Oseni et al. 2015).

While the ESR is our primary tool for addressing selection bias in impact estimation, we intentionally utilize OLS as the underlying estimator for the Blinder–Oaxaca decomposition. This choice is driven by the specific objective of the decomposition analysis, which serves as a descriptive 'accounting exercise' rather than a causal treatment-effect estimation. The standard Blinder–Oaxaca framework is mathematically built upon linear OLS specifications to partition observed earnings differentials into explained and unexplained components (Blinder 1973; Oaxaca 1973). Since our goal in this section is to quantify the descriptive role of e-commerce adoption in bridging (or widening) the existing gender earnings gap within the current labor market structure, the OLS-based decomposition remains the most transparent and theoretically consistent approach.

We designate the two groups of rural workers based on gender, labelling female workers as Group *F* and male workers as Group *M*. The mean real earnings difference to be decomposed corresponds to the difference in average real earnings between these two groups, denoted as $\overline{Y}_M$ for males and $\overline{Y}_F$ for females. Thus, the real earning gap is expressed as in Eq. (5.14), which forms the basis for the decomposition.

$$\Delta\overline{Y} = \overline{Y}_M - \overline{Y}_F = \overline{X}'_M \hat{\beta}_M - \overline{X}'_F \hat{\beta}_F \tag{5.14}$$

where $\overline{X}'_M$ and $\overline{X}'_F$ express the vectors of average values for observable characteristics for the female and male farmer groups, respectively, while $\hat{\beta}_M$ and $\hat{\beta}_F$ denote the corresponding vectors of estimated regression coefficients. E-commerce adoption is included as one of the observable characteristics, allowing the analysis to quantify how gender differences in digital participation contribute to the explained component of the earnings gap. Because Blinder-Oaxaca does not identify causal effects, the estimates should be interpreted as reflecting how observed differences in characteristics—including digital engagement—relate to differences in average earnings between men and women. Following Jann (2008), the expression in Eq. (5.14) can be denoted to represent the twofold Blinder-Oaxaca decomposition of the gender earnings gap as follows:

$$\Delta \bar{Y} = \left(\bar{X}_M - \bar{X}_F\right)' \hat{\beta}_M + \bar{X}_F' \left(\hat{\beta}_M - \hat{\beta}_F\right) \tag{5.15}$$

The first term on the right-hand side of Eq. (5.15) represents the portion of the earnings gap explained by differences in observed characteristics. The second term captures the unexplained portion. In this specification, following Jann (2008) and the pooled coefficient approach proposed by Neumark (1988), we adopt the pooled coefficient vector as the reference wage structure, such that the same pooled coefficient vector is used to evaluate the observed characteristics of both groups.

5.3 Results and Discussion

5.3.1 Determinants of E-Commerce Adoption and Determinants of Rural Earnings

The ESR estimates provide insight into both the determinants of e-commerce adoption and the earnings structures of adopters and non-adopters among rural employers and employees. Both the employer and employee models exhibit strong joint significance based on the Wald tests, indicating that the explanatory variables meaningfully predict the outcomes. In Tables 5.2 and 5.3, the estimated error-correlation parameters (ρ) differ across adopter and non-adopter regimes, providing evidence of selection on unobservable factors and thereby justifying the use of the ESR framework. The correlation coefficients, particularly ρ_2, are statistically significant, confirming the presence of selectivity bias arising from unobservable factors. In addition, the peer-adoption proportion serves as a strong and significant instrument in the selection equations for both groups, further supporting the validity of model identification.

As shown in Table 5.2, across both employers and employees, e-commerce adoption is shaped by a consistent set of socioeconomic factors. Education emerges as one of the strongest determinants, with the likelihood of adoption rising steadily from junior high school through university. These results confirmed the role of human capital in enabling digital engagement, particularly in navigating platforms, managing online transactions, and leveraging e-commerce for economic activities. Training participation also increases adoption for both groups, suggesting that digital or vocational exposure facilitates engagement with online platforms. This highlights the potential of capacity-building initiatives to overcome digital literacy barriers in rural areas and underscores the importance of structured interventions that equip rural workers with foundational skills and platform-specific knowledge.

Table 5.2 ESR estimation results: determinants of e-commerce adoption and determinants of rural earnings

Variable	Employer			Employee		
		Earnings			Earnings	
	Selection	Adopters	Non-adopters	Selection	Adopters	Non-adopters
Gender (female)	0.020**	−0.587***	−0.482***	0.030***	−0.317***	−0.473***
	(0.010)	(0.013)	(0.004)	(0.009)	(0.011)	(0.003)
Marital stat. (married)	0.022*	0.082***	0.060***	−0.045***	0.034**	0.061***
	(0.013)	(0.017)	(0.004)	(0.012)	(0.014)	(0.003)
Household members	−0.008**	−0.007	0.000	−0.015***	−0.006*	−0.010***
	(0.003)	(0.004)	(0.001)	(0.003)	(0.003)	(0.001)
Education						
Junior high school	0.219***	0.026	0.089***	0.191***	0.100***	0.131***
	(0.013)	(0.021)	(0.004)	(0.019)	(0.023)	(0.004)
Senior high school	0.350***	0.148***	0.171***	0.556***	0.297***	0.246***
	(0.013)	(0.022)	(0.005)	(0.017)	(0.022)	(0.004)
Vocational	0.368***	0.126***	0.164***	0.527***	0.348***	0.316***
	(0.018)	(0.026)	(0.008)	(0.020)	(0.023)	(0.006)
Diploma	0.620***	0.299***	0.292***	0.678***	0.464***	0.445***
	(0.035)	(0.040)	(0.020)	(0.024)	(0.029)	(0.010)
University	0.574***	0.421***	0.374***	0.731***	0.602***	0.591***
	(0.024)	(0.033)	(0.014)	(0.020)	(0.025)	(0.007)
Experience	−0.015***	0.031***	0.023***	−0.003**	0.045***	0.035***
	(0.001)	(0.002)	(0.000)	(0.001)	(0.002)	(0.000)
Experience sqr./100	−0.030***	−0.039***	−0.037***	−0.028***	−0.062***	−0.057***
	(0.003)	(0.004)	(0.001)	(0.003)	(0.004)	(0.001)
Training (trained)	0.262***	−0.016	−0.041***	0.128***	0.075***	0.115***
	(0.014)	(0.017)	(0.007)	(0.011)	(0.012)	(0.005)

(continued)

Table 5.2 (continued)

	Employer			Employee		
		Earnings			Earnings	
Variable	Selection	Adopters	Non-adopters	Selection	Adopters	Non-adopters
Sector (agriculture)	−0.810***	−0.032	−0.123***	−0.399***	0.117***	−0.073***
	(0.013)	(0.023)	(0.005)	(0.016)	(0.020)	(0.004)
Formality (formal)	0.086**	0.211***	0.276***	0.056**	0.413***	0.401***
	(0.040)	(0.042)	(0.018)	(0.024)	(0.024)	(0.008)
Working Hours	0.001***	0.009***	0.011***	0.004***	0.016***	0.017***
	(0.000)	(0.000)	(0.000)	(0.000)	(0.000)	(0.000)
Employment status						
Assisted by unpaid labor	0.033***	0.190***	0.124***	–	–	–
	(0.011)	(0.015)	(0.005)			
Assisted by paid labour	0.380***	0.593***	0.571***	–	–	–
	(0.037)	(0.040)	(0.017)			
Labour	–	–	–	0.321***	−0.166***	−0.140***
				(0.028)	(0.032)	(0.008)
Pandemic period						
During pandemic	0.290***	−0.233***	−0.055***	0.146***	−0.041***	0.014***
	(0.015)	(0.024)	(0.006)	(0.009)	(0.014)	(0.004)
Post-pandemic	0.476***	−0.277***	−0.047***	0.154***	−0.120***	0.004
	(0.016)	(0.026)	(0.007)	(0.012)	(0.016)	(0.005)
Peers proportion (IV)	3.118***	–	–	3.520***	–	–
	(0.035)			(0.032)		
Regional dummy	Yes	Yes	Yes	Yes	Yes	Yes
Constant	−1.854***	13.805***	13.431***	−3.363***	13.257***	13.187***
	(0.034)	(0.066)	(0.015)	(0.072)	(0.091)	(0.020)
Number of obs.	693,874	35,235	658,639	628,578	37,074	591,544

$ln\sigma_1$	–	-0.253^{***}	–	–	-0.419^{***}	–
		(0.011)			(0.010)	
ρ_{μ_1}	–	-0.070^{***}	–	–	−0.014	–
		(0.027)			(0.017)	
$ln\sigma_2$	–	–	-0.219^{***}	–	–	-0.410^{***}
			(0.003)			(0.003)
ρ_{μ_2}	–	–	-0.090^{***}	–	–	-0.020^{*}
			(0.029)			(0.011)

Note: The independent variable is the log of real earnings—robust clustered standard errors in parentheses.
$^{*}p < 0.05$, $^{**}p < 0.01$, $^{***}p < 0.001$. Survey weight was applied in the estimation.
Source: Author calculation

Table 5.3 ESR estimation results: determinants of e-commerce adoption and determinants of rural earnings across sectors

Variable	Agricultural employer			Non-agricultural employer			Agricultural employee			Non-agricultural employee		
		Earnings			Earnings			Earnings			Earnings	
	Selection	Adopters	Non-adopters	Selection	Adopters	Non-adopters	Selection	Adopters	Non-adopters	Selection	Adopters	Non-adopters
Gender (female)	−0.257***	−0.455***	−0.415***	0.056***	−0.591***	−0.530***	−0.150***	−0.299***	−0.403***	0.040***	−0.312***	−0.475***
	(0.032)	(0.067)	(0.006)	(0.011)	(0.013)	(0.005)	(0.041)	(0.048)	(0.005)	(0.010)	(0.011)	(0.004)
Marital stat. (married)	0.034	0.135***	0.069***	0.005	0.077***	0.060***	−0.054	0.057	0.084***	−0.042***	0.034**	0.048***
	(0.029)	(0.050)	(0.006)	(0.015)	(0.018)	(0.006)	(0.041)	(0.044)	(0.006)	(0.012)	(0.014)	(0.004)
Household members	−0.014**	−0.007	0.000	−0.008**	−0.007	0.002	−0.025**	−0.017	−0.011***	−0.014***	−0.006	−0.009***
	(0.007)	(0.013)	(0.001)	(0.004)	(0.005)	(0.002)	(0.011)	(0.012)	(0.002)	(0.003)	(0.004)	(0.001)
Education												
Junior high school	0.199***	0.027	0.084***	0.229***	0.030	0.092***	0.186***	0.092**	0.074***	0.194***	0.087***	0.143***
	(0.026)	(0.041)	(0.006)	(0.015)	(0.023)	(0.006)	(0.046)	(0.045)	(0.006)	(0.021)	(0.025)	(0.004)
Senior high school	0.300***	0.157***	0.163***	0.364***	0.152***	0.187***	0.404***	0.238***	0.152***	0.575***	0.293***	0.284***
	(0.027)	(0.043)	(0.007)	(0.015)	(0.026)	(0.008)	(0.049)	(0.046)	(0.007)	(0.019)	(0.023)	(0.005)
Vocational	0.346***	0.080	0.123***	0.375***	0.137***	0.197***	0.385***	0.216***	0.166***	0.545***	0.349***	0.363***
	(0.043)	(0.068)	(0.012)	(0.021)	(0.029)	(0.011)	(0.062)	(0.053)	(0.011)	(0.021)	(0.025)	(0.006)
Diploma	0.422***	0.209*	0.281***	0.648***	0.314***	0.334***	0.794***	0.419***	0.344***	0.682***	0.463***	0.500***
	(0.086)	(0.123)	(0.029)	(0.039)	(0.044)	(0.027)	(0.116)	(0.102)	(0.035)	(0.025)	(0.030)	(0.010)
University	0.539***	0.209**	0.334***	0.585***	0.455***	0.440***	1.176***	0.661***	0.449***	0.731***	0.602***	0.650***
	(0.051)	(0.090)	(0.019)	(0.028)	(0.036)	(0.020)	(0.084)	(0.082)	(0.026)	(0.021)	(0.027)	(0.007)
Experience	0.001	0.022***	0.017***	−0.016***	0.032***	0.029***	0.011**	0.018***	0.016***	−0.005***	0.046***	0.041***
	(0.003)	(0.005)	(0.001)	(0.002)	(0.002)	(0.001)	(0.005)	(0.006)	(0.001)	(0.001)	(0.002)	(0.000)
Experience sqr/100	−0.050***	−0.029***	−0.028***	−0.030***	−0.038***	−0.046***	−0.072***	−0.014	−0.027***	−0.022***	−0.064***	−0.067***
	(0.005)	(0.009)	(0.001)	(0.003)	(0.004)	(0.001)	(0.011)	(0.013)	(0.001)	(0.003)	(0.004)	(0.001)
Training (trained)	0.245***	0.022	−0.034***	0.263***	−0.019	−0.039***	0.173***	0.020	0.041***	0.127***	0.078***	0.122***
	(0.032)	(0.053)	(0.010)	(0.016)	(0.018)	(0.010)	(0.044)	(0.038)	(0.011)	(0.011)	(0.012)	(0.005)

Formality (formal)	0.228***	0.340***	0.332***	0.048	0.193***	0.256***	0.093	0.342***	0.346***	0.051**	0.421***	0.410***
	(0.084)	(0.111)	(0.027)	(0.045)	(0.043)	(0.024)	(0.062)	(0.061)	(0.015)	(0.026)	(0.026)	(0.009)
Working Hours	0.007***	0.011***	0.011***	−0.000	0.009***	0.011***	0.005***	0.011***	0.018***	0.004***	0.016***	0.017***
	(0.001)	(0.001)	(0.000)	(0.000)	(0.000)	(0.000)	(0.001)	(0.001)	(0.000)	(0.000)	(0.000)	(0.000)
Employment status												
Assisted by unpaid labor	−0.034	0.178***	0.133***	0.055***	0.192***	0.119***	–	–	–	–	–	–
	(0.022)	(0.038)	(0.006)	(0.013)	(0.016)	(0.006)						
Assisted by paid labour	0.319***	0.475***	0.595***	0.407***	0.605***	0.493***	–	–	–	–	–	–
	(0.077)	(0.109)	(0.023)	(0.042)	(0.040)	(0.023)						
Labour	–	–	–	–	–	–	0.271***	0.036	−0.032**	0.325***	−0.216***	−0.209***
							(0.068)	(0.063)	(0.015)	(0.031)	(0.036)	(0.010)
Pandemic period												
During pandemic	0.262***	−0.034	0.001	0.295***	−0.245***	−0.091***	0.206***	−0.117**	−0.005	0.143***	−0.037***	0.022***
	(0.044)	(0.110)	(0.009)	(0.016)	(0.025)	(0.007)	(0.042)	(0.053)	(0.007)	(0.010)	(0.014)	(0.005)
Post-pandemic	0.424***	−0.076	0.012	0.493***	−0.288***	−0.088***	0.311***	−0.289***	0.002	0.142***	−0.111***	0.005
	(0.045)	(0.110)	(0.010)	(0.017)	(0.027)	(0.009)	(0.046)	(0.056)	(0.009)	(0.013)	(0.017)	(0.006)
Peer proportion (IV)	3.483***	–	–	2.946***	–	–	3.988***	–	–	3.451***	–	–
	(0.058)			(0.043)			(0.085)			(0.034)		
Regional dummy	Yes	Yes	Yes	Yes	Yes	Yes	Yes	Yes	Yes	Yes	Yes	Yes
Constant	−2.920***	13.504***	13.394***	−1.807***	13.828***	13.293***	−3.815***	13.685***	13.232***	−3.360***	13.345***	13.226***
	(0.078)	(0.175)	(0.019)	(0.039)	(0.077)	(0.020)	(0.178)	(0.181)	(0.034)	(0.078)	(0.101)	(0.023)
Number of obs.	411,900	5285	406,615	281,974	29,950	252,024	177,207	2212	174,995	451,371	39,822	416,549
*lnσ*1	–	−0.246***	–	–	−0.257***	–	–	−0.660***	–	–	−0.411***	–
		(0.022)			(0.012)			(0.059)			(0.010)	

(continued)

Table 5.3 (continued)

Variable	Agricultural employer			Non-agricultural employer			Agricultural employee			Non-agricultural employee		
	Selection	Earnings		Selection	Earnings		Selection	Earnings		Selection	Earnings	
		Adopters	Non-adopters		Adopters	Non-adopters		Adopters	Non-adopters		Adopters	Non-adopters
ρ_{μ_1}	–	−0.068*	–	–	−0.066**	–	–	0.021	–	–	−0.010	–
		(0.038)			(0.033)			(0.039)			(0.018)	
$ln\sigma_2$	–	–	−0.201***	–	–	−0.251***	–	–	−0.493***	–	–	−0.387***
			(0.003)			(0.004)			(0.007)			(0.004)
ρ_{μ_2}	–	–	−0.197***	–	–	−0.034	–	–	−0176***	–	–	−0.029**
			(0.021)			(0.036)			(0.029)			(0.012)

Note: The independent variable is the log of real earnings—robust clustered standard errors in parentheses
$^{*}p < 0.05$, $^{**}p < 0.01$, $^{***}p < 0.001$. Survey weight was applied in the estimation
Source: Author calculation

In contrast, larger household size and longer work experience reduce the probability of adoption, suggesting that individuals with heavier domestic responsibilities or more established work routines may face constraints or weaker incentives to adopt new technologies.

Gender also appears to shape adoption patterns. Females are slightly more likely than males to adopt e-commerce in both groups. This may reflect increasing female participation in rural entrepreneurship and women's digital inclusion. Wihardja and Wibisana (2021) observed that the share of female entrepreneurs engaging in e-commerce rose from 2.7% in 2017 to 7.5% in 2020. Sectoral and contextual factors further shape adoption patterns. Agricultural workers—both employers and employees—are significantly less likely to adopt than those in non-agricultural sectors. This may reflect structural constraints such as limited digital infrastructure, limited digital skills, lower product digitizability, and weaker market linkages in agriculture (Akbar and Wijaya 2024; Loo et al. 2024; Smidt and Jokonya 2022). These findings underscore the need for sector-specific strategies to integrate rural farmers and agricultural microenterprises into digital ecosystems.

Adoption rates increased significantly during the pandemic, highlighting COVID-19 as a catalyst for digital engagement. Finally, the peer-adoption instrument shows a strong and positive influence in both models, underscoring the importance of local network effects in shaping individuals' decisions to adopt e-commerce. The increase in adoption rates persists after the pandemic, suggesting that COVID-19 catalyzed the digital transition, possibly due to movement restrictions and shifting consumer behaviour (Jílková and Králová 2021; Strusani and Houngbonon 2021).

The earnings equations reveal distinct patterns across employers and employees, as well as clear differences between adopters and non-adopters. Across both groups, gender remains a strong and persistent determinant of earnings: female workers consistently earn less than males in all regimes. The gender penalty is particularly pronounced among employer-adopters, while employee-adopters experience a slightly smaller but still substantial disadvantage. These findings reflect persistent gender earning gaps in rural Indonesia. Marital status generally raises earnings for both employers and employees—potentially capturing better productivity, greater household stability, or dual-income effects (Ahituv and Lerman 2007; Gray 1997)—though its effects tend to be stronger and more consistent among non-adopters.

Education is strongly associated with higher earnings for both adopters and non-adopters, among employers and employees alike. Higher levels of schooling are linked to progressively higher income, confirming the importance of human capital in determining earnings. Education also remains important for adopters, with particularly large returns at the diploma and university levels. In fact, the estimated effects of education are generally larger for adopters than for non-adopters, especially among employees. This suggests that e-commerce adoption does not weaken returns to schooling; instead, it complements formal education by enabling more educated individuals to better capitalize on opportunities in digital markets. Nevertheless, the estimates of the return to education could be subject to selection bias in our model due to unobservable characteristics, such as ability, that are not incorporated into the model (Kadir and Sukma 2019).

Experience positively affects earnings across all groups, aligning with human-capital expectations, though adopters and non-adopters differ in the magnitude of these gains. Sectoral effects also diverge. Working in agriculture is linked to lower earnings for non-adopters, both among employers and employees, reflecting the income disadvantage of rural and agrarian work. However, this negative effect disappears among employer-adopters and becomes positive among employee-adopters. This suggests that e-commerce adoption can reduce—and in some cases reverse—the earnings gap typically faced by agricultural workers by improving access to markets and income opportunities beyond traditional local channels, as confirmed by many studies, e.g., M. Liu et al. (2021) in rural China.

Overall, household size reduces earnings for both employer and employee adopters, as well as for non-adopter employees, while formality and longer working hours are associated with higher earnings for both employers and employees. Finally, the pandemic has a uniformly negative impact on earnings across all regimes, with adopters—especially among employers—experiencing sharper income declines. This indicates that although digital engagement expanded during the pandemic, the income streams associated with online activity were more vulnerable to broader economic disruptions.

The ESR results from the sectoral estimations in Table 5.3 are highly consistent with the pooled findings, offering nuanced insights into both the determinants of e-commerce adoption and the resulting earnings structures. The selection equations robustly confirm strong positive selection into e-commerce adoption, particularly among individuals with higher education and training. This highlights that digital readiness and access, often correlated with these socioeconomic factors, are crucial for entering the e-commerce space. Furthermore, the strong positive influence of the peer-adoption proportion instrument across all models underscores the importance of local network effects in the adoption decision process.

A significant pattern of consistency also emerges from the contrasting effects on earnings between adopter and non-adopter groups. Education is consistently associated with higher earnings, particularly in the non-agricultural sector and among employees in both sectors. Among agricultural employees with a higher education level (diploma and university), the effects are stronger for adopters than for non-adopters. These results indicate that the income returns to education are sector-specific and are more pronounced outside agriculture, while e-commerce adoption appears to enhance educational returns primarily in non-agricultural activities and wage employment. However, in agriculture, most education variables have weak or insignificant effects on employers' earnings, particularly among adopters, suggesting limited returns to schooling in agricultural self-employment. This finding suggests that once individuals adopt e-commerce, the impact of formal schooling on within-group earnings differences becomes less pronounced. In this sense, adoption acts as an equalising mechanism, reducing the explanatory power of traditional education for income differences among those already digitally engaged. This observation reaffirms that, in rural agriculture, unobserved ability and digital capability, rather than formal education alone, become the dominant drivers of the higher returns associated with e-commerce adoption. Our findings are supported by some studies, e.g., B. Liu and Zhou (2023), who found that the return to formal education is lower than the farmers' income gain from digital literacy in China.

Moreover, labor endowments—particularly work experience, working hours, formal employment arrangements, and the use of paid labor—consistently enhance earnings across both sectors. Importantly, earnings responses in the agricultural sector are not structurally rigid; rather, they are sensitive to the same labor and job characteristics, broadly mirroring patterns observed in non-agricultural activities. Nevertheless, a persistent gender earnings gap remains evident across all regimes, irrespective of e-commerce participation, underscoring deeply entrenched labor market inequalities. Finally, the negative earnings effects of the pandemic are more pronounced among adopters, suggesting that while e-commerce expands market access, it may also heighten exposure to macroeconomic shocks and offers only limited insulation against systemic disruptions.

5.3.2 Average Treatment Effect of E-Commerce Adoption

To gain an indicative picture of how e-commerce adoption affects the earnings distribution of rural workers, we estimated the density of the earnings distribution of employers and employees. Figure 5.1 presents kernel density plots of earnings by employment status and sector, disaggregated into six panels. Across all panels, the earnings distributions of e-commerce adopters are consistently shifted to the right relative to non-adopters, confirming that adopters earn more on average. The separation between the distributions is especially wide among agricultural employers and employees, suggesting that the income benefits of e-commerce are particularly pronounced in this group. In general, the density plots for employers are wider than those for employees, indicating that while the benefits of e-commerce are present for wage earners, they are somewhat more moderate compared to those for self-employed or entrepreneurial individuals.

The shapes of the distributions also suggest differences in variance. Among agricultural adopters, the earnings distribution appears not only shifted but also slightly more dispersed, suggesting a wider range of earnings outcomes. This could reflect the heterogeneous capacity of adopters to scale their operations or access premium markets through digital channels. In contrast, the distribution for non-agricultural employees shows a relatively compact shift, indicating that while e-commerce boosts earnings, the returns are more uniform and possibly constrained by wage structures or firm-level dynamics.

Figure 5.1 provides strong evidence that e-commerce adoption may increase employers' and employees' earnings in rural Indonesia. However, to confirm the causal impact of e-commerce adoption, we need to analyse the average treatment effect from ESR, PSM, and IPWRA methods. The estimated ATTs obtained from ESR, PSM, and IPWRA methods are presented in Table 5.4. Because earnings are expressed in logarithms, the estimated ATT values are interpreted as percentage changes using: $\%\Delta = (e^{ATT} - 1) \times 100$ (Halvorsen and Palmquist 1980. Our

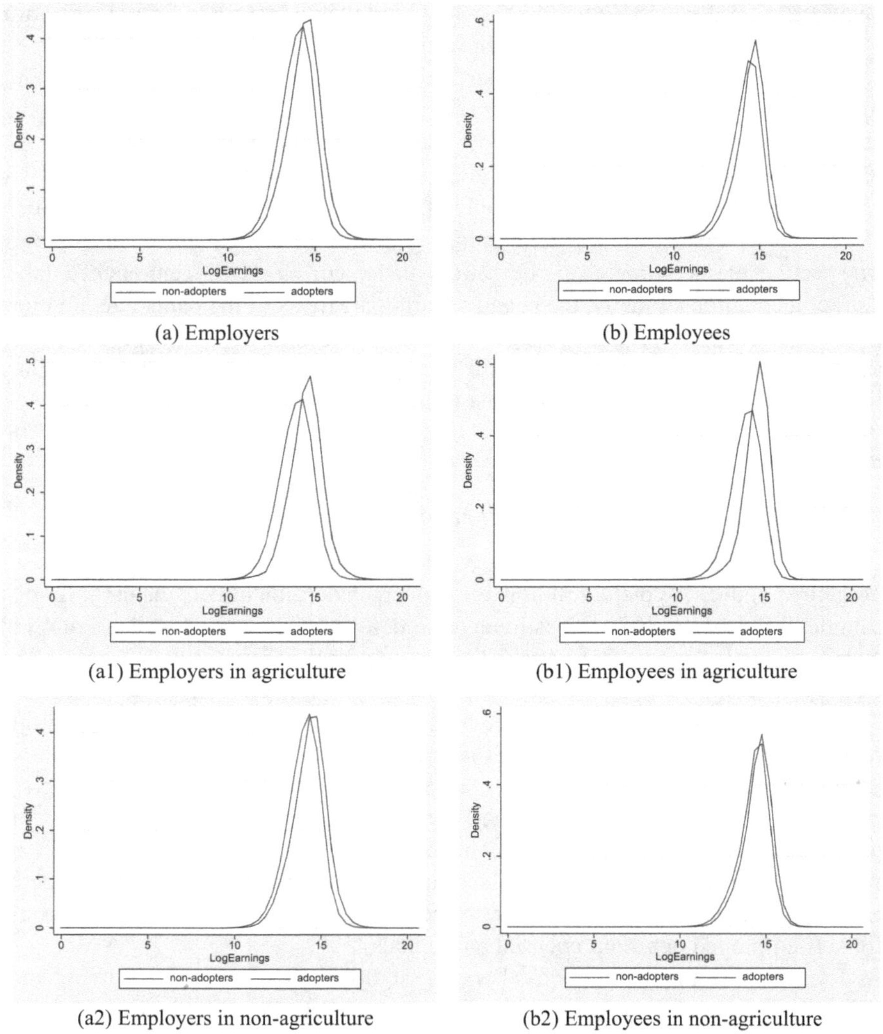

Note: the figure illustrates the distribution of earnings by plotting the kernel density function of log-transformed monthly earnings. The density is estimated using an Epanechnikov kernel with a fixed bandwidth of 0.3 to ensure an optimal balance between smoothing and the preservation of the distribution's underlying features (Van Kerm, 2003).
Source: Author calculation

Fig. 5.1 Kernel density distribution of log earnings by employment status and sector. (**a**) Employers. (**b**) Employees. (**a1**) Employers in agriculture. (**b1**) Employees in agriculture. (**a2**) Employers in non-agriculture. (**b2**) Employees in non-agriculture. Note: the figure illustrates the distribution of earnings by plotting the kernel density function of log-transformed monthly earnings. The density is estimated using an Epanechnikov kernel with a fixed bandwidth of 0.3 to ensure an optimal balance between smoothing and the preservation of the distribution's underlying features (Van Kerm 2003). Source: Author calculation

Table 5.4 Estimation results of the treatment effect of e-commerce adoption

	Employer earnings (log term)			Employee earnings (log term)		
Method	Adopters	Non-Adopters	ATT	Adopters	Non-Adopters	ATT
Pooled (agriculture + non-agriculture)						
ERS	14.279	13.969	0.310***	14.474	14.321	0.153***
PSM						
Neighbour (5) Calliper (0.005)	14.273	14.058	0.215***	14.566	14.357	0.203***
Kernel (Bootstrap with 1000 iterations)			0.240***			0.171***
IPWRA	14.345	14.116	0.229***	14.491	14.344	0.147***
Agriculture						
ESR	14.446	13.809	0.637***	14.563	14.133	0.431***
PSM						
Neighbour (5) Calliper (0.005)	14.434	14.073	0.361***	14.670	14.406	0.262***
Kernel (Bootstrap with 1000 iterations)			0.403***			0.300***
IPWRA	14.517	14.106	0.229***	14.587	14.260	0.327***
Non-agriculture						
ERS	14.249	14.023	0.226***	14.467	14.304	0.163***
PSM						
Neighbour (5) Calliper (0.005)	14.244	14.059	0.185***	14.553	14.350	0.197***
Kernel (Bootstrap with 1000 iterations)			0.208***			0.162***
IPWRA	14.318	14.118	0.200***	14.485	14.351	0.134***

Note: The independent variable is the log of earnings. ***$p < 0.01$, **$p < 0.05$, *$p < 0.1$; sampling weight was used in estimation. ESR and PSM used the same variables for the selection models. IPWRA used condensed control variables (only key variables) to ease the computation process.
Source: Author calculation

approximation is close to the percentage change calculated from the mean of the outcome level in original scale.

The ESR estimates indicate that e-commerce adoption substantially increases both employer and employee earnings. Our finding aligns with Chen et al. (2022), who investigated the impact of e-commerce adoption on rural household income in China. In the pooled sample, employers who adopt e-commerce earn about 36% more (ATT = 0.310), while employees earn approximately 17% more (ATT = 0.153) than their estimated counterfactual as non-adopters. The stronger effect among employers compared to employees aligns with theoretical expectations. Employers may leverage digital platforms more directly for business transactions, expanding market access and increasing operational efficiency (Guan et al. 2024; Liu et al. 2021; Zhang 2024). While the benefit remains statistically significant for employees, it may also reflect indirect advantages such as improved job matching or opportunities in digitally integrated firms.

Sectoral results reveal even stronger effects for agricultural enterprises. Employers in agriculture experience earnings gains of around 89% (ATT = 0.637), while employees benefit from a lower increase of approximately 54% (ATT = 0.431). These effects are substantially higher than those observed in non-agricultural settings, where employers earn about 25% more (ATT = 0.226), and employees earn around 18% more (ATT = 0.163). Our findings were supported by Liu et al. (2021), Chen et al. (2022), and Guan et al. (2024) in rural China. The higher impact of e-commerce adoption on earnings for the agricultural sector findings suggest that digital tools may be especially transformative for agricultural employers, who often face severe market access constraints, lower initial income levels, higher transaction costs, and weaker distribution networks (Guan et al. 2024; Markelova et al. 2009). By enabling direct market participation and broader customer reach, e-commerce mitigates many of these traditional barriers (Zhang 2024).

The PSM and IPWRA estimates behave as expected and confirm the positive effects of e-commerce adoption, though, with smaller magnitudes—particularly for employers—because they do not control for unobservable factors. For the pooled sample, PSM estimates indicate employer earnings gains of 24–27% and employee earnings gains of 19–23%. IPWRA results similarly show increases of about 26% for employers and around 16% for employees. Across both agricultural and non-agricultural subsamples, PSM and IPWRA consistently yield positive and statistically significant effects, though smaller than those produced by ESR. This pattern reinforces the robustness of the findings and highlights the added value of ESR in accounting for selection bias.

For employers, the ESR estimator yields larger treatment effects because it explicitly corrects for selection on unobservable factors (Ma et al. 2023). Enterprises that adopt e-commerce may possess advantageous but unmeasured characteristics—such as stronger managerial ability, better networks, higher technological readiness, or greater entrepreneurial drive—that influence both adoption and earnings potential. Unlike PSM and IPWRA, which adjust only for observable covariates, ESR jointly models the adoption decision and outcome equations, allowing the counterfactual earnings of adopters to reflect unobserved factors. When positive selection is present, ESR typically produces larger and more realistic estimates of the treatment effect.

Taken together, the results indicate that e-commerce adoption substantially improves earnings, with particularly pronounced effects in the agricultural sector, where digital platforms appear to alleviate long-standing market access constraints. The observed income gains can be attributed to enhanced supply chain performance driven by digital empowerment, as demonstrated by Wang et al. (2026) in the case of Taobao Village in China. The results also emphasize the significance of broader structural factors, such as education, training, and formal employment, in shaping the rural labor market outcomes in Indonesia. In general, the adoption of e-commerce not only increases earnings but also reshapes the agricultural mechanism toward modernization (Yang et al. 2025).

However, while our empirical results demonstrate that e-commerce adoption is positively associated with higher earnings, particularly among rural employers, the mechanisms driving these gains warrant further exploration. One likely channel is improved market access. Through e-commerce platforms, rural producers, especially in agriculture, can bypass traditional intermediaries and connect directly with broader consumer markets, including urban buyers (Guan et al. 2024). Another mechanism could be the reduction of transaction and operational costs. E-commerce platforms often provide integrated services, such as digital payment systems, logistics support, and customer service interfaces, which can streamline business operations, improve efficiency, and reduce transaction and operational costs, as found by Guan et al. (2024) in rural China.

Furthermore, e-commerce adoption may facilitate access to market information and feedback, thereby improving business decision-making. Real-time data on pricing trends, consumer preferences, and inventory management enables rural entrepreneurs to adjust supply and product offerings more responsively. This adaptability can lead to better resource allocation and higher revenue over time. However, these mechanisms may be unequally accessible depending on digital literacy, platform familiarity, and infrastructural constraints (Luo et al. 2025).

5.3.3 Heterogeneity of the Adoption-Earning Association Across the Earnings Distribution

The quantile regression results in Fig. 5.2 show that the association between e-commerce adoption and earnings is positive and statistically significant across the entire earnings distribution. However, the magnitude is not uniform: the association is strongest at the lower quantiles and gradually declines toward the higher end. This pattern indicates that low-earning rural workers—especially those in agriculture—are positioned to gain the most from digital participation. Our finding is supported by Guan et al. (2024) and Qiu et al. (2025) in rural China.

In the pooled sample, both employers and employees exhibit the largest adoption–earnings gaps at the 10th and 20th quantiles, with diminishing coefficients toward the median and upper quantiles. This suggests that e-commerce adoption is correlated with disproportionately larger relative earnings among low-income rural workers, supporting the view that digital tools may lessen structural constraints faced by marginalized groups. This also aligns with the concept of rural revitalization, where digital empowerment catalyzes high-quality economic development (You et al. 2025).

Sector-specific quantile regression results confirm this pattern. For agricultural workers, the association at the lower quantiles is substantially stronger than in non-agriculture. This reflects the role of e-commerce in improving market access and reducing transaction costs for small-scale rural producers and laborers. Overall, the quantile regression findings highlight distributional heterogeneity in the adoption–earnings relationship and complement the ESR results, which provide a causal interpretation.

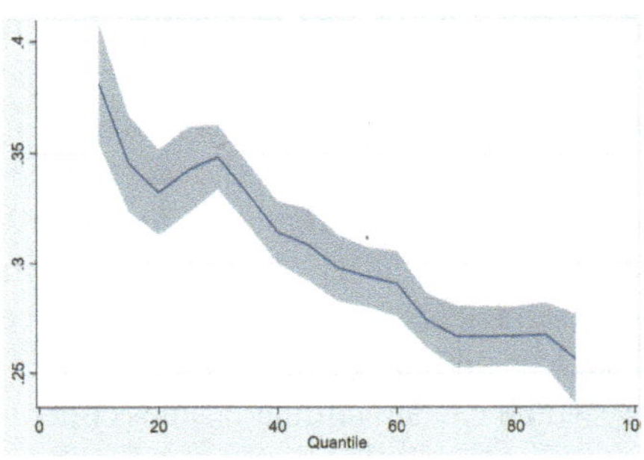

(a) Employers

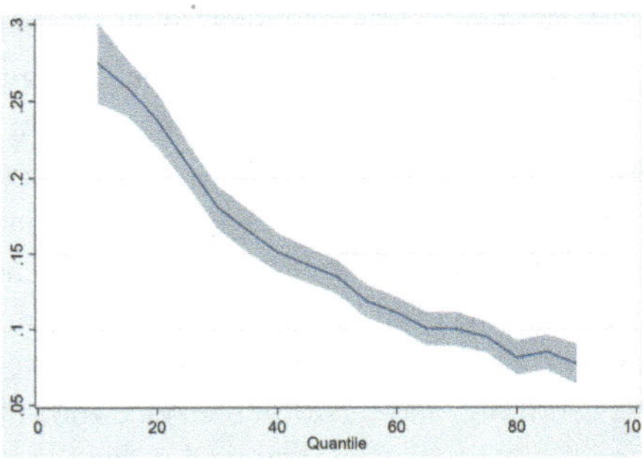

(b) Employees

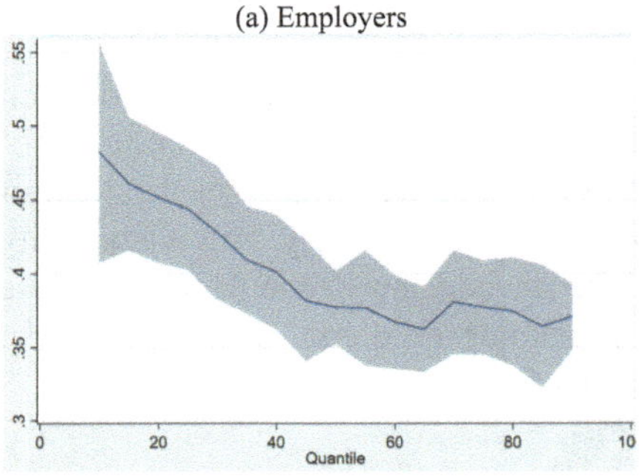

(a1) Employers in agriculture

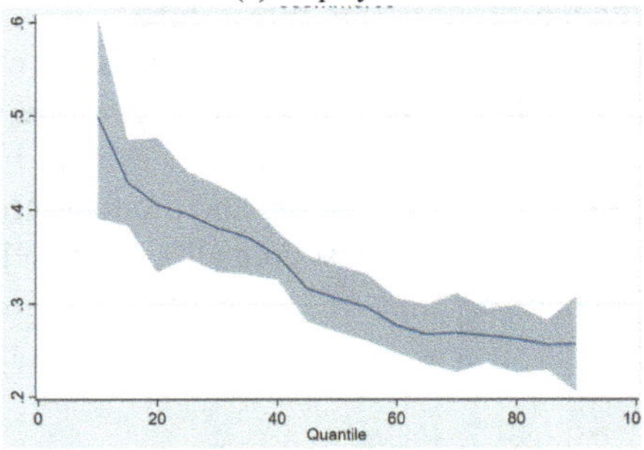

(b1) Employees in agriculture

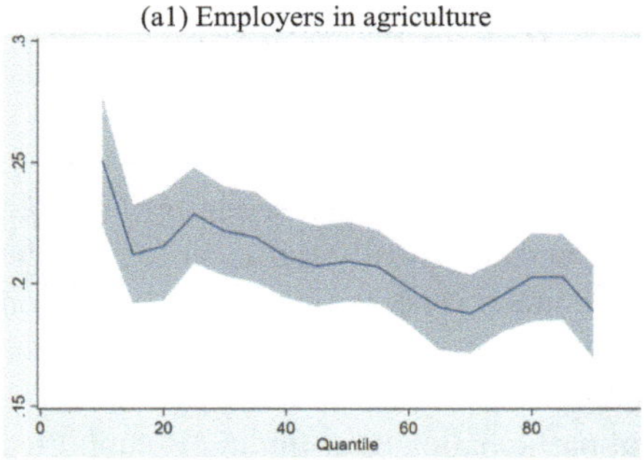

(a2) Employers in non-agriculture

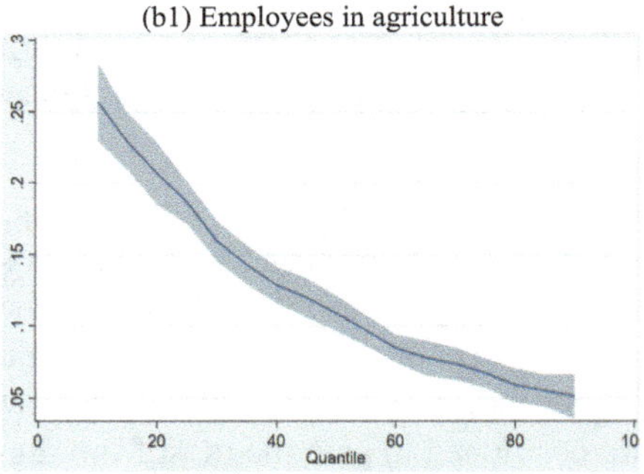

(b2) Employees in non-agriculture

Fig. 5.2 Estimation plots of the adoption-earnings association across the earnings distribution. (**a**) Employers. (**b**) Employees. (**a1**) Employers in agriculture. (**b1**) Employees in agriculture. (**a2**) Employers in non-agriculture. (**b2**) Employees in non-agriculture. Note: The figure presents the estimated coefficients for the e-commerce adoption variable across the conditional earnings distribution. These estimates are derived from the Quantile Regression (QR) specified in Eq. (5.13). The solid line represents the point estimates for each quantile, while the shaded area (or dashed lines) denotes the 5% confidence interval, allowing for an assessment of the statistical significance and the heterogeneous impact of adoption across different income levels. The independent variable is the log form of real earnings. The same control variables were applied to all regression equations: e-commerce adoption, gender, marital status, years of schooling, tenure, training, and formality status. All control variables are statistically significant at the 5% level. Sampling weight was used in estimation. Source: Author calculation

5.3.4 *Adoption Contribution to the Gender Earnings Gaps in Agriculture*

The previous ESR estimates in Table 5.3 confirm the presence of gender earnings gaps among rural workers. For employers, the gap remains larger among adopters than non-adopters, whereas for employees, the gap narrows substantially among adopters, indicating different patterns across employment types. Table 5.4 further shows that the earnings gains associated with e-commerce adoption are greater in agriculture than in non-agriculture. Moreover, Table 5.5 shows that these earnings gains are larger for women than for men among rural agricultural employees, while they are broadly similar across genders among rural agricultural employers. Taken together, these findings suggest that e-commerce participation could help narrow gender income disparities among rural agricultural workers.

However, the aggregate decomposition shows that only a small share of the gender gap is explained by differences in observed characteristics ("endowments"). For employers, endowments account for only 13% of the total gap, while for employees, they explain 19%. In contrast, the majority of the earnings gap—87% among employers and 81% among employees—is attributed to structural or "coefficients" effects, which capture differences in how the labor market rewards men's and women's characteristics. These structural effects point to systematic differences in returns to skills, sectoral roles, job placement, or possible gender-based constraints, highlighting that unequal treatment rather than unequal characteristics drives most of the gender earnings inequality. Our findings are supported by Sohn (2015) and Ruslan and Sukma (2025b), who found that the structural component explains the majority of the gender wage gap in Indonesia.

The detailed Oaxaca–Blinder decomposition results in Table 5.6 show that e-commerce adoption contributes only a small share of the explained gender earnings gap among rural agricultural employers and employees. Although men's slightly higher adoption rates are associated with higher overall earnings, the positive endowment effects—0.005 for employers and 0.003 for employees—indicate

Table 5.5 ESR estimation results: the treatment effect of e-commerce adoption by gender in agriculture

	Employer earnings (log term)			Employee earnings (log term)		
Group	Adopters	Non-Adopters	ATT	Adopters	Non-Adopters	ATT
Male	14.518	13.901	0.617***	14.607	14.216	0.390***
Female	13.814	13.212	0.602***	14.300	13.695	0.605***

Note: The independent variable is the log of earnings. ***p < 0.01, **p < 0.05, *p < 0.1; sampling weight was used in estimation.
Source: Author calculation

Table 5.6 Oaxaca-Blinder decomposition of gender earnings gaps among rural employers and employees in agriculture

	Employer		Employee	
1. Gender differential				
Mean male log(earnings)	14.055***		14.137***	
	(0.002)		(0.003)	
Mean female log(earnings)	13.457***		13.489***	
	(0.005)		(0.005)	
Log(earning) difference	0.598***		0.648***	
	(0.005)		(0.0052)	
2. Aggregate decomposition	Endowment	Structural	Endowment	Structural
Total	0.076***	0.522***	0.123***	0.525***
	(0.002)	(0.005)	(0.003)	(0.005)
Share of the total gap (%)	12.761	87.239	18.974	81.025
3. Detailed decomposition				
E-commerce	0.005***	−0.000	0.003***	−0.001***
	(0.000)	(0.001)	(0.000)	(0.000)
Control variables	0.072***	0.096***	0.120***	−0.052
	(0.002)	(0.033)	(0.002)	(0.069)
Constant		0.426***		0.578***
		(0.033)		(0.069)
Number of observations	411,900		177,207	

Note: Robust standard errors in parentheses (clustered at subdistrict level); ***$p < 0.01$, **$p < 0.05$, *$p < 0.1$; sampling weight was used in estimation.
Source: Author calculation

that e-commerce access helps narrow the raw earnings disparity only marginally. However, the predominance of structural factors indicates that although e-commerce enhances women's productive endowments, deeply embedded institutional, infrastructure, and market constraints continue to suppress their relative returns, thereby sustaining the earnings gap despite improvements in digital access. Similar constraints have been documented among smallholders in other developing contexts (Livondo et al. 2026), emphasizing the universality of these barriers.

5.4 Conclusion, Policy Implications, and Limitations

5.4.1 Conclusion

This study provides comprehensive evidence on the determinants and income effects of e-commerce adoption among rural employers and employees in Indonesia. Using nationally representative labor force data and a robust econometric framework—ESR, PSM, IPWRA, and quantile regression—we show that education, digital skills, gender, and sectoral affiliation strongly shape adoption patterns, with rural agricultural workers and women consistently lagging.

The empirical results demonstrate that e-commerce adoption is strongly associated with higher earnings, with the largest gains concentrated among rural employers and agricultural workers. The ESR estimates confirm substantial positive effects even after correcting for selection on unobservable factors, while PSM and IPWRA produce consistent but smaller gains. Quantile regression further reveals that the benefits are largest at the lower end of the rural income distribution, indicating that digital participation can play a meaningful role in reducing rural income inequality.

Gender disparities persist across rural labor markets, yet the results show that e-commerce adoption yields greater proportional income gains for female workers, especially in agriculture. While adoption does not eliminate gender earnings gaps, the Blinder–Oaxaca decomposition indicates that e-commerce contributes modestly to narrowing the gap, even though most inequality is driven by structural differences in labor-market returns rather than endowments. These findings highlight both the promise and the limits of digital inclusion as a pathway to gender-equitable rural development.

5.4.2 Policy Implications

The study's findings underscore that expanding e-commerce adoption can support rural income growth, but the distribution of gains depends heavily on structural conditions—particularly workers' education, digital capabilities, employment formality, and gender roles. Thus, policies should move beyond connectivity and address the deeper constraints that limit rural workers' ability to benefit from digital markets.

First, targeted digital skills development is essential. Tailored training programs that integrate digital marketing, online business management, and financial literacy into agricultural extension services and vocational centers can help small producers and informal workers convert digital participation into income gains. Supporting women through flexible training schedules, community-based delivery, and partnerships with women's cooperatives can further strengthen female digital entrepreneurship.

Second, improving rural digital and logistical infrastructure—including affordable broadband, local fulfillment hubs, and digital payment systems—will reduce operational costs and expand rural producers' market reach. Public–private partnerships can accelerate these investments, particularly in lagging agricultural regions.

Finally, regulatory and institutional support is needed to sustain digital engagement. Simplifying business registration procedures, encouraging the formalization of microenterprises, and expanding access to digital finance, microcredit, and logistics services can help rural workers scale their online activities.

While individual adoption is crucial, the long-term success of digital inclusion in Indonesia may require a comprehensive policy framework similar to the national demonstration projects in China, which have been shown to effectively bridge the urban-rural economic gap (Yu et al. 2025). By combining infrastructure development, capability building, and gender-responsive interventions, policymakers can ensure that digital participation becomes a more inclusive engine of rural earnings growth.

5.4.3 Limitations and Future Works

The limitations of this study fall into three main aspects: methodological constraints, measurement simplification, and scope limitations. First, the use of cross-sectional data limits the ability to capture dynamic or long-term effects and to address reverse causality fully. However, the ESR framework corrects for selection bias on unobservable factors (using peer adoption as an instrument), but the design cannot account for evolving unobserved household-level heterogeneity (such as resource allocation or joint decision-making). Second, the measurement of digital engagement is limited to a binary indicator (adopter vs. non-adopter), which fails to capture crucial variations in intensity, frequency, or the specific type of platform used. This simplification may mask the true range of impacts associated with different levels of digital involvement. Finally, the scope of outcomes is narrow, focusing exclusively on earnings and neglecting broader welfare dimensions. Future research should address these limitations using longitudinal data, more granular measures of digital intensity, and a broader array of welfare outcomes.

Acknowledgements This paper was presented in the session "E-commerce for Rural and Agricultural Development" at the International Conference on "Innovations for Sustainable Agriculture and Rural Development", held at the Asian Development Bank Institute (ADBI), Tokyo, Japan, on 22–24 September 2025. ADBI and Lincoln University, New Zealand jointly organized the conference. The authors gratefully acknowledge the valuable comments and suggestions from the participants, as well as travel support from ADBI.

We wish to express our sincere gratitude to BPS–Statistics Indonesia for providing access to the National Labour Force Survey (SAKERNAS) microdata, without which this study could not have been conducted.

We have no known conflict of interest to disclose.

Appendix 1: Falsification Test Results (Regression Among Non-Adopters)

	Employer		Employee	
Variable	Agriculture	Non-agriculture	Agriculture	Non-agriculture
Proportion of peer adopters	0.339	0.643	0.200	0.262
	(0.301)	(0.433)	(0.501)	(0.507)
Gender (female)	−0.420***	−0.554***	−0.391***	−0.467***
	(0.006)	(0.005)	(0.005)	(0.004)
Marital stat. (married)	0.061***	0.059***	0.086***	0.039***
	(0.006)	(0.007)	(0.006)	(0.005)
Household members	−0.002	0.000	−0.010***	−0.009***
	(0.001)	(0.002)	(0.001)	(0.001)
Education				
Junior high school	0.108***	0.147***	0.069***	−0.024
	(0.010)	(0.015)	(0.017)	(0.019)
Senior high school	0.212***	0.286***	0.144***	−0.052
	(0.017)	(0.028)	(0.033)	(0.037)
Vocational	0.177***	0.307***	0.148***	0.022
	(0.020)	(0.030)	(0.034)	(0.038)
Diploma	0.364***	0.514***	0.335***	−0.032
	(0.040)	(0.051)	(0.062)	(0.056)
University	0.478***	0.662***	0.460***	−0.151*
	(0.042)	(0.066)	(0.079)	(0.085)
Experience	0.023***	0.042***	0.014***	−0.018***
	(0.003)	(0.004)	(0.005)	(0.006)
Experience sqr./100	−0.027***	−0.044***	−0.025***	−0.065***
	(0.042)	(0.066)	(0.001)	(0.001)
Other control variables	Yes	Yes	Yes	Yes
Period dummy	Yes	Yes	Yes	Yes
Regional dummy	Yes	Yes	Yes	Yes
Constant	13.479***	13.502***	13.093***	12.088***
	(0.036)	(0.059)	(0.067)	(0.074)
Number of obs.	406,615	252,024	174,995	416,549
R-squared	0.201	0.271	0.426	0.322

Note: The independent variable is the log of real earnings—robust clustered standard errors in parentheses

*p < 0.05, **p < 0.01, ***p < 0.001. Survey weight was applied in the estimation

References

Abdullah, A. S. A. (2025). *The Impact of E-Commerce on the Growth of MSMEs in Indonesia* (pp. 3126–3130). https://doi.org/10.2991/978-94-6463-758-8_260

Ahituv, A., & Lerman, R. I. (2007). How do marital status, work effort, and wage rates interact? *Demography*, *44*(3), 623–647. https://doi.org/10.1353/dem.2007.0021

Akbar, F. (2022). Gender Wage Gap: Evidence from Employment in Informal Sector. *The Journal of Indonesia Sustainable Development Planning*, *3*(2), 104–117. https://doi.org/10.46456/jisdep.v3i2.301

Akbar, M., & Wijaya, G. (2024). Digital Literacy of Rural Areas in Indonesia: Challenges and Opportunities. *Proceedings of the 4th International Conference on Rural Socio-Economic Transformation, RUSET 2023, 1 November 2023, Bogor, Indonesia.* https://doi.org/10.4108/eai.1-11-2023.2344347

Amalia, R., Aini, R. Q., Paradita, J., & Mirza BR, A. D. (2025). Bridging The Digital Divide : The Role of Technology in Enhancing Rural SMES in Indonesia. *Jurnal Ilmu Manajemen Dan Bisnis*, *16*(1), 27–34. https://doi.org/10.17509/jimb.v16i1.82681

Ariansyah, K., Sirait, E. R. E., Nugroho, B. A., & Suryanegara, M. (2021). Drivers of and barriers to e-commerce adoption in Indonesia: Individuals' perspectives and the implications. *Telecommunications Policy*, *45*(8), 102219. https://doi.org/10.1016/j.telpol.2021.102219

Astuti, M., Ganefri, & Yulastri, A. (2023). Literature Review: The Influence of Demographics, User Experience and E-Commerce Platforms In The Digital Business World. *Indonesian Journal of Computer Science*, *12*(5). https://doi.org/10.33022/ijcs.v12i5.3444

Blinder, A. S. (1973). Wage Discrimination: Reduced Form and Structural Estimates. *The Journal of Human Resources*, *8*(4), 436. https://doi.org/10.2307/144855

BPS. (2023a). *Complete Enumeration Results of the 2023 Census of Agriculture—Edition 1.*

BPS. (2023b). *ICT Development Index (IDI).*

BPS. (2023c). Welfare Indicators - Volume 52, 2023.

Chen, S., Liu, W., Song, H., & Qing, Z. (2022). The Effects of E-Commerce on Rural Household Income: Evidence and Mechanism. *SSRN Electronic Journal.* https://doi.org/10.2139/ssrn.4174845

Fernandes, C., Borges, M. R., & Caiado, J. (2021). The Contribution of Digital Financial Services to Financial Inclusion In Mozambique: An ARDL Model Approach. *Applied Economics*, *53*(3), 400–409. https://doi.org/10.1080/00036846.2020.1808177

Fointuna, J. I., Susamto, A. A., & Afifah, E. N. (2025). The Effect of Internet Diffusion on Income Inequality: Cross-Regional Analysis In Indonesia. *Information Technology for Development*, *31*(4), 1222–1242. https://doi.org/10.1080/02681102.2025.2472079

Goldfarb, A., & Tucker, C. (2019). Digital Economics. *Journal of Economic Literature*, *57*(1), 3–43. https://doi.org/10.1257/jel.20171452

Gray, J. S. (1997). The Fall in Men's Return to Marriage: Declining Productivity Effects or Changing Selection? *The Journal of Human Resources*, *32*(3), 481. https://doi.org/10.2307/146180

Greene, W. H. (2012). *Econometric Analysis* (S. Yagan, D. Battista, A. D'Ambrosio, & J. Kolongowski, Eds.; 7th ed.). Prentice Hall.

Guan, X., He, L., & Hu, Z. (2024). Impact of Rural E-Commerce on Farmers' Income and Income Gap. *Agriculture*, *14*(10), 1689. https://doi.org/10.3390/agriculture14101689

Hadi, A. (2018). Bridging Indonesia's Digital Divide: Rural-Urban Linkages? *Jurnal Ilmu Sosial Dan Ilmu Politik*, *22*(1), 17. https://doi.org/10.22146/jsp.31835

Halvorsen, R., & Palmquist, R. (1980). The Interpretation of Dummy Variables in Semilogarithmic Equations. *The American Economic Review*, *70*(3), 474–475.

He, C., Hao, H., Su, Y., & Yang, J. (2024). A Study on Factors Influencing Farmers' Adoption of E-Commerce for Agricultural Products: A Case Study of Wuchang City. *Sustainability*, *16*(21), 9496. https://doi.org/10.3390/su16219496

ILO. (1993). *Revision of the International Classification of Status in Employment.*

ITU. (2022). *Measuring Digital Development: Facts and Figures.*

Jann, B. (2008). The Blinder–Oaxaca Decomposition for Linear Regression Models. *The Stata Journal: Promoting Communications on Statistics and Stata*, *8*(4), 453–479. https://doi.org/10.1177/1536867X0800800401

Jílková, P., & Králová, P. (2021). Digital Consumer Behaviour and eCommerce Trends during the COVID-19 Crisis. *International Advances in Economic Research*, *27*(1), 83–85. https://doi.org/10.1007/s11294-021-09817-4

Kadir, K., & Sukma, W. L. (2019). RETURNS TO EDUCATION AND WAGE DISTRIBUTION IN INDONESIA: A COMPARISON ACROSS GENDER GROUPS. *Jurnal Litbang Sukowati : Media Penelitian Dan Pengembangan*, *2*(2), 19. https://doi.org/10.32630/sukowati.v2i2.90

Kilay, A. L., Simamora, B. H., & Putra, D. P. (2022). The Influence of E-Payment and E-Commerce Services on Supply Chain Performance: Implications of Open Innovation and Solutions for the Digitalization of Micro, Small, and Medium Enterprises (MSMEs) in Indonesia. *Journal of Open Innovation: Technology, Market, and Complexity*, *8*(3), 119. https://doi.org/10.3390/joitmc8030119

Li, W., & He, W. (2024). Revenue-Increasing Effect of Rural E-Commerce: A Perspective of Farmers' Market Integration and Employment Growth. *Economic Analysis and Policy*, *81*, 482–493. https://doi.org/10.1016/j.eap.2023.12.015

Li, J., & Zhao, D. (2020). Analysis on the Development of Rural E-Commerce in Hubei Province under the Background of Rural Revitalization Strategy. *2020 International Conference on E-Commerce and Internet Technology (ECIT)*, 14–19. https://doi.org/10.1109/ECIT50008.2020.00011

Li, X., Xiong, H., Hao, J., & Li, G. (2024). Impacts of internet access and use on grain productivity: evidence from Central China. *Humanities and Social Sciences Communications*, *11*(1), 90. https://doi.org/10.1057/s41599-023-02546-5

Lian, X., Mu, Y., & Zhang, W. (2023). Digital Inclusive Financial Services and Rural Income: Evidence From China's Major Grain-Producing Regions. *Finance Research Letters*, *53*, 103622. https://doi.org/10.1016/j.frl.2022.103622

Lin, B., Wang, X., Jin, S., Yang, W., & Li, H. (2022). Impacts of cooperative membership on rice productivity: Evidence from China. *World Development*, *150*, 105669. https://doi.org/10.1016/j.worlddev.2021.105669

Liu, B., & Zhou, J. (2023). Digital Literacy, Farmers' Income Increase and Rural Internal Income Gap. *Sustainability*, *15*(14), 11422. https://doi.org/10.3390/su151411422

Liu, M., Min, S., Ma, W., & Liu, T. (2021). The adoption and impact of E-commerce in rural China: Application of an endogenous switching regression model. *Journal of Rural Studies*, *83*, 106–116. https://doi.org/10.1016/j.jrurstud.2021.02.021

Livondo, J. L., Maina, S. W., & Ombati, J. M. (2026). Infrastructure and Market Factors Influencing Implementation of Agri E-Commerce Platforms among Smallholder Potato Farmers in Kenya. *Global Journal of Agricultural Research*, *14*(1), 1–18. https://doi.org/10.37745/gjar.2013/vol14n1118

Lokshin, M., & Sajaia, Z. (2004). Maximum Likelihood Estimation of Endogenous Switching Regression Models. *The Stata Journal: Promoting Communications on Statistics and Stata*, *4*(3), 282–289. https://doi.org/10.1177/1536867X0400400306

Loo, M. K., Ramachandran, S., & Raja Yusof, R. N. (2024). Systematic Review of Factors and Barriers Influencing E-Commerce Adoption among SMEs over the Last Decade: A TOE Framework Perspective. *Journal of the Knowledge Economy*. https://doi.org/10.1007/s13132-024-02257-5

Luo, Y., Zhou, L., & Zhang, W. (2025). Can E-Commerce Bring Dividends to Rural Households? New Evidence from The Income Inequality Perspective. *Economic Analysis and Policy*, *86*, 363–379. https://doi.org/10.1016/j.eap.2025.03.036

Ma, W., Zhou, X., & Liu, M. (2020). What Drives Farmers' Willingness to Adopt E-Commerce in Rural China? The Role of Internet Use. *Agribusiness*, *36*(1), 159–163. https://doi.org/10.1002/agr.21624

Ma, W., Abdul-Rahaman, A., & Issahaku, G. (2023). Welfare Implications of Participating in Agri-Value Chains Among Vegetable Farmers in Northern Ghana. *Agribusiness*, *39*(3), 793–811. https://doi.org/10.1002/agr.21792

Markelova, H., Meinzen-Dick, R., Hellin, J., & Dohrn, S. (2009). Collective Action for Smallholder Market Access. *Food Policy*, *34*(1), 1–7. https://doi.org/10.1016/j.foodpol.2008.10.001

Market Research Indonesia. (2025, May 2). *Indonesia Rural Digital Inclusion: A Quiet Revolution.* https://marketresearchindonesia.com/insights/articles/indonesia-rural-digital-inclusion-revolution

Marschak, J. (1959). *Binary choice constraints on random utility indicators* (No. 74; Cowles Foundation Discussion Papers). https://ideas.repec.org/p/cwl/cwldpp/74.html

Neumark, D. (1988). Employers' Discriminatory Behavior and the Estimation of Wage Discrimination. *The Journal of Human Resources*, *23*(3), 279. https://doi.org/10.2307/145830

Oaxaca, R. (1973). Male-Female Wage Differentials in Urban Labor Markets. *International Economic Review*, *14*(3), 693–709. https://doi.org/10.2307/2525981

OECD. (2018). *Bridging the Digital Divide: Include, Upskill, Innovate.*

Onitsuka, K., Hidayat, A. R. T., & Huang, W. (2018). Challenges for The Next Level of Digital Divide in Rural Indonesian Communities. *The Electronic Journal of Information Systems In Developing Countries*, *84*(2). https://doi.org/10.1002/isd2.12021

Oseni, G., Corral, P., Goldstein, M., & Winters, P. (2015). Explaining gender differentials in agricultural production in Nigeria. *Agricultural Economics*, *46*(3), 285–310. https://doi.org/10.1111/agec.12166

Priyatna, M. (2022). Does Internet Usage Lead to An Increase in Household Incomes? Indonesian Rural Case Study. *Jurnal Ekonomi Indonesia, 11*(1), 13–24. https://doi.org/10.52813/jei.v11i1.69

Purevkhuu, S., & Munkhbold, J. (2021). Demographic and Cultural Factors Influencing the Adoption of B2C E-Commerce in SCO Region. *Eduvest—Journal of Universal Studies*, *1*(10). https://doi.org/10.59188/eduvest.v1i10.231

Qiu, H., Deng, H., Lu, M., Luo, L., Chen, X., & Wang, Z. (2025). The Impact of Rural E-Commerce on Farmers' Income Gap: Implications for Farmers' Sustainable Development. *Sustainability*, *17*(9), 3921. https://doi.org/10.3390/su17093921

Rainer, K., & Cegielski, C. (2011). *Introduction to Information Systems: Enabling and Transforming Business* (3rd ed.). John Wiley & Sons Inc.

Rogers, E. M. (2003). *Diffusion of innovations* (5th ed.). Free Press.

Rolando, B. (2025). The Impact of E-Commerce on the Growth of Micro, Small, and Medium Enterprises in Indonesia. *Jurnal Pendidikan Dan Kewirausahaan*, *12*(3), 1113–1127. https://doi.org/10.47668/pkwu.v12i3.1542

Rosenbaum, P. R., & Rubin, D. B. (1983). The Central Role of the Propensity Score in Observational Studies for Causal Effects. *Biometrika*, *70*(1), 41. https://doi.org/10.2307/2335942

Ruslan, K., & Sukma, W. L. (2025a). Decomposition of Post-Pandemic Gender Wage Gaps in Indonesia: an Analysis Across the Wage Distribution. *Jurnal Ketenagakerjaan*, *20*(2), 201–222. https://doi.org/10.47198/jnaker.v20i2.517

Ruslan, K., & Sukma, W. L. (2025b). Do The Sticky Floor and Glass Ceiling Phenomena Persist in The Indonesian Labour Force After The Pandemic? *Jurnal Ekonomi Indonesia*, *14*(2), 125–144. https://doi.org/10.52813/jei.v14i2.567

Selorm, O., Selorm, A., & William, G. (2022). Adoption of Electronic Commerce by Agribusiness Small Medium Enterprises in The Upper East Region of Ghana. *Journal of Development and Agricultural Economics*, *14*(3), 79–94. https://doi.org/10.5897/JDAE2022.1350

Smidt, H. J., & Jokonya, O. (2022). Factors Affecting Digital Technology Adoption by Small-Scale Farmers in Agriculture Value Chains (AVCs) In South Africa. *Information Technology for Development*, *28*(3), 558–584. https://doi.org/10.1080/02681102.2021.1975256

Sohn, K. (2015). Gender Discrimination in Earnings in Indonesia: A Fuller Picture. *Bulletin of Indonesian Economic Studies*, *51*(1), 95–121. https://doi.org/10.1080/00074918.2015.1016569

Strusani, D., & Houngbonon, G. V. (2021). *The Impact of Covid-19 on Disruptive Technology Adoption in Emerging Markets.* https://www.ifc.org/wps/wcm/connect/publications_ext_content/ifc_external_publication_site/publications_listing_page/disruptive-tech-adoption-covid-19

Valarezo, Á., López, R., & Pérez Amaral, T. (2020). Adoption of E-Commerce by Individuals and Digital-Divide. In *Applied Economics in the Digital Era* (pp. 103–134). Springer International Publishing. https://doi.org/10.1007/978-3-030-40601-1_4

Van Kerm, P. (2003). Adaptive Kernel Density Estimation. *The Stata Journal: Promoting Communications on Statistics and Stata*, *3*(2), 148–156. https://doi.org/10.1177/1536867X0300300204

Wang, M., Ding, X., & Cheng, P. (2024). Exploring The Income Impact of Rural E-Commerce Comprehensive Demonstration Project and Determinants of County Selection. *Humanities and Social Sciences Communications*, *11*(1), 1286. https://doi.org/10.1057/s41599-024-03785-w

Wang, J., Dou, N., & Nie, H. (2026). How Digital Empowerment Enhances Rural Supply Chain Performance: Evidence from Taobao Villages in China. *Frontiers in Sustainable Food Systems*, *10*. https://doi.org/10.3389/fsufs.2026.1732739

Wihardja, M. M., & Wibisana, P. S. (2021). *Gender Insights from the COVID-19 Digital Merchant Survey in Indonesia*. World Bank. https://thedocs.worldbank.org/en/doc/eea1f0e8ba5f015c5d7cf16ce54c1ba0-0070012021/world-bank-covid-19-digital-merchant-survey-on-gender-in-indonesia

Wihardja, M. M., Pradana, A. T., Wibisana, P. S., & Swarnata, A. (2024). *The Heterogeneous Impacts of Digital Transformation and Investment on Indonesia's Labour Market* (524; ERIA Discussion Paper Series).

Wirdiyanti, R., Yusgiantoro, I., Sugiarto, A., Harjanti, A. D., Mambea, I. Y., Soekarno, S., & Damayanti, S. M. (2023). How Does E-Commerce Adoption Impact Micro, Small, and Medium Enterprises' Performance and Financial Inclusion? Evidence from Indonesia. *Electronic Commerce Research*, *23*(4), 2485–2515. https://doi.org/10.1007/s10660-022-09547-7

Wooldridge, J. M. (2002). Inverse probability weighted M-estimators for sample selection, attrition, and stratification. *Portuguese Economic Journal*, *1*(2), 117–139. https://doi.org/10.1007/s10258-002-0008-x

World Bank. (2016). *World Development Report 2016: Digital Dividends*. Washington, DC: World Bank. https://doi.org/10.1596/978-1-4648-0671-1

World Bank. (2021). *Beyond Unicorns Harnessing Digital Technologies for Inclusion in Indonesia*.

Wu, M. (2025). Digital Inclusive Finance, Rural E-Commerce, and Urban-Rural Income Gap. *GBP Proceedings Series*, *3*, 35–43. https://doi.org/10.70088/7hvzt370

Yacob, S., Sulistiyo, U., Erida, E., & Siregar, A. P. (2021). The Importance of E-Commerce Adoption and Entrepreneurship Orientation for Sustainable Micro, Small, and Medium Enterprises in Indonesia. *Development Studies Research*, *8*(1), 244–252. https://doi.org/10.1080/21665095.2021.1976657

Yang, Q., Zhu, Y., Liu, L., & Wang, F. (2022). Land Tenure Stability and Adoption Intensity of Sustainable Agricultural Practices in Banana Production in China. *Journal of Cleaner Production*, *338*, 130553. https://doi.org/10.1016/j.jclepro.2022.130553

Yang, Y., Wang, F., & Tang, B. (2025). The Impact and Mechanism of E-Commerce on Rural Agriculture: Evidence from China. *NJAS: Impact in Agricultural and Life Sciences*, *97*(1). https://doi.org/10.1080/27685241.2025.2523380

Yin, M., Han, X., Yan, Y., & Wang, X. (2025). Can Farmers Increase Their Income by Participating in E-Commerce? Evidence from Rural China. *Frontiers in Sustainable Food Systems*, *9*. https://doi.org/10.3389/fsufs.2025.1597169

You, Q., Yuan, Z., & Yu, X.-S. (2025). High-Quality Development and Rural Revitalization: The Role of Rural E-Commerce. *Frontiers in Sustainable Food Systems*, *9*. https://doi.org/10.3389/fsufs.2025.1599629

Yu, Y., Tu, H., & Tian, Q. (2025). The Impacts of Rural E-Commerce on County Economic Development: Evidence from National Rural E-Commerce Comprehensive Demonstration Policy in China. *Journal of Theoretical and Applied Electronic Commerce Research*, *20*(3), 235. https://doi.org/10.3390/jtaer20030235

Zeng, Y. (2025). *Estimation and Inference of Average Treatment Effect in Percentage Points under Heterogeneity*.

Zhang, H. (2024). Research on The Effect of E-Commerce Adoption in Improving Farmers' Income and Welfare in The Context of Digital Economy. *Frontiers in Humanities and Social Sciences*, *4*(3). https://doi.org/10.54691/748sqj08

Zhang, Y.-F., & Zhao, H. (2025). The Effect of E-Commerce on Digital Inclusive Finance: Evidence from The E-Commerce Boom in Rural China. *Cogent Economics & Finance*, *13*(1). https://doi.org/10.1080/23322039.2025.2460082

Zhang, L., Sum, S. B. M., & Ramli, Z. B. (2025a). Evaluation of the Effectiveness of Government Policy Tools in Rural E-Commerce Poverty Alleviation. *Journal of Cultural Analysis and Social Change*, 4039–4055. https://doi.org/10.64753/jcasc.v10i4.3735

Zhang, Y., Wu, X., & Cai, R. (2025b). The Effects of Rural E-Commerce on Income Inequality: Evidence from the National Rural E-Commerce Comprehensive Demonstration Policy in China. *Economic Analysis and Policy*. https://doi.org/10.1016/j.eap.2025.05.052

Chapter 6
Policy- and Household-Level Challenges of E-Commerce for Smallholder Agriculture in Vietnam: Case Studies with Fruit Farmers in Peri-Urban and Rural Areas

Rachmat Mulia, Nghia Dai Tran, Thinh Nhu Le, Hai Trong Le, Heather Mackay, and Magnus Jirström

6.1 Introduction

E-commerce grows rapidly in Asia (Ganbold 2024; Kauth 2024). E-commerce is the sale and purchase of goods and services through electronic networks and the internet, encompassing a broad range of commercial activities (Bao et al. 2025). E-commerce can help developing countries transform their agriculture into a digitalized sector and reduce rural poverty (Li et al. 2023; Zhang and Fan 2023).

Vietnam is among Asian developing countries with steady e-commerce growth (Le and Tran 2020). In 2020, Vietnam's average annual growth rate for business-to-customer e-commerce revenue was nearly 19%, rising from USD5

R. Mulia (✉)
World Agroforestry (ICRAF) Vietnam,
HCMCC Tower, Thuy Khue Ward, Tay Ho District, Hanoi, Vietnam
e-mail: R.Mulia@landscapealliance.org

N. D. Tran
Division of Natural Resources and Environmental Economics Studies, Institute of Policy and Strategy for Agriculture and Rural Development (IPSARD),
Thuy Khue Ward, Tay Ho District, Hanoi, Vietnam

Food and Agriculture Organization of the United Nations,
Hanoi, Vietnam
e-mail: tran.nghia@FAO.org

T. N. Le
Fruit and Vegetable Research Institute (FAVRI),
Trau Quy, Gia Lam district, Hanoi, Vietnam
e-mail: lenhuthinhfavri@gmail.com

W. Ma et al. (eds.), *E-Commerce for Inclusive Rural and Agricultural Development*, Contributions to Economics,
https://doi.org/10.1007/978-981-92-5237-4_6

billion in 2016 to USD11.8 billion (IDEA 2021). The growth has been stimulated by several factors, including improved internet service and nationwide coverage, as well as the promulgation of national and sub-national policies targeting e-commerce development across all sectors (ITA 2024). Vietnam's e-commerce will continue to grow in the future, driven by the government's ongoing efforts to improve the support infrastructure, such as online payment systems and logistics services, and its ambition to transform all sectors, including agriculture, into digitalized ones (IDEA 2021; ITA 2024).

Despite these government policies and efforts, the impact of e-commerce on Vietnam's agricultural sector remains limited, particularly in smallholder agriculture (Nguyen et al. 2022; Trang et al. 2024). Smallholder farmers substantially contribute to Vietnam's agricultural production (Hoang 2020; Tran 2024). However, many farm households in Vietnam prefer to sell their agricultural products to middlemen or traders at the farmgate, although often with a limited bargaining power, resulting in relatively low prices and little incentive for farmers to improve product quality (Bui et al. 2021; USAID 2022). E-commerce can help farmers connect directly with urban customers, reduce their reliance on market intermediaries, and obtain fair prices (Bruckert et al. 2023; Stoeva et al. 2024).

From the consumers' side, most urban consumers in Vietnam still prefer to purchase agricultural products, especially fresh products, from traditional retail markets rather than modern outlets or online (Nguyen 2024). Several factors, such as more affordable prices and proximity to residences, have led to this preference. However, recent concerns over food safety may shift their attention to online food products, as they can directly access information on origin and production processes from producers through e-commerce platforms or social media (EC 2020). Concern over food safety has been triggered by increasing evidence of excessive use of chemical inputs in vegetable and fruit production in Vietnam (ADB 2023; Ngo et al. 2020). Approximately 60% of urban consumers in the country prefer labelled or certified agricultural products (Ha et al. 2021).

It is important to understand the challenges that prevent a stronger impact of e-commerce on smallholder agriculture because improved access to market opportunities and the use of new technologies, including digital ones, have been widely

H. T. Le
Division of Natural Resources and Environmental Economics Studies, Institute of Policy and Strategy for Agriculture and Rural Development (IPSARD),
Thuy Khue Ward, Tay Ho District, Hanoi, Vietnam
e-mail: lehai.ipsard@gmail.com

H. Mackay
Department of Human Geography, Lund University, Lund, Sweden

Department of Economics, Geography, Law and Tourism, Mid Sweden University, Östersund, Sweden
e-mail: heather.mackay@miun.se

M. Jirström
Department of Human Geography, Lund University, Lund, Sweden
e-mail: magnus.jirstrom@keg.lu.se

recognized as a sustainable way to enhance rural livelihoods and develop the agricultural sector (Fan and Gan 2025; Hoang 2020).

According to the government-technology-smallholder framework (Sun et al. 2024; Yuan and Sun 2024), apart from the support technologies such as e-commerce platforms or social media, a digital transformation of smallholder agriculture depends on the interlinkage between two key actors, namely, the government with its policies and smallholder farmers as agents of change. Perspectives of local stakeholders are also important to ensure that support policies are tailored to the specific and practical needs of farmers and to avoid top-down policies that risk ineffective implementation (Sun et al. 2024). However, studies reporting policy-level challenges of e-commerce for smallholder agriculture in Vietnam and their interlinkages with household-level challenges are scarce. Existing studies have focused only on household-level challenges (Dao et al. 2025; Nguyen et al. 2022; Tran et al. 2024) or on the effect of households' demographic or socio-economic conditions on farmers' participation in e-commerce (Hoang and Tran 2023; Tran et al. 2024).

This study aimed at investigating policy- and household-level challenges of e-commerce for smallholder agriculture in Vietnam and the interlinkage between them using fruit farmers in peri-urban areas of Hanoi City (hereafter referred to as 'peri-urban Hanoi') and the rural regions of Son La Province ('rural Son La') as case studies. Fruit products, whether fresh or processed, are significant agricultural commodities for Vietnam's domestic and export markets (USDA-GAIN 2021). The purchase of fresh and processed fruit products accounted for approximately 8–9% of the monthly food expenditure of urban households in Vietnam (Ha et al. 2021). The study compared peri-urban and rural areas because proximity to urban and market centres determines the selling profile and strategies of farm households (Hoang 2020). The investigation of policy-level challenges used support policies promulgated by Hanoi City and Son La Province between 2000 and 2022. The challenges farmers face in participating in e-commerce were identified through semi-structured household interviews. The perspectives of local stakeholders on how support policies can better facilitate farmers' participation in e-commerce were examined through focus group discussions (FGDs).

The study had three research questions: What are the focuses of policies supporting e-commerce development promulgated by Hanoi City and Son La Province? What are the production and selling profiles of fruit farmers in peri-urban Hanoi and rural Son La, and the challenges that they encountered in participating in e-commerce? And what are local stakeholders' perspectives on how support policies can better facilitate farmers' participation in e-commerce? The findings of this study will enrich the understanding of the crucial intertwining between local governments and farmers to boost e-commerce development for smallholder agriculture. They can also be used to develop targeted interventions to enhance the accessibility and integration of smallholder farmers into e-commerce opportunities.

The paper is organized as follows. Section 6.2 describes the study sites and research methodologies used to investigate the presence and focus of support policies, the barriers farmers encountered to participating in e-commerce, and stakeholder perspectives. Thereafter, the results (Sect. 6.3) and discussions, including suggestions for further studies (Sect. 6.4), were presented before the conclusions and policy recommendations (Sect. 6.5).

6.2 Materials and Methods

6.2.1 Study Sites

The selected study sites in peri-urban Hanoi and rural Son La are areas designated by local governments for high-value fruit production, mainly due to their favorable biophysical and climatic conditions for growing fruit trees. Additionally, they served as the study sites for the Fruit and Vegetable Research Institute (FAVRI), and the connection between local stakeholders and FAVRI facilitated the household interviews and FGDs conducted in the present study.

The study sites in peri-urban Hanoi were Chuong My and Quoc Oai districts. They are approximately 30 km from Hanoi's City centre, one of the country's largest urban and market centres. The two districts are known for producing pomelo (*Citrus maxima*) and longan (*Dimocarpus longan*). According to the General Statistics Office of Vietnam, Hanoi City contributed 10.3% of Vietnam's total pomelo production (GSO 2021), and Chuong My District had the largest pomelo cultivation area in the city. Hanoi City is also a major production area for longan, and 10.6% of the city's total longan cultivation area is in Quoc Oai District.

The study sites in rural Son La were Yen Chau and Moc Chau districts, which are located 200–250 km from the Hanoi City centre. The two districts are also fruit-producing areas, e.g., for plums (*Prunus domestica*) and mangoes (*Mangifera indica*). Yen Chau accounted for about 22% of Son La Province's total mango production (SLSO 2021). Approximately 28.6% of the plum cultivation area in Son La Province is in Moc Chau District (SLSO 2021).

6.2.2 Investigating the Presence and Focus of Support Policies

Policies supporting e-commerce development issued by Hanoi City and Son La Province were identified through consultations with policy experts from the Institute of Policy and Strategy for Agriculture and Rural Development (IPSARD), i.e., a think tank under the Ministry of Agriculture and Rural Development of Vietnam. The Google search engine was used for further exploration, and policy documents (in either English or Vietnamese) were obtained from several websites, including https://thuvienphapluat.vn. The focus of the support policies was examined by screening their full texts. According to Bao et al. (2025), the focuses of policies supporting digital transformation in agriculture are usually further development of support infrastructure and services (e.g., internet coverage in rural areas), legal and regulatory frameworks to provide a conducive environment for both businesses and consumers, cyber security (e.g., related to online transaction and payment system), trade facilitation and logistics, or human capacity to engage in digital technology.

6.2.3 *Household Interviews*

The interviews were conducted with pomelo, longan, mango, and plum farmers in Chuong My, Quoc Oai, Yen Chau, and Moc Chau districts, respectively. Considering the COVID-19 pandemic situation in Vietnam in 2021 and the resources available for the study, a stratified purposive sampling approach (Campbell et al. 2020) was employed, with consultation with farmer associations at the district level to select two communes per district with large fruit tree cultivation areas.

The associations were also asked to recommend 50–60 households from each of the two communes in each district for interviews. The households should represent the variety of fruit farmers in terms of, e.g., socio-economic status (i.e., poor, near-poor, average, or better-off households, according to the local government's income standard) and landholding size. The two selected communes were Tran Phu and Nam Phuong Tien in Chuong My District; Dai Thanh and Hoa Thach in Quoc Oai District; Sap Vat and Chieng Hac in Yen Chau District; and Tan Lap and Moc Chau Commune in Moc Chau District. Based on the list of recommended households from the farmer associations, 89 and 110 households in peri-urban Hanoi and rural Son La, respectively, were available for interviews (Table 6.1). Several recommended households were either unavailable or unwilling to be interviewed during the intermittent relaxation period of social distancing related to the COVID-19 pandemic. Considering the pandemic situation, additional households recommended for interviews by the farmer associations were not sought.

A semi-structured questionnaire, divided into four sections was used for the interviews. Section 1 collected brief information about the demographic and socio-economic profiles of the households (e.g., ethnicity, family size, and

Table 6.1 Number of respondents in the household interviews (the respondents represented different households)

Respondents	No. of respondents (people)	Districts
Peri-urban areas of Hanoi City		
Pomelo farmers	49	Chuong My
Longan farmers	40	Quoc Oai
Total	89	
Rural areas of Son La Province		
Mango farmers	54	Yen Chau
Plum farmers	56	Moc Chau
Total	110	

Source: Authors

socio-economic status). Section 2 focused on the farming practices (including fruit tree cultivation) that households managed, and Section 3 investigated buyers of their fruit products and household participation in online selling activities. Section 4 focused on several issues, including the impacts of COVID-19 on fruit production, which were relevant at the time of the household interviews. The household interviews were conducted by a group of experts from FAVRI and IPSARD between October 2021 and March 2022 at households' residences or communal houses. The responses from the interviewed households were immediately recorded on the questionnaire forms.

6.2.4 Focus Group Discussion with Local Stakeholders

The FGDs were conducted in Moc Chau District, rural Son La, in July 2022, and in Chuong My District, peri-urban Hanoi, in October 2022. One FGD was conducted per site, and each involved around 15 participants representing local authorities at the district and commune levels especially the Department of Agriculture and Rural Development (DARD), the Farmers' and Women's Union, and farmer cooperatives. The FGD in Moc Chau was attended by local stakeholders from the two selected districts in rural Son La and that in Chuong My by those from the two selected districts in peri-urban Hanoi.

The experts from IPSARD led the discussion by first presenting the results of the investigation into the presence and focus of support policies, as well as the barriers farmers encountered to participating in e-commerce. Thereafter, all participants were asked to share their perspectives on how support policies can better facilitate farmers' participation in e-commerce. In the two FGDs, all participants' inputs were recorded on A0-sized paper and displayed during the discussion.

6.2.5 Data Analysis

The information collected during the household interviews was entered into Microsoft Excel for analysis. The Chi-Square statistic (Turney 2023) was used to test for a significant difference in proportion among the four selected districts, e.g., the proportion of households with certified fruit products. The Marascuilo Procedure (Wagh and Razvi 2016) was used as a post hoc test following a significant Chi-Square test, with a Bonferroni correction (Hayes 2024) applied for multiple pairwise comparisons. The Chi-Square and post hoc tests were conducted in Microsoft Excel.

The local stakeholder perspectives recorded on A0-sized papers during the FGDs were transferred into Microsoft Word for analysis. No weighting-of-opinions exercise with the FGD participants was conducted, nor was the level of importance assigned to different perspectives from local stakeholders during the data analysis.

6.3 Results

6.3.1 Presence and Focus of Support Policies

Hanoi City, the capital of Vietnam and one of the largest urban and market centres in the country, issued at least 9 policies supporting e-commerce development. Most of their policies were promulgated between 2016 and 2021 (Table 6.2) and focused on improvements in infrastructure, services, cybersecurity, and human capacity. For example, regarding human capacity, the E-commerce Development Plan of Hanoi City for 2021 (72/2021/KH-UBND) targeted that at least 2000 business actors, households, government officials, and students in the city would increase their e-commerce skills through training activities.

The earliest support policy issued by the city between 2000 and 2022 was the Planning on Agricultural Development of Hanoi City to 2020, with an orientation to 2030 (17/2012/QĐ-UBND) issued in 2012. It mentioned the need to develop branding for agricultural products. In the document detailing the implementation of the Planning, the People's Committee of Hanoi City highlighted that branding was a stepping stone towards e-commerce for agricultural products. The Planning was followed by two supporting policies in 2018 and 2019, before the promulgation of the E-commerce Development Plan 2021–2025 of Hanoi City (169/2021/KH-UBND) in 2020. The Plan aimed to transform traditional transactions into digital transactions across all sectors by encouraging the further development of support infrastructure, services, and human capacity. Several policies were enacted in 2021 and 2022 to implement various tasks outlined in the Plan, including the E-commerce Development Plan of Hanoi City for 2021 (72/2021/KH-UBND), which encouraged stronger integration between e-commerce businesses and 'safe' agricultural products.

Son La Province has at least three policies supporting e-commerce development. The Trade Development Plan of Son La Province, issued in 2010 (1078/2010/QĐ-UBND), highlighted the need to develop modern forms of commercial activity across all sectors. The Plan to Develop E-commerce in Son La Province 2021–2025 (2934/2020/QĐ-UBND), enacted in 2020, encouraged the development of

Table 6.2 Polices supporting e-commerce development in Hanoi City and Son La Province by promulgation year

	Support policies promulgated by	
Promulgation year	Hanoi City	Son La Province
2000–2005	–	–
2006–2010	–	1
2011–2015	1	–
2016–2020	3	1
2021–2022	5	1
Total	9	3

Source: Authors

infrastructure and human resource capacity to boost the participation of local communities, including farm households, in e-commerce. Decision No. 2312/2021/QD-UBND issued in 2021 highlighted the need to produce safe fruits and vegetables for traditional and online markets.

Among the 12 support policies promulgated by Hanoi City and Son La Province, none was enacted specifically for the agriculture sector. All policies support e-commerce development in all sectors. Furthermore, only those enacted relatively recently, i.e., since 2020, mentioned e-commerce for smallholder agriculture.

6.3.2 Household Fruit Production and Selling Profile

The interviewed households had multiple years of experience in growing fruit trees, e.g., about 8 years on average for mango farmers and 21 years for pomelo farmers (Table 6.3). Income from fruits contributed 40–60% of total household income. In all districts studied, 2–3 family members per household participated in managing fruit tree cultivation.

Among buyers, the interviewed households in peri-urban Hanoi sold their fruit products to different types of traders (i.e., collectors, retailers, or wholesalers) or directly to consumers, e.g., through local markets (Fig. 6.1a, b). An interviewed household could sell to more than one type of buyer. Only a few households in Chuong My district sold pomelos before the 2021 interviews. Due to the COVID-19 pandemic, the interviews could only be conducted before the 2021 pomelo harvesting season. On the other hand, those in rural Son La sold their fruits mainly to collectors, i.e., middlemen who bought fruits from farmers at the farmgate (Fig. 6.1c, d).

Related to selling channels (i.e., online or offline), 4–25% of the interviewed households in the selected districts have ever sold their fruits online (Table 6.3). However, they could only sell in relatively small quantities, namely, 2–100 kg per household. They used Zalo or Facebook to sell fruits online. Information about the online buyers was not collected during the interviews. However, informal discussions with several households that participated in online selling revealed that the buyers were mainly traders or supermarkets. For example, Mr. Nguyen Hai Son, a pomelo grower in Chuong My District, sold 100 kg of his pomelo fruits online to a supermarket in Hanoi City's centre. Mrs. Vu Thi Van, a farmer in Moc Chau district, sold plums to traders from other provinces who contacted her on Facebook.

By combining data from two associated districts, fruits produced by approximately 40% of interviewed households in peri-urban Hanoi were certified, compared with 11% ($p < 0.001$) in rural Son La (Table 6.3). More households in peri-urban Hanoi than in rural Son La participated in farmers' cooperatives ($p < 0.001$), and most farmers with a VietGAP certificate were members of cooperatives (Table 6.3).

Table 6.3 Fruit production and selling profile of interviewed households in peri-urban areas of Hanoi City and rural areas of Son La Province

		Selected districts in peri-urban Hanoi		Selected districts in rural Son La	
	Unit	Chuong My (Pomelo farmers)	Quoc Oai (Longan farmers)	Yen Chau (Mango farmers)	Moc Chau (Plum farmers)
No. of households (HHs) interviewed	HHs	49	40	54	56
Average no. of family members per HH involved in fruit tree cultivation	People	2.5	2.4	2.3	2.4
Average years of experience in fruit tree cultivation	Years	13.5	21.1	8.2	19.5
Average fruit tree cultivation area per HH	Ha	0.8	0.3	1.5	1.8
Average fruit productivity per HH	Ton/ha	37.8	15.6	6.9	12.9
Average fruit production per HH	Ton	27.3	3.4	10.7	21.2
Income from fruit selling to HH income in 2020	%	57	43	54	61
HHs with certified fruit products*	%	43[a]	38[a, b]	11[b]	11[b]
HHs participated in cooperatives*	%	71[a, c]	95[a]	22[b]	57[c]
HHs with certified fruit products and members of cooperatives	%	83	94	83	89
HHs sold fruits online in 2019	%	4	8	7	20
HHs sold fruits online in 2020	%	10	10	13	23
HHs sold fruits online in 2021	%	0**	8	13	25

Source: Authors

*Percentages with different superscripts among the four study districts differ significantly according to the Marascuilo Procedure with 5% confidence interval explains the a,b,c

**Only a few households sold pomelo fruits before the interviews in 2021 (due to the COVID-19 pandemic, the interviews could only be conducted before the pomelo harvesting season in 2021), and among them, none sold online

6.3.3 Reasons Not to Participate in E-Commerce According to Interviewed Households

In peri-urban Hanoi and rural Son La, 'no information about e-commerce' and 'not familiar with e-commerce technology' were the two main reasons mentioned by the

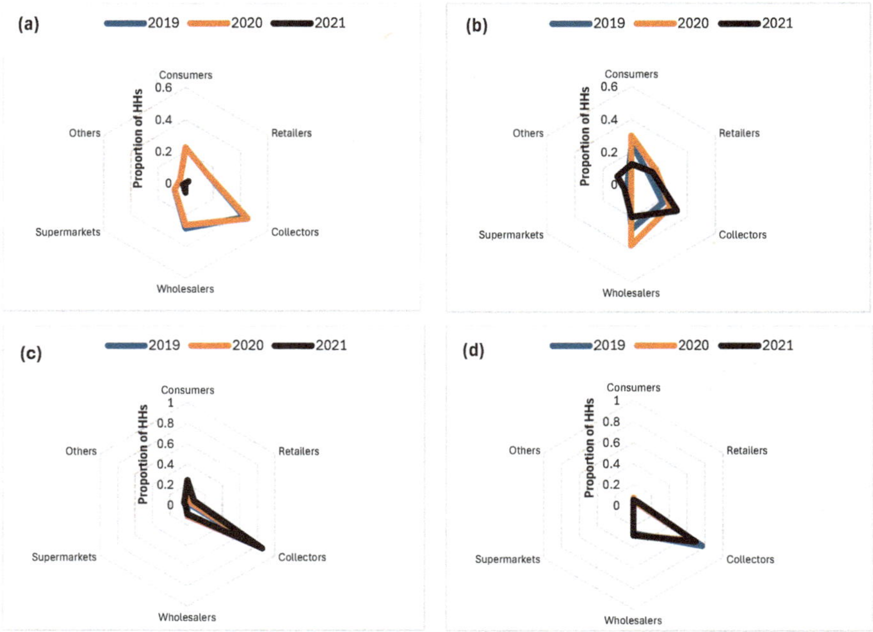

Fig. 6.1 Buyers of (**a**) pomelo fruits produced by interviewed households in Chuong My district, (**b**) longan in Quoc Oai, (**c**) mango in Yen Chau, and (**d**) plum in Moc Chau district between 2019 and 2021. Source: Authors

interviewed households in the selected districts, for not participating in e-commerce (Fig. 6.2). These two reasons represented knowledge and technical challenges, respectively. The households also mentioned a preference for keeping current offline channels, such as selling to traders at the farmgate, and not having a smartphone, as reasons. There were other various reasons mentioned by fewer households, such as a lack of family members or being illiterate, and they were grouped into ‘other reasons’ in Fig. 6.2. An interviewed household could have more than one reason.

6.3.4 Local Stakeholder Perspectives

According to stakeholders in peri-urban Hanoi and rural Son La who participated in the FGDs, barriers that local farmers encountered in participating in e-commerce relate to the presence, focus, and implementation of support policies. For example, regarding support policies, they highlighted the absence of a policy specifically enacted for the agricultural sector (Table 6.4). They argued that sector-specific policies can help ensure the allocation of public resources and implementation of policy measures that benefit smallholder farmers.

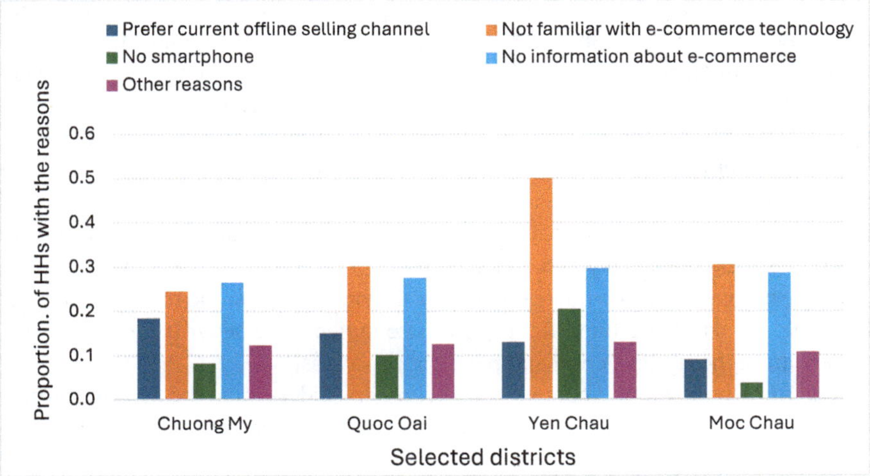

Fig. 6.2 Reasons hindering participation in e-commerce according to household interviews. Source: Authors

Table 6.4 Local stakeholder perspectives on how the support policies can better facilitate farmers to participate in e-commerce (x means the perspective of the stakeholders in the corresponding study area)

Stakeholder perspectives	Peri-urban Hanoi	Rural Son La
In terms of presence of support policies		
Need of support policy enacted specifically for the agricultural sector to help ensure the allocation of public resources and implementation of policy measures	x	x
Need of policies which can provide better support for smallholder farmers to develop safe fruit tree cultivation and meet product quality standards to respond to urban consumers' concern over food safety and attract online customers		x
In terms of focus		
Policies should have more refined regulations to build a strong farmer-urban customer trust	x	x
In terms of implementation		
Need a strict implementation of sanctions and penalties for any fake order or fraud in e-commerce	x	x
Improvement in the implementation of government's capacity development programs	x	x
Local governments need to better involve private and business entities in policy implementation	x	

Source: Authors

In terms of policy focus, while appreciating policies that encouraged the further development of support infrastructure, services, and human capacity to boost e-commerce in Hanoi City and Son La Province, stakeholders underlined the need for policies that build strong trust between farmers and urban customers by countering fake orders and fraud. They highlighted the absence of a legal procedure to verify the identity of online customers and to allow regular inspections by relevant government agencies of local e-commerce activities and transactions. Additionally, they underscored the lack of regulations on 'e-receipt' that can serve as proof when buyers or sellers breach any agreement on product quality, e.g., when there is inconsistency in appearance or quality between the delivered and advertised products. Stakeholders also underlined the need to strengthen cybersecurity to protect data privacy throughout transaction and payment processes.

Regarding policy implementation, stakeholders underscored the need to improve the application of the government's capacity development programs (Table 6.4). They claimed that many farm households, including those living in relatively remote areas, still lack knowledge of e-commerce and the technical skills necessary to use e-commerce platforms or social media for online selling. Additionally, stakeholders expected strict enforcement of sanctions and penalties for any fake orders or fraud in e-commerce, and greater involvement of private and business entities in implementing support policies, as they are at the forefront of digital technology advancements and market trends.

Although not directly related to support policies for e-commerce development, stakeholders in rural Son La also highlighted the absence of policies that can better support smallholder farmers in developing safe fruit tree cultivation (i.e., with fewer chemical inputs) and meeting product quality standards, such as VietGAP, to address urban consumers' concerns over food safety and attract online customers.

6.4 Discussions

6.4.1 E-Commerce for Smallholder Agriculture in the Recent Support Policies

The recent support policies promulgated by Hanoi City and Son La Province mentioned e-commerce for smallholder agriculture. This could be triggered by experiences during the COVID-19 pandemic, when many urban consumers sought fresh agricultural products online. Lockdown policies worldwide restricted people's physical access to food stores, and e-commerce was considered an effective solution because it could minimize direct person-to-person contact (Guo et al. 2022). In addition, the Vietnamese government likely learned from the case of fruit farmers in Bac Giang province, in the country's Northeast region, who sold more than 8000 tons of lychee to over 63 provinces and cities nationwide during the COVID-19 pandemic via the Postmart and Voso e-commerce platforms (VP 2021). It was the result of strong coordination between the national and local governments and e-commerce platform enterprises, which actively promoted local lychee fruits from the province through online channels and facilitated shipping services during the pandemic. Although it took place during a special occasion, the achievement indicated that smallholder farmers could be well connected with urban customers through the strong role and coordination of the government and e-commerce platform enterprises.

The local stakeholders in the study sites who participated in the FGDs appreciated the recent policies. However, they argued that policies enacted specifically for e-commerce development in the agricultural sector remain necessary to ensure the allocation of public resources and the implementation of policy measures that benefit smallholder farmers. In addition, they underlined that sector-specific policies could be more effective than cross-sectoral policies because the former directly address the unique challenges faced by specific target groups, such as smallholder farmers.

As part of policy-level challenges, the government-technology-smallholder framework also highlighted that insufficient attention has been paid to smallholder agriculture in policies supporting e-commerce development, including in Asia's developing countries, and that there is a lack of effective policies and public investment to develop rural digital infrastructure (Yuan and Sun 2024). Support policies enacted specifically for the agriculture sector might address this challenge, provided they align with cross-sectoral policies to avoid conflicting outcomes. The success of sectoral policies often relies on complementarity with other policies (SD 2025). For example, the success and effectiveness of support policies enacted specifically for the agriculture sector will depend on and are intertwined with complementary policies in the broader business and service sectors.

6.4.2 Need for Support Policies that Build a Trustworthy E-Commerce System

The focus of policies supporting e-commerce development in Hanoi City and Son La Province includes further development of legal and regulatory frameworks, infrastructure and services, cybersecurity, trade facilitation and logistics, and human capacity. The local stakeholders who participated in the FGDs underscored that these focuses can create conducive digital ecosystems, but support policies should also aim to make the e-commerce systems trustworthy. Apart from a secure payment system, buyer-seller trust in e-commerce can be achieved through, e.g., transparency and credibility in buyer-seller contact information, authentic customer reviews as social proof, consistency in the appearance and functionality between delivered and advertised products, and reliable after-sales systems in case of any issue with delivered products (Slezak 2024).

E-commerce systems in many developing countries often lack trustworthy features. Online buyers and sellers in these countries often hesitate to engage in e-commerce due to concerns about data privacy, payment fraud, and product authenticity (Lafuente and Sallan 2024). Vietnam is likely not an exception, in which online buyers and sellers, including smallholder farmers, face numerous issues with fake orders and various forms of fraud, especially when using cash on delivery (COD), the most popular payment method for online orders in the country (Le 2024). E-commerce platform enterprises and Vietnamese authorities need to strengthen their collaboration on mitigation measures and ensure an effective implementation (Le 2024).

The local stakeholders proposed several measures to enhance farmer-urban customer trust in e-commerce, and the fact that a trustworthy feature remains lacking in the Vietnam's e-commerce system calls for further studies on a thorough policy review that evaluates the relevance, inclusiveness, and effectiveness of measures to mitigate or avoid various forms of fraud in e-commerce introduced in the current national or local support policies.

6.4.3 Knowledge and Technical Challenges for Farmers to Participate in E-Commerce

The knowledge and technical challenges that restricted fruit farmers' participation in e-commerce in peri-urban Hanoi and rural Son La were also found in other regions of the country, where farmers grow other crops. For example, these challenges were reported by farmers who managed various crops and livestock in Quang Tri, Tuyen Quang, Thai Nguyen, Lang Son, and Cao Bang Province (Dao et al. 2025; Tran et al. 2024) and by tea farmers in Thai Nguyen, Cao Bang, Tuyen Quang, and Phu Tho Province (Nguyen et al. 2022).

According to Vietnam's Ministry of Trade and Industry (VN 2024), a lack of knowledge, technical skills, and interest in online selling is a common barrier to smallholder farmers' participation in e-commerce. These challenges persist despite efforts by the Vietnamese government to increase awareness and capacity among Vietnamese society, including farmers, in e-commerce through capacity development programs and supportive policies. For example, at the national level, Article 7 of the Decision No. 52/2013/NĐ-CP issued in 2013 encouraged the application of the national e-commerce development program to "strengthen public information and raise awareness on e-commerce", "train and develop capacity of human resources involved in e-commerce", and "build management capacity and organize activities to support e-commerce development". There is a need for studies that investigate the implementation and effectiveness of the government's capacity development programs promoting e-commerce in the country.

When comparing peri-urban and rural areas, the government's capacity development programs on e-commerce might need to prioritise rural areas. This is because farmers in peri-urban areas likely have greater opportunities for direct, in-person interactions with various types of urban traders. In the present study, among the four districts studied, significantly higher e-commerce participation was observed in Moc Chau District ($p < 0.001$), located about 200 km from the Hanoi City centre. However, this was not observed in Yen Chau, the other studied district in rural Son La. As also indicated by the present study, farmers living farther from urban and market centres tended to participate more in online selling activities due to limited market opportunities and greater reliance on middlemen (Hoang 2020).

6.4.4 Challenges for Farmers to Comply with Product Quality Standards

Along with the growing concern among urban consumers in Vietnam about food safety, strategies to better engage them in e-commerce should focus on improving product quality, providing reliable information on key product attributes and branding, and attractive packaging (VIR 2024). Although not all online consumers may search for a product's attributes, providing such information can give advertised products a competitive advantage (Maaya et al. 2020). Online agricultural products that meet quality standards and feature attractive packaging and branding, such as those associated with a 'green lifestyle' or the One Commune One Product (OCOP) program, have drawn attention from urban consumers in Vietnam and could generate substantial income for smallholder farmers (HT 2024; USAID 2022). The recent policies mentioning e-commerce for smallholder agriculture promulgated by Hanoi City and Son La Province also indicated that only safe agricultural products have a promising future in e-commerce.

However, many farmers in Vietnam still face difficulties in complying with all product quality standards (ADB 2023). This persists despite efforts by national and sub-national governments to promulgate support policies and facilitate numerous technical training sessions for local extension workers and smallholder farmers across the country (ADB 2023). The local stakeholders in the study sites who participated in the FGDs highlighted several factors that can stimulate farmers to comply with the VietGAP, which include the availability of market incentives (i.e., higher prices or better access to the market) for certified products and more detailed technical guidance for farmers to better comply with all VietGAP requirements. Additionally, they underscored that local governments should encourage farmers to join local cooperatives. In the present study, more than 83% of interviewed households with product certificates were members of local cooperatives. Such membership can often help farmers comply with product quality standards (ADB 2023).

6.5 Conclusions and Policy Recommendations

6.5.1 Conclusions

Hanoi City promulgated at least nine support policies, and Son La Province promulgated at least three policies between 2000 and 2022 for e-commerce development across all sectors. These policies encouraged further improvements in legal and regulatory frameworks, support infrastructure, services, human resource capacity, and cybersecurity. Among the 12 support policies, none was specifically enacted for the agriculture sector, and only those issued since 2020 mentioned e-commerce for smallholder agriculture. At the household level, farmers faced knowledge and technical constraints that prevented them from participating in e-commerce. Additionally, they faced challenges in meeting product quality standards to better attract online urban customers. However, farmers in peri-urban areas had greater opportunities for direct and in-person interactions with urban traders. The local stakeholders in the study sites identified ways the support policies can better facilitate farmers' participation in e-commerce.

6.5.2 Policy Recommendations

In line with the perspectives of local stakeholders in the study site, the main recommendations to address policy-level challenges include: (1) promulgate support policies specifically for the agricultural sector which are in harmony with other existing policies to ensure complementarity and avoid conflicting outcomes, (2) amend the existing or issue new policies which can build a strong farmer-urban costumer trust in e-commerce, (3) amend the existing relevant policies to help farmers comply with product quality standards to attract online urban customers, and (4) strengthen the implementation of sanctions and penalties to counter fake orders or frauds in e-commerce.

To address the knowledge- and technical-level challenges, there is a need for local governments to (1) improve the implementation of capacity development programs to substantially enhance the knowledge and technical skills of smallholder farmers in e-commerce and (2) provide more technical guidance for farmers to better comply with the requirements set by product quality standards.

Acknowledgement This paper was presented in the session "E-commerce for Rural and Agricultural Development" at the International Conference on "Innovations for Sustainable Agriculture and Rural Development", held at the Asian Development Bank Institute (ADBI), Tokyo, Japan, on 22–24 September 2025. ADBI and Lincoln University, New Zealand, jointly organized the conference. The authors gratefully acknowledge the valuable comments and suggestions from the participants, as well as travel support from ADBI.

The authors would like to thank Doan Thu Huong, Nguyen Thu Hang, Le Huy Huan, Le Quynh Dung, Nguyen Thi Nga, Nguyen Thai Thinh, Pham Thanh Van, and Le Thi Ha for their contributions to data collection through household interviews and focus group discussions with local stakeholders at the study sites.

Funding This study was part of the Challenge 4 of AgriFoSe2030 program (phase II): https://www.slu.se/en/collaboration/international/slu-global/agrifose/. The program is funded by the Swedish International Development Cooperation Agency (Sida) (no grant code).

Data Availability The datasets used and/or analysed during the current study are available from the corresponding author on reasonable request.

Competing Interests There are no potential competing interests associated with this research. Furthermore, the authors confirm that neither this manuscript nor any part thereof has been previously published or submitted for publication elsewhere.

Ethical Statement The ethical aspects of the research methodologies applied in the present study were thoroughly assessed by the board members of FAVRI and IPSARD, as government institutions under the Ministry of Agriculture and Rural Development of Vietnam, before each research activity involving household interviews or focus group discussions on the case study sites. The approvals were granted through the issuance of documents signed by the directors of the two institutions (e.g., No. 81-VRQ-KH by FAVRI and No. 322/GM-CSCL-TNMT by IPSARD) to support local authorities in the case study sites in providing administrative permission. The assessment by FAVRI and IPSARD was to ensure that the study did not collect sensitive personal data, did not experiment on animals or humans, and did not involve children. This process complied with the legal procedures in Vietnam for research activities conducted with local communities in any province of the country.

Informed Consent from the Study Participants Verbal informed consent has been obtained from all the study participants. In the local social and political context of Vietnam, oral approval to participate in an interview and the option to decline to answer specific questions are appropriate, while requesting signatures on paper does not align with the intended and declared anonymity of presenting results. The interview procedure conformed to existing regulations and ethical standards of FAVRI and IPSARD. The date, time, and location of the participants' verbal consent were recorded on the data collection forms.

Author Contributions RM: Conceptualisation, Data curation, Formal analysis, Investigation, Methodology, Project's administration, Resources, Software, Supervision, Validation, Visualisation, Writing—original draft, Writing—review & editing. NDT: Conceptualisation, Data curation, Formal analysis, Investigation, Methodology, Project's administration, Resources, Supervision, Validation, Writing—review & editing. TNL: Conceptualisation, Data curation, Formal analysis, Investigation, Methodology, Project's administration, Resources, Supervision, Validation, Writing—review & editing. HTL: Conceptualisation, Data curation, Formal analysis, Investigation, Methodology, Project's administration, Resources, Validation, Writing—review & editing. HM: Conceptualisation, Data curation, Funding acquisition, Methodology, Project's administration, Resources, Supervision, Validation, Writing—review & editing. MJ: Conceptualisation, Data curation, Funding acquisition, Methodology, Project's administration, Resources, Supervision, Validation, Writing—review & editing.

References

ADB (2023) Imperatives for improvement of food safety in fruit and vegetable value chains in Vietnam. Manila, the Philippines. https://www.adb.org/publications/food-safety-fruit-vegetable-value-chains-viet-nam

Bao M, Latif S, Bao D, Latif Z, Lu J (2025) Overcoming e-commerce barriers in developing markets: A review of data-driven strategies for sustainable growth. Sustainable Futures 10: 101408. doi:https://doi.org/10.1016/j.sftr.2025.101408.

Bruckert M, Lepiller O, Sautier D, Nguyen TTL, Nguyen TS (2023) Studying the impact of e-commerce on the sustainability of food systems in Vietnam. In: Valette E, Blay-Palmer A, Intoppa B, Battista AD, Roudelle O, Chaboud G (Eds) Evaluating Sustainable Food System Innovations, London: Routledge, pp. 118–143.

Bui TN, Nguyen AH, Le TTH, Nguyen VP, Le TTH, Tran TTH, Nguyen NM, Le TKO, Nguyen TKO, Nguyen TTT, Dao HV, Doan TNT, Vu THN, Bui VH, Hoa HC, Lebailly P (2021) Can a short food supply chain create sustainable benefits for small farmers in developing countries? An exploratory study of Vietnam. Sustainability 13(5), 2443. doi:https://doi.org/10.3390/su13052443

Campbell S, Greenwood M, Prior S, Shearer T, Walkem K, Young S, Bywaters D, Walker K (2020) Purposive sampling: Complex or simple? Research case examples. J Res Nurs 25: 652–661. doi:https://doi.org/10.1177/1744987120927206.

Dao TH, Nguyen MH, Cao TPT, Hoang TTH (2025) Digital capacity education for young farmers in the Northeast region, Vietnam: A study of agricultural product consumption. Journal of Education, Learning, and Management, 2(2), 316–323. doi:https://doi.org/10.69739/jelm.v2i2.1039

EC (2020) The food and beverage market entry handbook Vietnam. Luxembourg. https://rea.ec.europa.eu/publications/food-and-beverage-market-entry-handbook-vietnam_en

Fan D, Gan W (2025) Does the adoption of Internet digital technologies improve farmers' fertilizer management performance? An empirical analysis based on the China Rural Revitalization Survey. International Journal of Agricultural Sustainability, 23(1). doi:https://doi.org/10.1080/14735903.2025.2467619

Ganbold S (2024) E-commerce in the Asia-Pacific region. https://www.statista.com/topics/7121/e--commerce-in-asia-pacific/#topicOverview. Accessed 28 June 2024.

GSO (2021). Statistical Summary Book of Vietnam 2020. Hanoi, Vietnam. https://www.gso.gov.vn/en/data-and-statistics/2021/07/statistical-summary-book-of-viet-nam-2020/

Guo J, Jin S, Zhao J, Wang H, Zhao F (2022) Has COVID-19 accelerated the e-commerce of agricultural products? Evidence from sales data of e-stores in China. Food Policy 112, 102377. doi:https://doi.org/10.1016/j.foodpol.2022.102377.

Ha TM, Shamim S, Do PHK (2021) Food risk in consumers' eye and their consumption responses: Evidence from Hanoi survey. J Asian Bus Econ Stud 28: 86–100. doi:https://doi.org/10.1108/JABES-12-2019-0126/FULL/PDF.

Hayes A (2024) What is the Bonferroni test (correction) and how is it used? https://www.investopedia.com/terms/b/bonferroni-test.asp. Accessed 2 August 2024.

Hoang GH (2020). Determinants of the adoption of mobile phones for fruit marketing by Vietnamese farmers. World Dev Perspect 17, 100178. doi:https://doi.org/10.1016/J.WDP.2020.100178.

Hoang GH, Tran HD (2023) Smallholder farmers' perception and adoption of digital agricultural technologies: An empirical evidence from Vietnam. Outlook Agric 52: 457–468. doi:https://doi.org/10.1177/00307270231197825.

HT (2024) Authorities and businesses team up to boost Vietnamese e-commerce. https://hanoitimes.vn/authorities-and-businesses-team-up-to-boost-vietnamese-e-commerce-327489.html. Accessed 30 July 2024.

IDEA (2021) Thương mại điện tử Việt Nam 2020. Hanoi, Vietnam. https://idea.gov.vn/file/66d4f658-3e94-4abc-b50f-d9da0e616b82

ITA (2024) Assessment of current buyer behavior in market. https://www.trade.gov/country-commercial-guides/vietnam-ecommerce. Accessed 7 July 2024.

Kauth J (2024) APAC is leading the e-commerce charge. https://hellopartner.com/2024/03/21/apac-is-leading-the-e-commerce-charge/. Accessed 27 June 2024.

Lafuente E, Sallan JM (2024) Digitally powered solution delivery: The use of IoT and AI platforms in business models. Technological Forecasting and Social Change. doi:https://doi.org/10.1016/j.ijpe.2024.109383

Le L (2024) Cash-on-delivery fraud is a nightmare for gig workers in Vietnam. https://restofworld.org/2024/cash-on-delivery-fraud-vietnam/. Accessed 07 December 2025.

Le DB, Tran TP (2020) Digital economy and digital transformation in Vietnam. Hanoi, Vietnam. https://www.economica.vn/Content/files/PUBL%20%26%20REP/EVFTA%20and%20Digital%20Economy%20in%20Vietnam%20ENG.pdf

Li J, Yan X, Li Y, Dong X (2023) Optimizing the agricultural supply chain through e-commerce: A case study of Tudouec in Inner Mongolia, China. Int J Environ Res Public Heal 20. doi:https://doi.org/10.3390/ijerph20053775.

Maaya L, Meulders M, Vandebroek M (2020) Online consumers' attribute non-attendance behaviour: Effects of information provision. Int J Electron Commer 24(3): 338–365. doi:https://doi.org/10.1080/10864415.2020.1767429

Ngo HM, Liu R, Moritaka M, Fukuda S (2020) Urban consumer trust in safe vegetables in Vietnam: The role of brand trust and the impact of consumer worry about vegetable safety. Food Control 108, 106856. doi:https://doi.org/10.1016/J.FOODCONT.2019.106856.

Nguyen M (2024) Retail foods annual. USDA and GAIN. Ho Chi Minh City, Vietnam. https://www.fas.usda.gov/data/vietnam-retail-foods-annual-0

Nguyen KD, Long D, Nguyen NQ (2022) Tea farmers' intention to participate in livestream sales in Vietnam: The combination of the Technology Acceptance Model (TAM) and barrier factors. J Rural Stud 94: 408–417. doi:https://doi.org/10.1016/j.jrurstud.2022.05.023.

SD (2025) Cross-sectoral policy alignment. https://pollution.sustainability-directory.com/term/cross-sectoral-policy-alignment/#:~:text. Accessed 14 July 2025.

Slezak A (2024) Trust in e-commerce: How to build it and increase sales. https://business.trustedshops.com/blog/building-trust-in-ecommerce. Accessed 05 December 2025.

SLSO (2021) Son La Statistical Yearbook 2020. Hanoi, Vietnam. https://thuvienthongke.com/nien-giam-thong-ke-son-la-2020/v7468.aspx

Stoeva S, Van Gompel R, Van den Bossche L, Rogge E, Slavova P, Grivins M, Mileiko I (2024) Understanding collaboration in short food supply chains: a focus on collaborative relationships, interaction mechanisms and relational benefits. Agric Econ 12, 49. doi:https://doi.org/10.1186/s40100-024-00344-4

Sun Y, Miao Y, Xie Z, Wu R (2024) Drivers and barriers to digital transformation in agriculture: an evolutionary game analysis based on the experience of China. Agric. Syst. 2024, 221, 104136. doi:https://doi.org/10.1016/j.agsy.2024.104136

Tran PP (2024) Impact investment in agricultural sustainability: Driving positive social and environmental change in Vietnam's farming sector. https://www.aimr.asia/impact-investing/impact-investment-in-agricultural-sustainability/#:~: Accessed 5 February 2026.

Tran CU, Limnirankul B, Kramol P, Kramol P, Gia HH, Da TNT (2024) Digital technology adoption among smallholder farmers in Vietnam: Implications for digital agricultural extension strategies. J. Int. Dev. 37: 351–370. doi:https://doi.org/10.1002/jid.3904.

Trang H, Do T, Vo H (2024) Adoption of e-commerce in the agricultural business sector in Vietnam. JEFMS 7 (12). doi:https://doi.org/10.47191/jefms/v7-i12-21

Turney S (2023) Chi-Square (X2) tests: Types, formula & examples. https://www.scribbr.com/statistics/chi-square-tests/. Accessed 26 June 2024.

USAID (2022) Utilizing e-commerce to increase rice sales. https://www.usaid.gov/vietnam/program-updates/oct-25-2022-utilizing-e-commerce-increase-rice-sales. Accessed 10 August 2024.

USDA-GAIN (2021) Vietnamese fruit production and exports confront the challenges of salinity intrusion and COVID-19. Ho Chi Minh City, Vietnam. https://fas.usda.gov/data/vietnam-vietnamese-fruit-production-and-exports-confront-challenges-salinity-intrusion-and

VIR (2024) Agricultural produce seeks to conquer e-commerce market. https://vir.com.vn/agricultural-produce-seeks-to-conquer-e-commerce-market-110668-110668.html. Accessed 23 October 2024b.

VN (2024) More than two million agricultural households trained in digital skills. https://vietnamnews.vn/economy/1655592/more-than-two-million-agricultural-households-trained-in-digital-skills.html. Accessed 17 August 2024.

VP (2021) Vietnam aims to connect 5 million farming households to e-commerce platforms. https://en.vietnamplus.vn/vietnam-aims-to-connect-5-million-farming-households-to-e-commerce-platforms-post206400.vnp. Accessed 2 August 2024.

Wagh ST, Razvi NA (2016) Marascuilo method of multiple comparisons (an analytical study of Caesarean section delivery). IJCMR 3: 1137–1140.

Yuan Y, Sun Y (2024) Practices, challenges, and future of digital transformation in smallholder agriculture: Insights from a literature review. Agriculture 14 (12): 2193. doi:https://doi.org/10.3390/agriculture14122193

Zhang X, Fan D (2023) Can agricultural digital transformation help farmers increase income? An empirical study based on thousands of farmers in Hubei Province. Env Dev Sustain 26: 14405–1443. doi:https://doi.org/10.1007/s10668-023-03200-5.

FSC
www.fsc.org
MIX
Papier | Fördert gute Waldnutzung
FSC® C083411

Kolibri 360 GmbH
Ferdinand-Jühlke-Straße 7
99095 Erfurt, Deutschland
produktsicherheit@kolibri360.de